CANADIAN
INCOME
FUNDS

CANADIAN INCOME FUNDS

*Your Complete Guide to
Income Trusts, Royalty Trusts,
and Real Estate Trusts*

PETER BECK
&
SIMON ROMANO

John Wiley & Sons Canada, Ltd.

This book consists of general information that is provided solely for informational and educational purposes and is not to be construed as an offering or solicitation of securities, as advice in respect of securities, general or specific, or as advice as to the investing in or the buying or selling of securities, express or implied. This book is intended to provide general information, and is not intended to assist in the making of investment decisions, which should generally be made only in consultation with a financial advisor or dealer.

The securities mentioned in this book may not be suitable for all types of investors; their prices, value and/or income they produce may fluctuate and/or be adversely affected by exchange and interest rates, among other things. This publication does not take into account the investment objectives, financial situation or specific needs of any particular investor. Before making an investment decision in any security, an investor should consider whether such security is appropriate given the investor's particular investment needs, objectives and financial circumstances. The authors suggest that, prior to investing in any security, you contact a registered dealer or a registered advisor in your jurisdiction to discuss your particular circumstances.

This book is not to be construed as providing tax advice, express or implied. As with any transaction having potential tax implications, investors should consult with their tax advisors.

The information and any statistical data contained herein were obtained from sources that we believe to be reliable, but the authors do not represent that they are accurate or complete, and they should not be relied upon as such. All estimates and opinions expressed herein constitute judgements as of the date of this publication and are subject to change without notice.

John Wiley & Sons Canada Ltd
6045 Freemont Boulevard
Mississauga, Ontario
L5R 4J3

Library and Archives Canada Cataloguing in Publication
Beck, Peter, 1955-
        Canadian income funds : your complete guide to income trusts, royalty trusts and real estate investment trusts / Peter Beck, Simon Romano.

Includes index.
ISBN 0-470-83495-1

        1. Mutual funds--Canada. 2. Fixed-income securities--Canada. I. Romano, Simon, 1959- II. Title.

HG5154.5.B42 2004   332.63'27   C2004-904833-3

Production Credits
Cover: Kyle Gell Design
Interior text design: Interrobang Graphic Design Inc.
Printer: Transcontinental Printing
Printed in Canada
10 9 8 7 6 5 4 3 2 1

To my father, on his 95th birthday.
—Peter Beck

I would also like to dedicate this book to Emma and Colin Romano.
—Simon Romano

Contents

Acknowledgements

The authors wish to thank Chris Hunt of Swift Trade and John Lorito and Jennifer Estrela of Stikeman Elliott LLP for their assistance. All errors are our own.

Introduction

Sitting outside on a shady patio on a warm day having a light lunch is one of summer's greatest joys. On the corner of Roxborough and Yonge street in Toronto, Café Doria has a beautiful patio, capable of seating 20 to 25 people under the natural shade of a large oak tree. On this particular July Saturday I was having lunch with my dad, who had come to visit us from Hungary. The fact that he's 93 years old certainly didn't prevent him from enjoying some of the simple luxuries of life, such as having a meal on a patio with his only son, whose latest book on hedge funds had been written up in the *National Post* that morning. William Hanley's article, *Hedge Funds for the Masses*, was on the main page of the business section of the paper. Dad was very proud to see my picture, and although his English is not as good as it used to be, he managed to read the whole article right after breakfast. By the time we arrived at the restaurant for lunch, he had read it three more times and could have recited paragraphs from it by heart.

Café Doria is mostly frequented by regulars who live in the neighbourhood. On weekends, they come in for a late morning coffee and croissant and a dose of the written news. At a quarter to twelve, when we sat down, many of the late risers were still reading their papers and sipping their lattes. I counted three *National Post*s, three *Globe and Mail*s, and one *Toronto Star*. I could hardly contain a big smile when I noticed that two people with the *Post* were reading my article. Though vanity has never been one of my weaknesses, I could not escape feeling just a bit smug.

A large bottle of cold San Pellegrino arrived immediately after we placed our orders. I poured some and turned to my right, spotting a smiling face at the table next to us looking at me.

"That's you in the paper," the man said, pointing at the business section of the *Post* that he had been reading a minute before. He promised he would buy the book and read it, although he said he was really not interested in investing in hedge funds. He explained that most of his investments were concentrated in his RRSP as, being young and single, he would rather invest the money in himself and continue to enjoy the finer things in life than put it into an investment vehicle that he knew nothing about.

"You know, what I really would like to learn about is income trusts. Almost every day I read or hear about them and I have no clue what they do." He said this as the waitress was approaching with the steaming plates. "My broker has been suggesting that I convert some of the mutual funds in my RRSP into income trusts, but even he couldn't tell me what they are or how they work." By this time the lasagna had landed in front of me and my concentration shifted towards satisfying a less conversational instinct. The man bade me goodbye, and folding his papers under his arm, walked inside to take care of his bill.

It was not until the middle of the next week, when I was talking to my friend and corporate counsel Simon Romano, that I suddenly remembered the conversation. "You have structured many income trusts, haven't you?" I asked. I remembered that Simon was one of the foremost experts on the subject in the country. I told him about my encounter with the man in the café. "How many other people must be out there with the same questions?" he asked. "Tens of thousands, if not hundreds," I answered. "You and I should write a book on the subject."

We wasted no time discussing the validity of writing such a book and went straight to how we could find the time to do it along with all of our other commitments. After thinking about it for a few days, we decided to write a book about Canadian income trusts.

We approached John Wiley and Sons Canada Ltd., who did such an excellent job of publishing and promoting my first book, *Hedge Funds for Canadians*, co-authored with Miklos Nagy. They loved the idea, and the rest is history. You are holding a copy of our labour in your hands.

Our goals in writing this book were simple: to make this complex and popular investment vehicle easy to understand, to take some of the legal and business mumbo-jumbo out of income trusts, and to explain them in a way that my friend in the café, and you, my dear reader, can easily understand. So jump right in—we promise it will be informative, enjoyable, and an invaluable tool for deciding if income trusts should become part of your investment portfolio.

Peter Beck

What Are Income Trusts Anyway?

TODAY'S INCOME TRUST LANDSCAPE

In late July of 2004, there was speculation that the Ontario government was considering an initial public offering for the Liquor Control Board of Ontario (LCBO), the world's largest wine and spirit buyer. The transaction, if it goes ahead, could value the business at several billion dollars.

For the Finance Minster, this could mean a serious reduction of the Ontario government debt without having to raise taxes. For investors in the proposed public offering, it could mean a steady, reliable investment that yields an average of 7–8 percent—more than three times as much as the best current savings account rates. This is a rather spectacular example of what this book is about. You see, the Ontario government may be considering turning one of its most profitable businesses—one that is reported to have put C$1.04 billion into the coffers for the year ending March 31, 2004—into an *income trust*.

With over 150 trusts currently trading on the Toronto Stock Exchange at a combined value of about C$91 billion, this relatively new vehicle, the income trust, is one of the hottest tickets on the Canadian investment landscape today. Indeed, of the C$4.6 billion generated from initial public offerings (IPOs are when a company sells shares to the public for the first time), C$3.8 billion was from income trusts last year in this country.

Between January, 2000, and December, 2003, the Canadian income trust market performed very well indeed, with total returns of over 150 percent, meaning that $100 invested in 2000 would be worth over $250 by December 2003, making income trusts one of the best-performing classes of investments over that period. Compare that to the under 10 percent return of the S&P TSX Composite Index over the same period! Note that we said *Canadian*. This is because income trusts, and the unique way in which they are structured, are a peculiarly Canadian animal. A number of attempts to export similar investment vehicles to the United States have been made, albeit with limited success to date.

So what is going on? How are these investments able to outperform other, more traditional ones? Is this some kind of loophole that is being exploited? Somebody must be on the losing end *somewhere*, right? Are they a fad? Can you invest in them? What are the risks? How much should you invest? How do they work? Where can you find information? So many questions. In this book we will examine the specifics of income trusts, and attempt to demystify some of the misconceptions and confusion surrounding them. But first, some of the basics.

THE BASICS: WHAT IS A TRUST?

In its simplest form, a trust means holding property for the benefit of others. Sound complicated? It's not. Imagine the following scene.

In a hospital, a healthy baby girl is delivered. Later on the immediate family gathers in the hospital room, and the paternal grandfather pulls out a ring that has been a family heirloom for centuries. Handing it to the little girl's father, he says, "Give this to her when she is old enough to wear it." By saying these words, and handing over the ring, a *trust* is created. The proud father is holding the ring for the benefit of his daughter or "holding property for the benefit of others." This is one of the simplest forms of trust, and it does not have to be in writing for it to be legally enforceable in a court of law, although having a legal document makes the enforcement of it considerably easier.

In a trust, property changes hands in exchange for a promise to hold it for a third person. This creates a separation between the ownership of property and the benefit of that ownership. This is different from a simple contract, such as buying a loaf of bread, where the benefit of ownership, in this case taking the bread home and eating it, is simply a matter of paying the specified price. If the little girl's father were to buy the ring in a jewelry store under such a contract, for instance, he would have the ownership and the benefit of that ownership as well. He could break it, sell it, melt it down—do whatever he wanted. But in our example of a trust, once he accepted the ring from the grandfather, he has the ownership but no benefit of that ownership. Those benefits belong to his daughter, to be received in the future.

Income trusts are based on this simple structure, and the concept of a trust has been around for quite some time—since the fall of the Roman Empire to be exact.

THE HISTORY OF TRUSTS

Rome at its height controlled the (then) known world, and its military legions were stationed all over Europe, the Mediterranean, and Asia, assuring complete compliance with the wishes of the capital. Unprecedented wealth was gathered in the Eternal City, and signs of it are still visible to this day. This wealth was not just represented by land, but also by minted coins that served as a universal representation of goods and services. The Romans also had a sophisticated legal system that to this day provides the basis for laws in a large number of European countries.

But things must come to an end, especially an empire whose basic economic engine was built on slavery. By the middle of the fifth century, the Western Roman Empire was no more, and many small kingdoms were created by people in territories it had once occupied in Europe. The Eastern Roman Empire survived for almost another thousand years, with Constantinople as its capital.

As no central government was in place in Europe, there was no longer any reliable minting of coins acceptable in the many kingdoms that sprang up after the Romans retreated. So the representation of wealth shifted toward the ownership of land. Land allowed people to produce food, one of the basic necessities of life. Rulers sought to enlarge their kingdoms by taking land from other kingdoms, since more land represented more food production and thus more wealth. However, these monarchs were not that keen on tending the land themselves—cultivating in those days with crude equipment was very hard work—and, in any case, they were too busy fighting for more land.

Consequently, the kings had to find others to cultivate their land. Since minted coins or paper money were not an acceptable representation of real value, they could not easily hire labourers to plow the land. Even if they could pay some kind of gold or silver coins for the work, there were no markets where peasants could buy food with coins. With land the main representation of wealth, it had to be the consideration for services. But how could land represent payment for services? This is where we bring a third party into the picture.

As you can imagine, these kings did not just brawl outside taverns to decide who was going to control a village. They gathered arms and soldiers, and fought large-scale battles. Those who joined them were not (contrary to Hollywood's many interpretations) just in it for the valour and victory of battle; once new lands were occupied, these soldiers expected to be paid for their services. So the ruler gave them some of the land they had just conquered. The deal was that the soldier would own the land as long as he was loyal to the king, and prepared to fight future battles for him.

The soldiers were no more eager to tackle the drudgery of cultivating the land than the kings. So they simply became landlords—the word itself originated at this time—and parcelled up the land among tenants, giving each a piece to work on. When the harvest was collected, the tenants, known as peasants, gave a certain percentage of it to the landlord and kept the rest. Thus the economic engine of the feudal system was created and the soldiers, known as vassals, accepted land in exchange for military service.

Being at war all the time is not exactly safe work, and as vassals died, the question of ownership of their land became an issue. People had many children in those days, and the question of how to divide the property amongst them was complicated. To keep the estate intact, the custom of the day was that the oldest son inherited everything, and the rest were out of luck. Girls had to get married to survive or become chambermaids, servants, etc., and the other boys sought the service of another king to obtain their share of land from the spoils of war.

Some forward-looking vassal fathers thought a little differently. They wanted not only to take care of their oldest sons, but others in the family as well. Dividing the estate into small pieces was not efficient—over generations, parcels would become minuscule—so these progressive fathers came up with the concept of trusts. This is how it worked: the father left the land to his eldest son, who promised to take the payments from the tenants (a percentage of produce collected each year after the harvest) and divide it among all of the brothers and sisters, including himself. Thus he held the property, for the most part, for the benefit of others. However, he was also a beneficiary in receiving part of the payments.

The system worked, and as similar structures became more popular, the concept of the trust found its way into the law books. Today, many countries have laws to accommodate the creation and existence of trusts to achieve any number of personal and business goals.

THE PLAYERS IN A TRUST: WHICH ONE IS THE INVESTOR?

One of the simplest trusts is the one described earlier, where the happy father accepts a ring for his newborn daughter to be held by him in trust until she gets old enough to wear it. To get an idea of where the modern investor fits into the picture, let's examine the players and their roles in a little more detail.

The grandfather pulled out the ring that had been a family heirloom for generations. At that point in time he owned the ring. It was his, and he had full title to it. This gave him the right to do whatever he wanted with it. He could pawn it, sell it, melt it down or frame it and hang it on the wall. But he chose to follow the family tradition, and seeing that his first grandchild was a girl, he found it appropriate to give it to her. However, the granddaughter could not even hold on to it yet, let alone put it on her little finger. So, the next best thing was to hand the ring to someone who would be there when the time came that she would be able to wear it. And in this case, the most logical person for the task was her father.

So by saying the words "Give this to her when she is old enough to wear it," the grandfather creates a trust, and becomes what is known as the settlor of that trust. The settlor is the individual (or other legal entity) that owns an asset and is willing to transfer it into a trust. So the pivotal moment in creating the trust is when the son agrees to the request and accepts the ring. At this point, the title of the ring transfers to the father—it is legally his. However, unlike the grandfather, he can't pawn it, sell it or melt it down. He can do only one thing; he must hold on to the ring until his daughter is old enough to wear it and then give it to her. Of course, he could frame it and put it on the wall until that day—that would not be a violation of the trust agreement. Thus, our happy dad has become the trustee, or the individual who keeps ownership of the trust property until the trust comes to its conclusion. In this case, that will be when the girl is old enough to wear the ring.

But hold on for a second; nobody asked the little girl if she wanted the ring in the first place—the decision was made without her. This is another important point; a trust can be set up without the agreement of the beneficiary, in this case the little girl. Only an agreement between the settlor and the trustee is needed to set up a trust for a beneficiary. This is very like the role of today's investor in an income trust. The investor is, much like the little girl, the beneficiary of the trust.

REASONS FOR SETTING UP A TRUST

A trust may be set up for personal reasons such as estate preservation or asset protection, or for business reasons. Income trusts are set up by corporations and businesses. But why? What are the advantages of setting them up and allowing the public to buy into them? One of the main reasons comes down to one of the two certainties in life—taxes.

Tax Mitigation

Under Canadian tax law, the general principle is that any profits a trust makes are not subject to taxation so long as those profits are distributed to the beneficiaries each year. The beneficiaries may well have to pay income tax on the moneys received based on their personal tax bracket, but the trust itself will not pay tax. This is in stark contrast to corporate taxation. A corporation has to pay income tax on any profit it makes before it can distribute the leftovers to its shareholders as dividends. These dividends are then taxed again at the personal level, though at a lower rate than regular income. The combined percentage of these two taxes is higher than the single income tax one would pay at the personal level as the beneficiary of a trust.

Let's look at a very simple example. Mr. Jones, a practising lawyer, lives in Ontario, and holds 100 percent of the shares of a public corporation that owns a number of apartment and office buildings. The company collects rent, and pays the expenses for running and maintaining the buildings. Mr. Jones' share of the profit is $800,000 a year. The company then pays about 36 percent of that $800,000 as combined federal and provincial taxes, or roughly $288,000. So when all is said and done, there is $512,000 profit left over to pay out to Mr. Jones as a dividend. Surprise, surprise—next April he has to pay about another 31 percent of tax on the dividend. Thus, another $158,720 is sent to Revenue Canada. From his initial share of the profit of $800,000, Mr. Jones is left with a measly $353,280.

Now let's see what would happen if those buildings were in a trust, with Mr. Jones as one of the beneficiaries. The rent will still be collected by the trust, and all expenses paid just as in the case of the corporation, so Mr. Jones' share of the profit is still $800,000 at the end of the year, and this entire amount is paid to him. As we discussed earlier, as long as the money is distributed to the beneficiary, no tax is payable by the trust.

However, our successful lawyer friend still has to pay income tax on the $800,000. Because he lives in Ontario, his combined federal and provincial tax rate is approximately 46.4 percent (his professional income already put him in the highest tax bracket), so he will send $371,200 to the government and end up with $428,800.

Let's compare this to our first example, where a corporation owned the buildings. The math is pretty simple. $428,000 – 353,000 = $75,520. That's a lot of money to give to the government if Mr. Jones doesn't have to. We firmly believe (and we are sure you will agree with us) that we could find better ways to spend our own money.

This tax advantage of trusts over corporations gave birth to the idea of income trusts, and we will examine these advantages in the next chapter. But for the moment, we need to understand one very important point: As long as a trust distributes all of its profits — after expenses—through the trust, it does not pay income tax on those profits. This is one of the fundamental reasons trusts are set up. Investors buy units in the trust, which act much like stocks (more on this later), and the investors in the units are paid distributions based on the cash flow from the company. As we will see later, there are a number of different ways in which this arrangement can work.

A Possible Downfall: Liability

As we discussed earlier, any type of asset or property can generally be placed into a trust. A business is an asset, for instance, as it is a going concern that hopefully creates a profit every year. With the preferential tax treatment for trusts, why do we still find most of the businesses operating under the corporate makeup? One issue is liability. Owners of corporations have limited liability while a trust beneficiary may not. Let's go back to Mr. Jones and see how this would affect his properties.

As Mr. Jones was a very successful individual, he and his family took five to six vacations a year; they avoided most of the popular holiday destinations and preferred unusual locations instead. During a particularly cold January, they decided to spend two weeks on the island of Mauritania, in a resort that catered to the rich and provided complete seclusion. There was no TV, radio, phone or Internet—just sunshine, the beach, great books, and unbelievable food.

Unbeknownst to Mr. Jones, two days into their vacation, Toronto, where his buildings were, was hit by one of the worst cold spells in history. The superintendent in one of his apartment buildings decided it was just too much for him and purchased a last-minute package to Cuba for a week at an all-inclusive resort. The next day he was gone. He tried to contact Mr. Jones to tell him of his decision—the vacation time was owed to him—but, of course, he could not get through. As a result, no one replaced him for that week.

The cold spell had been preceded by a stint of warm weather, and the resulting deep-freeze made the sidewalk in front of a particular building a skating rink. As there was no one to clear the ice of this busy area, over the next three days eight separate individuals fell and sustained numerous injuries. At the end of it all, the city had cleared the sidewalk, and sent a huge bill to Mr. Jones. As he could not be reached at his island paradise, Mr. Jones was surprised when he returned to find a class-action lawsuit filed on behalf of the eight victims by one of the sharpest litigators in town. The litigator was claiming damages in excess of $15,000,000, and should he succeed, that money would have to be paid.

Now, let's see what would happen to the $15 million in a case where the buildings were owned through a corporation, assuming that it has $1 million in insurance. A corporation is a legal entity that is created by a registration process, and, as such, is legally entitled to own property, run a business, etc. It can also be sued, as it would be in this case, and should the plaintiffs succeed, the company would have to pay the $15 million. The company would then sell all the buildings it owns along with any other assets for which it would receive, let's say, $9.5 million. This sum, plus the insurance proceeds of $1 million, would be paid out to the plaintiffs, and no more. The corporation would go bankrupt, and the remaining $4.5 million would never have to be paid, even though Mr. Jones, the sole shareholder, has lots of other assets. This is because the liability rests with the corporation, and does not include the shareholder. Once the corporation pays all it can, the story ends. True, Mr. Jones loses all of his buildings, but that is it—he pays no further damages, and keeps his own personal wealth.

Now let's see what would have happened if Mr. Jones had set up a trust to own his buildings, of which he was the sole beneficiary, and a third party, perhaps a friend, was the trustee. The sharp lawyer would have sued the trustee and the beneficiary as well, and *both* may have been held fully liable.

Let's assume that the trust was set up in such a way that the buildings can be sold, and the $9.5 million—plus the $1 million in insurance proceeds—paid out for the damages. That equals $10.5 million, the same as in the case of the corporate ownership. However, in this case, the remaining $4.5 million could still be owed by Mr. Jones personally. And because he owns all kinds of other assets—his big house, a large stock portfolio, a cottage up north, etc.—he would likely have had to liquidate some or all of these assets to pay the balance.

The big problem with the trust structure in this case is that the beneficiary may have *unlimited liability*. And as businesses can always run into unforeseen problems, and accidents can always happen, most business owners would rather take the less advantageous tax situation that comes with owning that business through a corporation, and enjoy the limited liability that a corporation provides, than set up a trust model.

The obvious question that comes to mind is, "Do I have unlimited liability as an investor in an income trust?" Don't worry; as you will see in the following chapters, this issue has been thoroughly addressed by some of the best legal minds in the country.

THE BASIC STRUCTURE OF AN INCOME TRUST

Before we get into the specifics of taxation, types of trusts, and more complex issues, we will give you an example of how the whole trust structure is set up.

Setting up a Trust Structure

Let's imagine that, through a wholly owned company (owned entirely by yourself), you own a rental property that is mortgage-free. Assume that it cost $250,000 to buy, and that municipal taxes are $2000 per year, and that utilities, maintenance, and other expenses are $8000 per year. Your company rents it out for $3000 per month, inclusive of utilities, for a total of $36,000 per year.

This means that the company's profit before income taxes is:

$36,000 (rent) − $8000 (utilities, etc.) − $2000 (municipal taxes) = $26,000 per year

If we assume that the company pays combined federal and provincial income tax of 40 percent, it will pay $10,400 in income tax on this $26,000, and net $15,600 per year after tax. It will pay you this in dividends, on which you will pay tax.

Step One: Add a Bank Mortgage

Now let's assume that there is a $50,000 bank mortgage on which the company is required to pay interest at 6 percent—or $3000 per year. Now, the company's profit before income taxes is:

$36,000 (rent) − $8000 (utilities, etc.) − $2000 (municipal taxes) −
$3000 (bank interest) = $23,000 per year

Again, if we assume that the company pays combined federal and provincial income tax at 40 percent, it will pay $9200 in income tax on this $23,000 and therefore net $13,800 per year after tax.

The reason for this is that, as long as the money borrowed is used to earn income, the mortgage interest costs are generally deductible against income for tax purposes, so the amount of tax payable is reduced.

Step 2: Add a Second Mortgage to Your Cousin Vincent

Now let's assume that, in addition to a $50,000 bank mortgage at 6 percent, the company has a second mortgage owing to your cousin Vincent, who lent the company money in the amount of $190,000 at 12 percent or $22,800 per year.

Now, the company's profit before income taxes is:

$36,000 (rent) − $8000 (utilities, etc.) − $2000 (municipal taxes) −
$3000 (bank interest) − $22,800 (interest to Vincent) = $200 per year

Again, if we assume that the company pays combined federal and provincial income tax at 40 percent, it will pay $80 in income tax on this $200 and net a mere $120 per year after tax! Wait a minute: Where is all the money going? It's going to your cousin Vincent, to the tune of $22,800 per year, and *he* is the one who has to pay tax on it.

Step 3: Vincent Becomes a Trust!

Now let's see what happens if we turn Vincent into a trust that doesn't pay taxes. Let's call it the Vincent Income Trust. Since as a trust, Vincent won't pay taxes and can live forever, it has avoided the two inescapables of death and taxes. Not bad!

The Vincent Income Trust has great financial statements. It owns a $190,000 second mortgage at 12 percent that, in good times, pays it $22,800 per year. Let's take it one step further and make the Vincent Income Trust the sole shareholder of your company, meaning that the Vincent Income Trust indirectly owns the rental property itself through the company, and directly owns the second mortgage.

Figure 1.1

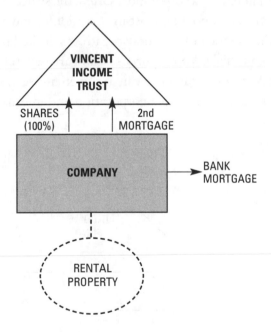

In this case, if the property appreciates in value, the Vincent Income Trust indirectly benefits, since it's the owner. If things go swimmingly, and you can raise the rent, then the company will make extra money, on which it will pay corporate income tax, and then pay dividends to the Vincent Income Trust.

If things go badly, of course, and the city raises taxes, or the house needs a new roof or furnace, or the bank won't renew the mortgage in three years or raises the rates, it will come out of the money that would otherwise have been interest on the second mortgage. In that case, the Vincent Income Trust will earn less.

OTHER STRUCTURES

Increasingly, income trusts are being structured using limited partnerships, rather than a corporation. Often, the structure involves the income fund on top, a holding trust in the middle, and a limited partnership carrying on the business underneath. As limited partnerships are pass-through vehicles for tax purposes, and are generally not subject to capital tax, these structures can be even more tax-efficient than the traditional model using a corporation and internal leverage.

Figure 1.2

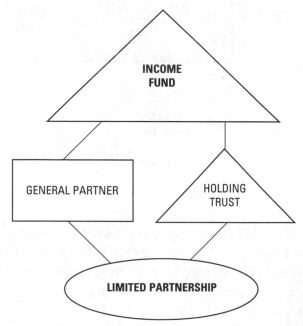

In the traditional model, if profits increase dramatically, corporate income tax may be payable on the increase. Also, capital tax, though apparently on the way out, applies to many corporations. As a result, some trusts are converting into the more tax-efficient structure. The limited liability protection available in a limited partnership is generally not as strong as that provided by a corporation, however.

THE ECONOMIC CLIMATE:
FUEL FOR THE RECENT BOOM

So what triggered the recent boom in income trusts? After all, back in the good old days of the stock market bubble, most of us hadn't even heard the term "income trusts." Didn't they exist back then? One of the first income trusts, as we know them today, was created in 1997 when oil company Norcen Energy Resources Ltd. hired Scotia Capital Inc. to sell a small stake in Iron Ore Co. of Canada. After some considerable financial engineering, the *Labrador Iron Ore Royalty Trust* was created and sold to retail investors. A few more followed, but there was really no large appetite at the time. After all, those were the days when you could make $50,000 a day by buying a dot-com stock at market open and selling it just before 4 p.m. on the same day—it was hard to compete with those kinds of returns. Even just dumping your money into an equity mutual fund could give you better than 10 percent yearly, not to mention the fact that the money you made on the increase in share prices was taxed at a much lower rate—that of capital gains—rather than the regular income tax paid on money coming in from a trust.

But all good things must to come to an end, and when the tech bubble burst around April of 2000, it was all downhill from there. Equity mutual funds could no longer make the same returns, and the exodus of capital began. Investors started pulling their money out of equities at an alarming rate, no longer having any faith that they would appreciate at the rates they did in the late 90s. The stock market sensed the unavoidable: that the economy was simply going to get worse. And it did. Public companies were making less money, and some of them started losing huge amounts quarter after quarter. To offset this effect, the U.S. Federal Reserve and the Bank of Canada started cutting interest rates, hoping to spruce up the failing economy.

Disillusioned with the declining markets, investors who were withdrawing money from mutual funds and selling their stock holdings were having an increasingly difficult time finding new homes for their money. Real estate was one bright spot, and certainly lots of money went into it. But owning a property is much more work than simply owning stocks or mutual funds—it has to be rented or leased, tenants will call you at 5 a.m. when the pipes freeze—should we go on? It is definitely not for everyone.

Putting money into a bank, GICs, or some sort of money market instrument seemed rather lame as well. Interest rates were declining, and by the time you paid tax on that income it didn't even cover inflation, let alone give you a decent return. The market was ready for a new instrument that could suck up all that money sitting on the sidelines.

The picture was not much rosier down on Bay Street. On the investment banking side of the street, the boys and girls had gotten used to making tons of money due to all the initial public offerings of stock (IPOs), and huge mergers and acquisitions that took place during the bubble years. That was no more. No mergers, no IPOs, no acquisitions, and thus, no fees. They needed something new, something that could generate those juicy fees again. They had to come up with something that the public *needed*. After all, there was an awful lot of money sitting out there, and they knew it.

Income trusts were the right solution. The Bay Street folks realized that the public wanted a return and that they were sick and tired of waiting for share prices to appreciate. They wanted cash, every month, month after month, at rates that even after paying tax would outpace inflation. So the financial advisors got busy, and started bringing more and more trust products to the market. They sold extremely well from the get-go, and continue to do so.

So now you have a basic idea of what trusts are, where they come from, and the advantages they can provide their beneficiaries. In the following chapters, we will examine all of the basics in greater detail, and look much more specifically at the different kinds of income trusts, and what to look for as an investor. This book has been designed for a wide audience, from small investors to business owners seeking to form their own trusts, so you can either read straight through, or skip to the section that you are most interested in. We will explore the nuts and bolts of Canadian income trusts. What are they? What are the types of income trusts? How are they and the investors in them taxed? Why do people invest in income trusts? What should you look for in an income trust? How can you assess the risks related to a particular income trust? How are income trusts created? What is a fund of funds?

Finally, we will look at what a business owner needs to know when considering converting his or her business to an income trust. At the end of the book, we provide a comprehensive list and description of current trusts available in the Canadian market.

You will see a lot of "may," "could potentially," "possibly," and other seemingly vague phrases throughout this book. There is a good reason for this: No investment is a sure thing, and as attractive as income trusts' returns look today, you will learn that they still, like any investment, are not without often substantial risks. We hope though, that by thoroughly describing what income trusts are, what types of them are out there, and how they are structured and work, you will gain the knowledge to prudently assess any investment decision you may make in income trusts.

The Different Types of Income Trusts

HOW DOES AN INCOME TRUST DIFFER FROM A REGULAR PUBLIC COMPANY?

To understand the different types of trusts, it is important to understand the differences between them and other investments. Units—the term used instead of shares in these vehicles—of an income trust have two distinct differences from common shares of a regular public company. These differences relate to, first, the amount of anticipated distributions, and second, their tax-effectiveness.

As we saw in our first simple example, first and most importantly, an income trust should distribute all or most of its available cash flow to investors on a regular, usually monthly, basis. This is very different from most Canadian public companies, which often distribute either none, or a small portion, of their available cash flow to shareholders as dividends. Cash flow is usually either reinvested in the business, or spent on acquisitions—sometimes with bad results if management makes poor decisions! An income trust, however, lets you make your own reinvestment or spending decisions, which also may be good or bad, by giving you the cash. Thus, as an investor, you can, unless there are unforeseen problems, anticipate receiving proportionately much more in the way of distributions from an income trust than from owning common shares of most ordinary Canadian public companies.

Second, and also key, is that an income trust is intended to be structured to either minimize or avoid the taxation of income that usually occurs at profitable companies. The main difference here is that public companies must pay income tax on their profits before distributing any excess to shareholders, who are then taxed again on that income. Since income trusts do not pay this first tax, distributions are generally higher than they would be if the income trust had to pay income tax on them first.

Thus, as a holder of income trust units, in addition to anticipating more substantial distributions than ordinary public companies, you should also anticipate that they will be increased, or juiced up, through tax planning at the income trust level.

In certain cases, distributions will also include a substantial return of capital component, which is not immediately taxable, thus providing another significant tax deferral advantage. We will discuss this in greater detail in Chapter 3.

THE TYPES OF INCOME TRUSTS

Income trusts can be broken down into five main categories. As we discussed before, almost any asset or property can be put into a trust, and so there are a number of industries which seek to adopt this model. Currently, the five main types of trusts are:

1. Business Trusts

2. Trademark Royalty Trusts

3. Oil and Gas Royalty Trusts

4. Real Estate Investment Trusts (REITs)

5. Funds of Income Funds

Business Trusts

This is the broadest category of income trusts, and one of the easiest to understand. As we have seen from our previous examples, a business can convert itself into a trust, realize significant savings on income tax, and distribute profits to its investors (the beneficiaries). The question is: Does any kind of business qualify to be part of an income trust? Theoretically, yes. But—and there is always a *but*—we know that the investors want a steady payout month after month, year after year. You have to remember that the only way the company can pay the interest on the loan it has with the trust is if it makes money. If it does not, then those payments will start dwindling. As any outstanding loans from banks usually have precedence (the trust loan is subordinated), they must be paid first before those interest payments can be made. We cannot emphasize this enough: Just as with public shares, if the company starts making less money, it will pay out less in distributions.

Here are some of the criteria that can make a business a strong candidate for the business trust model:

A. It has to make money. The reason for this, and for any public company, is that no income for the company means no distributions to the unit holders.

B. It needs a track record. As investors expect to get paid year after year, a business that can demonstrate years of consistent profit or cash flow behind it will be more likely to continue that performance. The best types of candidates are ones that are not unduly affected by economic cycles. Coffee companies, for instance, can still sell a cup of java in an economic downturn. By contrast, a high-end winery can be adversely affected by a slump.

People will generally spend less on commodities like fine wine in a down market.

C. The business must be relatively well established. As all or most of the cash flow is designed to be taken out of the company and distributed to the unit holders, there is really no money left to invest in new infrastructure for growth. Some of the cash flow can also be held back to cover so-called maintenance capital expenditures, in order to maintain things much as they are.

Business trusts are the new kid on the block. They have really come into their own in the 2000s. In theory, just about any stable, mature, cash-generating business may be a suitable candidate for a business trust, and a vast number have emerged, including in the areas of telephone directories, telephone companies, power generation, manufacturing, customs brokerage, entertainment, fisheries, and transportation. Not all of the new business trusts that have emerged have proved to be ideal income trusts, although many have been very good performers to date. Things to watch out for are trusts with major capital expenditure needs, trusts that pay out over 100 percent of their available cash (this is not sustainable), and trusts that use bank loans to keep their distributions level, among others.

Trademark Royalty Trusts

Trademark royalty trusts are a little different than regular business trusts, since instead of buying the whole business, you are in effect just buying the right to a portion of its cash flow. They do start out the same way. A trust is created, and money is raised from the unit holders. It's what comes after that is dissimilar.

The difference is that the trust does not lend money to the company, but rather it buys the company's trademark, and licenses it back for a fee on each product sold. Sound complicated? It's not really. Let's look at a real-life example: the A&W root beer and hamburger chain.

The company owns the name A&W, and it is trademarked. This means that no one can use it without the company's permission. That permission is not given for free— you have to pay a fee for the right to use the trademark, and even then, only in specific situations. This is one of the rights you get if you buy a franchise.

In the case of A&W, the corporation sells franchises to business people for a fee, who then run the restaurants. Every month, each restaurant pays a royalty for every burger, root beer, and anything else the restaurant sells. This percentage of the franchisees' sales represents the revenue for the corporation. Once the franchises pay this percentage and all other costs, they should end up with their own profit.

By buying the trademark, the trust can then license it back to head office in much the same way as head office then sub-licenses it to the franchisees. For example, if A&W head office collects—let's say—6 percent royalties on all sales from the individual restaurants, it will pay 3 percent royalties to the trust for licensing the name. The remaining 3 percent will pay for A&W's office overhead and all other expenses. The trust will then distribute any income to the unit holders, usually on a monthly basis. If A&W opens new restaurants, the trust pays 92.5 percent of the expected revenue stream from the royalty, so it gets a modest discount on the expected value of new restaurant openings.

So what kinds of businesses have potential for this trademark structure? The number one consideration is the underlying business model. Does it have longevity; is it recession proof? Will it still provide royalties if there is an economic downturn? If the answers are yes to all of these, this is a great model. In the case of A&W, you might ask yourself whether the latest trend towards health food might hurt the business, for instance.

Oil and Gas Royalty Trusts

This is the second oldest form of income trust, and differs from others in exactly what is done with the money that is raised from the selling of units. To understand this, let's examine how oil and gas

companies earn money. The business can be divided into two segments, *exploration* and *production*. Exploration is the process that finds
new wells from which the company can draw the gas or oil. Production is the process of selling the oil or gas.

Once a new well is found, measurements are made of how much
oil or gas is there (how much it will produce before it runs dry). The
richer the well, the more money it will make for the company. Let's
say a gas company has a couple of dozen wells, and during the lifecycle of those wells they estimate that they can extract about 200 million cubic feet of gas. This is considered the *inventory* of the company.
If, during the production phase of these wells, the company does
not find new wells through exploration, it will eventually run out of
gas to sell, as all the wells will be empty. So it is paramount that part
of the company's revenue goes towards financing exploration, to find
new inventory. Exploration is a rather unpredictable undertaking,
however. Sometimes months or even years go by before a new, and
viable, resource can be found—and in some cases new inventory is
never found at all! Long periods of time with no cash flow are not
the kind of activity that fits into the business model of a trust. On
the other hand, the production side of the business has a predictable,
steady cash flow, with controlled expenses—not bad for a trust.

With that in mind, oil and gas trusts work like this: The trust
acquires the oil or gas in the ground from the company, up front,
and usually at discounted prices. Then, as production proceeds the
profits are paid to the trust and distributed to the unit holders. Prior
to closing the deal (converting into a trust), the oil or gas company
will often spin off the exploration business into a different company,
that will be independently operated— another story altogether. There
are thus two main considerations here that we have to look out for:
commodity prices and inventories in the ground.

Profits and payouts can be greatly affected by changing oil and
gas prices. Weather affects gas prices, while geopolitical changes can
alter the price of oil and gas. A cold winter can push gas prices up,

while a mild one can make them drop like a stone. A war in the Middle East may make oil prices climb through the roof, or a weak U.S. economy paired with a strong dollar can make them drop. That is why this sector of income trusts is the most volatile, and due to this volatility generally offers the best yield on your investment. Volatility always means risk, and investors want higher returns for that risk.

The second consideration is more serious. Since the trust buys the inventory in the ground, there is a finite life expectancy for the revenue stream, except in the case of the oil sands trust which has enormous reserves. This differs greatly compared to, for example, a trademark royalty trust, where as long as there is a demand for the underlying product or service, the unit holders will likely get paid. With oil and gas, the only way the revenue stream can be maintained is if the company finds new inventory, and as it is not in the exploration business any more (it "spun off" that business, remember?), the only thing it can do is to buy other companies or wells that have existing inventory. But since most, if not all, of the profits are distributed to unit holders, the only way to finance the purchases is by selling more units or taking out a loan. In an increasing commodity price situation such as we have experienced in the early 2000s, that can easily be done. Should commodity prices start to decline, however, this may be a more difficult task to execute and the value of the oil and gas trusts may decline significantly.

As well, oil and gas trusts can take the form of either a business trust by using a loan, or a royalty trust in which the trust holds royalty in an underlying oil and gas well.

Real Estate Investment Trusts (REITs)

You have probably heard of these. One of the oldest forms of income trust in Canada is the real estate investment trust. REITs have been around for about two decades, and are designed to allow investors to have an interest in a diversified package of income-producing real estate without the headaches of managing the property themselves. REITs can specialize in office buildings, shopping centres, or residential apartment buildings, among other sectors. In most cases, the managers of the REIT will acquire, dispose of, and manage properties on behalf of investors; of course, they are compensated—sometimes very well. Most of the rental income (the cash flow), after expenses, will usually be distributed to unit holders, and much of the distributions may be in the form of a return of capital for tax purposes, thus avoiding immediate tax. It will have to be paid ultimately— you can't avoid the taxman, you can just put him off.

The REIT will be responsible for insuring its properties, paying property taxes, getting and keeping tenants, maintaining the properties, ensuring that utility bills are paid, and all the myriad other things that come from owning an income-producing property— including clearing snow in the winter! The REIT may contract some or all of these services out to others, but the REIT, and not the unit holder, will have to deal with them. The trust will generally own a portfolio of properties, thus providing the benefits of diversification. In other words, if one building falls on hard times, hopefully the others will not. It may have buildings located in just one town, or in many towns, which provides further diversification benefits in case one area is depressed economically.

As with all investments, REITs are not without their potential downsides. Office and commercial properties can be greatly affected by the state of the economy. Should a recession hit, and vacancy rates climb, there may not be enough income left to pay unit holders. As well, with residential properties, low interest rates can cause problems, because home ownership may become more attractive than renting. The same is true for government regulation such as rent control, which can freeze or even reduce income from residential properties.

Funds of Income Funds

For investors who like the concept of income trusts, but don't want to have to go through the process of selecting which ones to invest in, there are funds of income funds that focus on the income trust sector. In return for a management fee, you can leave the selection process to someone else, and end up with a more diversified and professionally managed portfolio of income funds. In a way, these are similar to mutual funds.

It works like this: If you have a limited amount of money to invest, you will not be able to buy units in more than maybe one or two income trusts. This is not diversification, and you are subject to the fortunes or misfortunes of only one or two trusts and their underlying businesses. Should one of them go bad, it could drastically affect your investment. But if, on the other hand, you put the same amount of money into 30, 40, or 50 different income trusts, you are suddenly diversified. This can be done by buying units in a fund of funds, which spreads your money over a wide range of income trusts. By buying these units, you are no longer subject to the fortunes of one or two companies or economic sectors. Now, you are relying on the power of a professionally managed investment vehicle, which is not only diversified, but has managers who should be constantly monitoring the trusts, and who will, hopefully, dump the potentially bad ones before they can really hurt your investment, or avoid them in the first place. Since the fund of funds will likely hold a large number of trust units of income funds with underlying businesses operating in a variety of different industries, your units in that fund mean that you are investing in a wide range of businesses. The advantage of diversifying your investment is that you are not putting all of your eggs in one basket. The concept is that if one or more of the income funds or other securities in the investment portfolio were to perform badly at a given time, the losses can be offset, or more than offset, by gains in other funds or securities in the portfolio that are doing well in the same time period.

For example, if a fund holds units in both a processed-meat based fund, as well as a real estate investment fund, the investor could see losses due to the bovine spongiform encephalopathy (BSE, or mad cow disease) scare on one side, but benefit from continued low interest rates and demand from the other fund at the same time.

It is unlikely that all of the underlying components of the investment portfolio will perform badly at the same time. Investing in a fund of funds is therefore theoretically a safer bet because you won't risk losing your entire investment in one underlying income fund should that income fund perform badly. On the other hand, you have also reduced the gains that would come from a star performer—large profits from a single REIT investment will be reduced by the losses from the processed meat trust, for instance.

Flexibility

Funds of funds are flexible in that they can be designed to invest in the income funds in a particular category, or they can be structured to hold the securities of several income funds in a number of different categories. Because income funds come in many different varieties such as REITs, Oil and Gas, Power Generation, etc., it is possible, through a fund of funds, to get exposure to many sectors of the income trust universe for less of an investment than would be required for you to invest in each one of these separately yourself.

Depending on the terms of the declaration of trust, a fund of funds may also have more than one type of security. The option of setting up different classes of securities —debt instruments as well as equity units can be used—provides a fund of funds with the flexibility of offering its unit holders different tax treatment depending on the units acquired.

Credit facilities may also be used to enhance returns by using leverage, giving further flexibility to the fund of funds.

Management by a Professional Investment Manager

Another advantage to investing in a fund of funds is the reassurance that the investments made will likely be carefully selected by a professional investment manager. Having someone with the time and expertise to drill down into the details of individual income funds and select the best ones is a definite advantage, and is a more hands-off type of investing. Some people like doing their own due diligence, but for those who don't and would rather leave things up to a pro, a fund of funds may be the way to go.

Management Fees

One downside of the fund of funds structure is fees. In return for the benefits of professional management and diversification, purchasers of funds of funds must also indirectly bear the cost of paying the fund manager to manage the investment portfolio. There is also the ongoing cost of operating and administering the whole thing. These expenses are usually paid before any distributions are made to the unit holders of the fund of funds.

Fluctuations in Value of the Underlying Income Funds and Distributions

The value of the units of a fund of funds will vary according to the performance of the underlying income funds or other securities. The amount of distributions available for payment to unit holders of the fund of funds depends directly on the amount of distributions paid by the underlying income funds or other securities included in the portfolio.

Composition of the Investment Portfolio

The performance of a fund of funds will vary depending on the make-up of its investment portfolio. The composition of the portfolio may vary widely from time to time, and may also at times be concentrated in a certain type of security, commodity, or industry, resulting in the portfolio being more or less diversified than an investor anticipated. More or less diversification could translate into more or less cash available for distribution to unit holders of the fund of funds, depending on performance, and could also increase or decrease the amount of associated risk.

Alternative Approaches to Asset Diversification

Some funds of funds, often called growth and income funds, have taken a different approach to further diversify their assets. The approach involves permitting the investment manager of the fund to invest in different classes of assets such as common shares, dividend-paying shares, other closed-end income funds, or high-yield debt, as well as income funds. By more widely diversifying investments in this manner, unit holders may benefit from capital appreciation as well as stable or increased distributions.

Split Share Funds of Funds

Split share funds of funds have all the characteristics of a typical fund of funds in that they hold the securities of other income funds and are managed by a fund manager. However, instead of offering one class of units to the public, split share funds of funds offer two or more classes. A recent example of a split share fund of funds is the Strata Income Fund, which completed a public offering on December 23, 2003. Under the IPO, Strata offered two classes of units to the public: units with a fixed rate of return, and units that do not have a fixed rate of return.

One of the main advantages of investing in a split share income fund is the ability to invest in one or more types of securities of the same fund, each of which may be subject to different tax treatment. Using this concept, you can determine what type of tax treatment would best complement the investments you already hold, and select the type and quantity of securities that fit your mould. Often, split share funds of funds have a pre-set portfolio of underlying investments rather than being actively managed.

Equal Weight Funds of Funds

Another type of fund of funds is an equal weight fund of funds. This type of income fund also has the typical characteristics of a fund of funds. However, it is considered to be a well-diversified fund that invests in various income funds across various industries. The strategy is to invest the same amount of money in each and every income fund it purchases. The theory behind this is that the poor performance by one income fund will be offset by a strong performance from the other income funds in the portfolio, especially since the amount invested will be, at least initially, equal across all the funds.

Although the amount initially invested in each income fund is equal at the outset, over time, as the value of the securities of each income fund fluctuates, the value of the amount of money invested in each income fund will also fluctuate. At regular intervals, usually once a year, the fund manager may re-balance the investments in the fund to make sure that the value invested in each of the income funds is equal.

A recent example of an equal weight income fund is the Brompton Equal Weight Income Fund, which made an IPO of its units on June 25, 2003.

RISKS

Before we move on to a more detailed analysis of income trusts, there is one important thing to remember. While they are often perceived to be like a very high-yielding government bond, the distributions paid out (generally monthly) on income funds are generally far less secure. Income fund investments have a risk profile that is similar to that of equities. Distributions can go up or down, and are by no means certain. Similarly, the price of the units themselves can go up or down based on many factors, including distribution levels, interest rates, and issues at particular trusts.

Tax Matters

INTRODUCTION

We have discussed the fact that the Canadian tax system plays a vital role in the existence and popularity of income trusts. For every dollar of income earned by a Canadian public corporation, it pays tax on that income of approximately 35 cents, depending on the type of income and the province in which it is earned. When the corporation distributes as dividends the 65 cents it has left to its shareholders, they also pay tax on those dividends. While there is something called the *dividend tax credit* that gives the shareholder some relief, this credit is not equal to all of the tax paid by the corporation, and so the shareholders still pay about another 20 cents of tax on the dividend. This leaves the shareholders with 45 cents after tax, so that the total tax paid on the original dollar is about 55 cents. If the shareholders had earned the dollar of income directly, they would pay about 45 cents of tax, leaving 55 cents after tax or approximately 10 cents more than where the income was earned through a corporation.

Obviously, if this excess tax could be eliminated, the value of the shareholder's interest in the corporation could be increased significantly. So how can the corporate tax be eliminated? As we have seen, one way is to eliminate the corporation from the equation completely and use a trust to carry on the business. This is because under the Canadian tax system, trusts are essentially *not taxable*. Instead, the unit holders of the trust pay tax on the income of the trust as if they earn the income *directly*. So, if we converted public corporations to trusts, we would eliminate that extra level of tax. This does not have the benefit of limited liability as does a corporation in case of trouble (remember Mr. Jones, from Chapter 1?), the considerable savings are very attractive.

There are other tax issues involved if we try to operate publicly owned businesses through trusts, however, and these are important to understand as an investor. Many Canadian stocks are owned by registered retirement savings plans (RRSPs) as well as other deferred plans and Canadian pension plans. In order to be a suitable investment for these plans, an interest in a public entity must be a qualified investment and not foreign property. Under the Canadian tax system, RRSPs and other deferred income plans may only invest in securities that are defined as qualified investments. In addition, such plans and pension plans are limited in the amount of foreign property that they can own, so it is not desirable for such plans to invest in a partnership or trust that carries on business in Canada when the interest in that partnership or trust is foreign property.

In order to be a qualified investment that is not foreign property the trust must qualify as a mutual fund trust for tax purposes. To qualify, the trust cannot carry on a business *directly*. Rather, the trust can only own shares or debt of a corporation that operates a business. This satisfies the tax act's stipulations, and allows income trusts to be eligible for RRSP and other deferred income plans.

You should now ask, "But I thought the goal was to eliminate the corporation. If we have a corporation back in the structure, how do we avoid the corporate level tax?" The answer to this question is leverage, or the degree to which a business or investor utilizes borrowed money (its debt).

DEBT AND EQUITY

Debt is generally understood to mean a liability or obligation to pay money or something else of value to another person. Debt can be long term, where the amount of the debt outstanding does not need to be repaid for a long period of time, generally over a year or more, or debt can be short term, where it must be repaid in less than a year's time.

Equity is a more difficult term to define, as it can have slightly different meanings in different contexts. Generally, it refers to an ownership interest. It can also sometimes refer to a shareholder's ownership interest in a corporation in the form of shares of the corporation. In a real estate context, however, as discussed in this chapter, equity in a piece of real estate usually refers to the difference between the fair market value of the property (what it is worth on the market) and the amount of debt (possibly in the form of a mortgage) that the owner owes on the property at a given time. If, for instance, you own a $250,000 home, but still owe, say, $175,000 on the mortgage, your equity would be in the $75,000 range.

In the case of an income trust, its equity owners are its unit holders, and the trust usually does not itself have debt outstanding. In turn, the income trust is usually both an equity holder and a debt holder in the underlying business.

FINANCIAL LEVERAGE

Financial analysts often refer to debt as leverage, which may seem a little odd. The reason for this is that financial leverage enables you to benefit, at greater risk, however, to a greater extent from increases in the underlying value of property.

Sound complicated? It's not. Imagine that you only have $10 in the bank. If you invest that $10 in something that will give you a 20 percent return, you will make $2. That's the best you can do. However, if you *borrow* $90, and invest it and your $10 in the same instrument, you will make $20 ($120 − $90 [minus your original $10] = $20 before interest). You have just doubled your original $10! The leverage can magnify your gains by *10 times*.

Figure 3.1

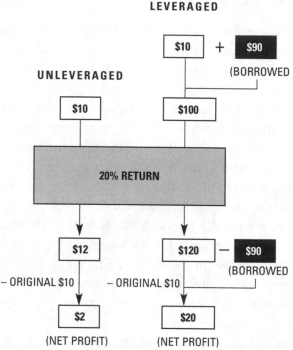

Let's use another simple example. If a property is purchased for $250,000 without any debt, and goes up in value to $350,000, you have made $100,000, or 40 percent, pre-tax, of your initial $250,000 investment.

On the other hand, if it was funded half with *debt*, then your initial equity investment of $125,000 has now turned into a profit of 80 percent! You have still only made $100,000, but the value of your original investment has increased by a greater amount. Assuming that you had the same $250,000 to invest, and could borrow another $250,000, you could buy two similar properties. If they both went up in value, then before interest cost the overall increase is $200,000, or 80 percent of your $250,000 investment.

Figure 3.2

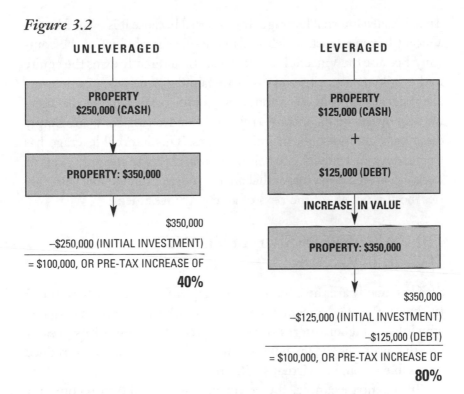

If it sounds too good to be true, it is! The downside of leverage is risk. If a $250,000 property funded without debt loses $100,000 in value, you have lost $100,000 or 40 percent of your original value. If two $250,000 properties funded half with debt go down $100,000 each in value, you must still repay the debt in full, and so your original $250,000 investment is now worth only $50,000, for a loss of 80 percent before interest. The lender gets his loan amount back, and your equity is magnified by the loan so that both gains and losses are greater. The debt levers your equity investment, allowing a smaller amount of equity to produce both greater overall returns or losses.

INTERNAL LEVERAGE

Let's go back to our cousin Vincent, from Chapter 1. The leverage represented by the second mortgage owned by the Vincent Income

Trust is called internal leverage. It is internal because it is owned by the Vincent Income Trust, which is also the sole shareholder of the company. Because the Vincent Income Trust also indirectly owns the equity in the building, its gains and losses remain the same—you can't leverage yourself with your own money! So, for financial purposes the internal debt owned by the income trust in the underlying company simply disappears, and does not magnify returns. This internal leverage has tremendous tax benefits (see below), but no ability to magnify gains or losses. However, don't forget that an investment in an income trust carries most, if not all, of the risks of an equity investment!

THE TAX BENEFITS OF LEVERAGE TO THE INVESTOR

So what exactly are the benefits of leverage for an income trust then? In the case of the Vincent Income Trust, it's the second mortgage, which has a higher interest rate (12 percent) because of its greater risk that provides the tax benefits. It enables the company to reduce its taxable income to virtually nil. How?

In our first example, the company paid $10,400 in income tax and netted $15,600 per year after tax, and your cousin Vincent got nothing. In the last example, the company paid $80 in income tax and netted $120 per year after tax, and the Vincent Income Trust earned $22,800 tax-free per year. The cash distributable to beneficiaries in the company or in the trust has gone up by an amazing 46 percent, from $15,600 to $22,800!

Now as we know, one of the quid pro quos is that to stay tax-free, the Vincent Income Trust must distribute all of its income each year. Again, this is a very important thing to remember. If you were to own all the units in the Vincent Income Trust, it would distribute all of the $22,800 to you. These distributions keep the nature of the income as ordinary income for tax purposes, and not dividends. Dividends can provide an additional tax credit to the recipient.

In this case, if you pay tax at a combined federal/provincial rate of 40 percent on your $22,800, you would pay $9,120 as tax, and you would net $13,680 after that. That is less tax than both you and the company would pay without the second mortgage. That's the first tax advantage. And here's an extra benefit—if you hold your interest in the Vincent Income Trust in your RRSP, *then all of the money will go in on a tax-deferred basis*. So, it may be more beneficial from an income perspective to hold units of the Vincent Income Trust inside your RRSP or other deferred plan rather than outside them.

These tax benefits are one factor that has helped drive up the price of income trusts relative to corporations. In fact, immediately following the conversion of a corporation into an income trust, shares in that company tend to go up by a substantial amount, often 20–30 percent. Sometimes, even saying you are *thinking* about such a conversion in public can lead to an increase, as CI Fund Management and Manitoba Tel have shown. Immediately after the proposal to convert Manitoba Tel into an income trust was tabled, the stock price went from $45.23 to $50.61 in only six trading days.

RETURN OF CAPITAL AND OTHER TAX NUANCES

Another tax advantage that income trusts have over corporations is their ability to pass through certain payments having the same tax character as the payments received by the trust—capital gains as capital gains, for instance, which are taxed at a lower rate than regular income. In addition, if an income trust is a REIT and holds property that is benefiting from capital cost allowance (CCA—a form of depreciation used for income tax purposes), then it can essentially pass the benefit of that CCA through to its unit holders.

When you buy a building, the value of the structure can depreciate over time, usually about 50 years. So if you pay $10 million for an office building and the land value accounted for $4 million of this, you could theoretically have a maximum depreciation of $6 million, should the building be worth nothing. Since depreciation is a non-cash expense for tax purposes, the trust will have that cash in its pocket. This money can be distributed to the unit holders, who also would not have to pay tax on it.

The result is that, even if they are taxable, the unit holders receive payment as a return of capital and thus pay no immediate tax on that portion. Rather, the amount of the payment is deducted from the cost basis of their units for tax purposes, meaning that if and when they sell their units they will have a greater capital gain. The neat thing about this is that what would otherwise be current income is effectively being both deferred and ultimately converted into a capital gain, which is taxed at a reduced rate. This double benefit of both capital gains treatment and deferral makes REITs quite attractive to investors with large tax burdens.

Similarly, certain oil and gas royalty trusts benefit from other deductions that allow a portion of their distributions to be treated as a return of capital. Most business trusts, on the other hand, have relatively limited return of capital treatment, and thus generate primarily income rather than capital payments.

IS THERE AN EFFECT ON OVERALL GOVERNMENT TAX REVENUES?

You may also have heard some concerns recently about income trusts and government tax revenues. It seems reasonable to think that because people who invest in income trusts are not paying as much income tax— and the industry is worth over $90 billion to date— maybe the government is making less money. The fact is, though, that the effect of income trusts on overall Canadian government tax revenues is difficult to quantify. Obviously, corporate income taxes are reduced substantially when a corporation converts into an income trust. However, these taxes and maybe more, due to the conversion of dividends into ordinary income and the loss of the associated dividend tax credits, are paid in turn by the unit holders, unless they are tax-exempt. So one of the main issues is how much of the money in income trusts is coming from tax-exempt entities such as RRSPs, RRIFs, registered pension plans, and the like, and being deferred for lengthy periods.

Another factor, however, is that even the conversion transactions themselves are often taxable to shareholders, which increases the current tax owing. As well, the improving quality and size of the companies that are becoming income trusts, for example, the Yellow Pages™ Income Fund, as well as the recent passage of limited liability legislation in Alberta in 2004 and Québec several years ago, and the expected passage of similar legislation in Ontario shortly, are seen as likely to encourage more institutional investors. Pension funds, for instance, have been holding back on income trust investments, in part out of liability concerns—again, remember Mr. Jones from Chapter 1. The strengthening of underlying businesses in income trusts will likely lead to more institutional involvement and perhaps an increased overall current drain on tax coffers.

As a result, in the 2004 budget, the Canadian government announced that pension fund investment in business trusts, but not REITs or resource royalty trusts, would be capped. If this change were enacted, it could make larger conversions of existing public companies into income trusts more difficult. However, in the face of substantial opposition from pension funds, who argued that this change created an unlevel playing field and that pensioners would be harmed, this proposal was put on hold during the 2004 federal election. The federal government is now contemplating what to do, but is still suggesting that something must be done to curb the possibility of substantial pension fund involvement in the income trust sector.

And what about provincial governments? All the potential benefits from turning the LCBO in Ontario into a trust are certainly attractive, but there are some concerns here, especially for smaller provinces. If a major publicly traded company in a smaller province was to become an income trust, and most of the investors in it were based in the larger provinces, then the corporate tax paid by the company to the home province would be replaced by tax paid by unit holders to the larger provinces. This could be potentially harmful to the treasuries of the smaller provinces. In the future, if this becomes an issue, we could at some point see government action to further limit the attractiveness of income trusts from a tax perspective.

However, prior to the 2004 budget, the Canadian government had not discouraged income trusts. In fact, for 2001 and 2002, they were almost the only deals that kept Bay Street going. More recently, income trust limited liability legislation in Ontario and Alberta has been supportive of income trusts. The future remains to be seen, however.

IDSs, IPSs AND OTHER PRODUCTS

Other products, similar in some ways to income trusts, have also been offered, including "income deposit securities" (or "IDSs", which were developed primarily by CIBC World Markets) and "income participating securities" (or "IPSs", which were first offered by BMO Nesbitt Burns). An example of an IDS is Volume Services America, and an example of an IPS is Medical Discoveries. In October, 2004, B&G Foods Holdings Corp. completed a similar offering of about U.S. $260 million of "enhanced income securities", or EISs. These structures tend not to use trusts on top, but rather to "paper-clip" together a share and a debt instrument, so that investors buy a "unit" consisting of two securities (a share and a subordinated note) that can be, although will generally not be, separated. The underlying businesses of these types of products tend to be U.S.-based businesses, with the result that there are more complex tax considerations. For example, in the U.S., among other things, it is possible for the Internal Revenue Service to treat what seems to be debt as equity, thus disallowing an interest deduction and exposing the underlying business to much more tax than was anticipated. Advance tax rulings are generally not obtained and, although it may be unlikely, if such a tax reassessment were to occur and be upheld, there could as a result be significantly lower distributions, and U.S. withholding taxes may also apply, among other adverse effects. The tax disclosure in prospectuses relating to these sorts of transactions should be reviewed by investors with particular care. Note that usual "will" tax disclosure may be replaced by "should", which is a lower level of comfort from the tax experts.

How to Choose an Income Trust

FIRST AND FOREMOST: DUE DILIGENCE

Investigate before you buy—makes perfect sense, doesn't it? We'd like to relate a true-to-life story for you to drive the concept home. It involves an actual acquaintance—we'll call him Mr. Smith.

One day Mr. Smith and his wife realized they needed a new dishwasher. Because they were careful individuals when it came to spending their money, on the following Saturday they visited three different stores to compare brands and prices. Mr. Smith spent considerable time the following week checking out the different manufacturers' websites to examine the technical attributes of each model in great detail. Finally, a week later they bought one of the dishwasher models for $489.95. The plumber charged a further $50 to install it. The Smiths were very pleased, knowing that by doing their homework, they got the best possible deal.

Three weeks later Mr. Smith received a call from his broker with great news. He had managed to get a small allocation of a hot IPO that was expected to make big money when it started trading.

The broker had a quota and received only 5000 shares. Since Mr. Smith was one of his best customers, he was willing to give him 1500. The rest he wanted to allocate to some of his other customers. The broker explained that the price would be around $18–20, and was going to be oversubscribed so there was a chance that they may even cut his allotment back, meaning that the 1500 could become 1200.

Our friend recognized what he thought was a good deal and jumped forward with both feet. Not only did he take the 1500, but also persuaded the broker to give him another 200. As it turned out, the IPO was not oversubscribed and Mr. Smith got all of his 1700 shares, priced at $18, costing him a total of $30,600.

Unfortunately, when the shares hit the market, the price dropped 70 cents on the first day and the decline continued in the weeks ahead. The stock finally settled around the $15 mark and stayed there for a long time, until Mr. Smith finally dumped the 1700 shares after two years for $16.80, losing a total of $2040, not to mention the opportunity cost of having $30,000 tied up in something that didn't give any return.

The question here is how can someone spend so much time investigating a $500 purchase and then put $30,000 into a stock he had never heard of without even thinking about it? It doesn't seem to make any sense. You are right to think so, but unfortunately, we have seen many similar cases. This is why—probably to your irritation—we constantly preach about *due diligence*. And not just with income trusts. Any kind of financial instrument you are thinking of putting your money into should be investigated *thoroughly*. After all it's *your* money and nobody will watch out for it as well as you! This book will help guide you in practising due diligence in evaluating income trusts.

THE STAGES OF YOUR INVESTMENT LIFE

Before we begin looking at how to assess an income trust, it is important to evaluate your own investment criteria—why, in this world of literally hundreds of investment products, would you want to put your money into an income trust? This depends partly on where you are in your investment lifecycle. As we travel through life, from the first dollar we save to the last one we spend, our investment objectives can change considerably. For instance, there is nothing further from the mind of an average 21-year-old than his or her retirement, and even further than that is the concept of saving for it. Certainly there can be exceptions, but for the majority this is the rule.

So let's look at the different stages of this cycle and their corresponding investment goals. Again, these stages are not meant to describe everybody, but more to represent how a group of individuals tends to behave, based on historical trends. Our investment objectives change as we pass different milestones in our lives. Generally speaking, these milestones are represented by the following:

Graduation

Getting Married

Kid(s) Arrive(s)

Kid(s) Leave(s) Home

Retirement

Graduation

Very few people are able to save enough money prior to graduation to invest in anything at all. After all, if you have anything left over from paying your tuition and general living expenses, there are an awful lot of other areas where that money can be spent. Liquid assets, the type they serve at the local pub, are more likely to interest this age bracket than investments. Following graduation comes the first job, and although the pubs still may seem as attractive as before, there might be money left over to do something with. If there is, this is the time when most people are willing to take risks. At this stage, people often do not look for a safe bank deposit, but rather a one-time home-run investment in a junior mining company or the newest technology play. Retirement seems so far away and life has so much to offer that income and safety are not real considerations for them. Young adults want gain, and lots of it, *fast*. They are often active traders, who try to carve out a large chunk of profit from the market with limited funds.

Getting Married

Once the wedding bells ring, the local pub may not be as attractive, and thoughts turn more to saving for a house and starting a family. Saving money for a down payment while taking high risks with your funds is not only dangerous for your future, but could even be dangerous for the well-being of the marriage itself! Rather, your money must go into something relatively safe, generally a high-interest savings account or similar instrument, where it can be easily accessed as soon as the right opportunity comes along.

Kid(s) Arrive(s)

Kids, mortgage payments, credit card payments, day care and activity costs, educational costs, home repairs, taxes—should we continue? Can anyone save and invest at this point? Fortunately, and hopefully, things usually improve. Equity increases in your home, promotions bring in more income, and suddenly there is money to be invested. And then it hits you: one day you'll retire and will need money. So you start contributing to an RRSP. However, as you still have many years to go, there is time to be a little more aggressive. Most people in this situation will play the market a bit, by looking into higher-risk, higher-return investment vehicles. This is the second major group of active traders.

Kid(s) Leave(s) Home

After the kids leave home, you may become one of the empty nesters. You are still working, and the house is paid off, and can be sold to buy a condo or a smaller retirement home. This brings in excess cash that can be invested. Retirement is getting ever closer though, so it is important to be more conservative and build up that nest egg, hopefully your income is larger than what is required to maintain your lifestyle. Saving becomes much easier in the years leading up to 65, and if the money is well invested, it can grow.

Retirement

Finally, it happens. You have retired. Golf everyday? Hmmm ... Your nest egg has to support your lifestyle for the coming years of well-earned rest and relaxation. Income becomes very important at this point, and capital gains much less so. The larger the percentage of return on your portfolio, the better you can enjoy the so-called golden years.

The above descriptions are generalizations based on the Canadian population, and may not reflect your position as an individual. So where do income trusts fit into these life stages? Currently, Canada's largest demographic segment is the baby boomers. They are, at the time of writing this book, between the ages of 40 to 55, placing them somewhere into the mid-to-later cycles of raising kids or kids leaving home. They are still raising their children, having had them later in life than their parents did for the most part, and are looking forward to at least another 10 years of productive working. You would think that this would make them pass over the steady, relatively reliable cash flow that income trusts provide in favour of growing their nest egg. However, something happened in the late

1990s that made them very leery of portfolio growth—the tech stock/dot-com bubble.

Many of the boomers in the late 1990s and early 2000s were planning to retire at 55, not build a nest egg, because they were expecting to be, or on paper anyway already were, filthy rich because of an investment in a high-flying dot-com company or a mutual fund that was returning 50 percent a year. They thought it would never end. Sadly, they were terribly mistaken. Now we all know that bubbles eventually burst. Investments tanked, portfolios were shredded, and the boomers started frantically pulling billions out of their mutual funds, whose returns had dwindled into the low single digits (or less) in many cases. As a result, this segment is very gun shy, and the last thing they want is a repeat of losses. Hoping for the big payday is no longer attractive, and the boomers have opted for steady, above-average returns with as little perceived risk as possible. Enter the income trust, whose popularity has been fuelled by this large demographic and their experiences.

Regardless of where you are in your life cycle, if you want a steady payout on your investment, a high-quality income trust can be a good investment for you. There are other considerations as well that make these investments attractive.

SOME ECONOMIC CONDITIONS TO CONSIDER

There are a number of economic conditions that can affect investments of all kinds, including income trusts. The following are a few examples of general conditions to pay attention to when considering investment.

Today's Interest Rate Climate

One of the main reasons income trusts have become so popular in the past few years is the low interest rate environment we live in at the present time. When the banks pay 2 percent on GICs, and government bonds give you around 4.5 percent, an 8–12 percent yield, or higher, on investment from an income trust can be very attractive. At the time of writing this book, we are experiencing the lowest rates in the last 40 years, and should these low rates continue, income trusts may well continue to be in great demand. But how long will these low rates last, and what will happen to income trusts if they start going up? Is the recent Bank of Canada increase in the prime lending rate, with the speculation of more to come in the fall of 2004, something to be worried about?

Interest rates and inflation usually move in parallel to one another. And since we are experiencing a very low inflation rate, we can probably expect interest rates to stay relatively low as well for the near future. The general state of the economy also affects interest rates. So the real question is what are the chances of an increase in the inflation rate in North America? The scope of this book is much too limited to explore underlying economic influences that may affect the future (we don't purport to have a crystal ball; if we did, we'd be rich), so let's start by discussing the second part of the question: What will happen to income trusts if interest rates go up?

To answer this question, we will need to ask one first. As a rational individual, how would you invest your money if you could get the same 9 percent yield on either a government bond or an income trust? Remember, government bonds should pay regardless of the economic situation, but payments from income trusts can be greatly affected by changing economic conditions. The answer is easy; the risk is much lower in government bonds, so you'd put your money there—we hope! Since the majority of investors will think like this—and so they should—the same income trust that pays 9 percent would have to yield at least 13–15 percent to compete with a 9 percent or higher rate of return.

Now, if the underlying businesses in the income trusts are unable to increase payouts as quickly as interest rates rise, the increased yield needed to satisfy investors will have to come from lower unit prices. So an income trust unit that was trading at $10 and was paying 90 cents yearly might still be paying the 90 cents, but the price of units might drop to, say, $6.42. Unit holders will receive a 14 percent return, but a unit holder just lost $3.58 from the $10 he or she paid for the units.

Rising interest rates also generally reflect overall economic health, so the underlying business may perhaps throw off more cash, by giving higher distributions and causing an increase in the unit price.

The upshot of this is that we do not believe that higher—as long as they are still reasonable—interest rates will necessarily kill income trusts as mainstream investment vehicles, but their unit price may suffer to reflect new economic realities. On the flip side, if interest rates were to decline further, the price of units of many income trusts may well increase. Beware, however; we are experiencing the lowest rates in the last 40 years, and the recent, albeit small, increases are an indication that it is highly unlikely that rates will drop back to their recent lows.

Expectations of a sharp increase in interest rates may lead you to decide to sell some susceptible income trusts, and buy them back later—hopefully at a lower cost.

Equity Market Outlook

The second reason that income trusts have done so well in the last four years is the vicious bear market—it is extremely difficult to make money in declining markets. As equity mutual funds kept losing through the beginning of the 21st century, investors were taking their money out and desperately trying to find a new home for it. Income trusts have been one of the few bright spots in these dark times.

There have been many predictions that, once the economy turns around and we enter a bull market, investors will dump income trusts and invest in equities, as growth can be more attractive than income.

We have never really shared that fear. From March 2003 to the end of the year, the major equity indexes in North America went up anywhere from 25–50 percent. Still, during the same time we experienced an unprecedented boom in income trusts. Contrary to predictions, people were not dumping their trust holdings and getting into high-growth equities, but kept on buying more trusts. More and more products came to the market and the existing trusts, for the most part, enjoyed strong appreciation.

So do we believe that rising equity markets would negatively affect the unit prices of income trusts? Not really. In our opinion there is a demand for *both* equity appreciation and a steady monthly return. They satisfy different needs, so they can exist in harmony. Even if equities appreciate as spectacularly in the years ahead as they did in 2003, the chances are their success will not have a negative effect on the prices of income trusts.

Exchange Rate Considerations

In today's increasingly global economy, people are doing more and more business with more and more countries. Here in Canada, our major trading partner is the United States. When a Canadian company sells its products or services south of the border, they are paid in U.S. dollars, and the exchange rate from U.S. to Canadian dollars can greatly affect the profitability of that organization. So companies that sell to the United States prefer a low Canadian dollar—they can make money on the exchange rate—while enterprises that buy from the United States prefer a strong one.

This means it is imperative to examine, before we invest, the potential effects of exchange fluctuation on a trust. In 2003 the U.S. dollar fell 22 percent against its Canadian counterpart. That kind of fluctuation can be either devastating or very good for a business. As an example, let's say Canadian company X sells widgets to customers in the United States. In 2002 they sold US$127 million worth of widgets. At the then current average exchange rate of 64 cents, that represented a Canadian dollar revenue of over $198 million. As a result, in 2003 they opened 14 new accounts and increased their sales to US$141 million; the U.S. dollar unit price of the widgets did not change in that time frame. However, the average exchange rate for the year was up to 74 cents, giving them an equivalent of C$190 million. That's $8 million less than the year before. And because they sold more widgets, they had to produce more. Larger production meant larger expenses, meaning that there was less profit at the end of the year. If this company was an income trust, it is conceivable that distributions would have to be reduced. So this is another environmental issue for consideration. The company could be doing very well, and management could be excellent, but payouts might be adversely affected by external circumstances.

Certainly the flip side also can be true. A company that relies on buying products or raw materials from the U.S. can have a windfall during a period of increasing dollar values.

Some income trusts have hedged their interest rate exposure by buying, usually from banks, currency contracts to lock in today's rates, much like you would lock in a floating rate mortgage. That can help, but is only a short-term solution. At some point, the contracts will expire, and the reality of the interest rate environment will kick in.

In summary, before you invest find out the company's potential vulnerability to the exchange rate. With this knowledge you can react quickly if you see danger signs on the horizon. And remember: it takes a few months for events like this to start affecting payouts. As long as you understand what the likely effect can be, you can react by making an intelligent decision either to stay in or sell your holdings. And don't forget, you can always buy them back later. In this day and age, the price of making a trade is relatively low, so trading fees should not be a major consideration when it comes to selling and buying back a security. For those who are not fond of managing investments, seek out income trusts that are not affected by exchange rate fluctuations.

Commodity Price Outlook for Oil and Gas

An issue that affects oil and gas trusts is the price of their products. As we discussed earlier, oil and gas prices are sensitive to different circumstances. Gas prices generally depend mostly on the weather, and oil on geopolitical situations, for the most part. Of course, supply and demand factors also affect prices. The last two bitterly cold winters have seen natural gas prices climb considerably. Oil prices have also risen due to the war in Iraq, the renewed tension in the Middle East, and the global fight against terrorism, among other things.

As oil and gas trusts rely on selling the raw material before refining, these kinds of price changes can greatly affect their businesses. As well, these commodity prices are denominated in U.S. dollars, and the exchange rate can also play a major part in the profitability of these trusts. These are the main reasons they are the most volatile of all the trusts. Our widget company, in the example above, could increase productivity or move some of its production offshore, where labour costs are lower, to seek to offset the negative effect of an exchange difference. But in the case of oil and gas trusts that depend on a commodity-driven price, there are few mitigating elements. These two factors— commodity prices and exchange rates—can positively or negatively affect the trust, and subsequently its distributions. So before you invest in one of these oil and gas trusts—they can be very attractive due to their high yields—please realize the potential commodity-related risks involved.

UNDERSTANDING THE UNDERLYING BUSINESS

You must also seek to understand the business attributes of the trust you are considering investing in. Why is that so important? After all, if it has a good track record of paying monthly distributions, why should you have to understand the business? Because otherwise you will not know what affects its distributions and unit price.

Imagine owning units in a trust that is in the dog food business. If you don't know that the company uses beef to produce its products, you won't be prepared for the negative consequences of a U.S. beef import ban after mad cow disease was discovered in Canada. A thorough knowledge of the trust's underlying business can sometimes give you an edge, and can help you analyze in advance how an event or piece of news might affect your investment.

Stability of Distributions

This is definitely one of the most important considerations when investing in income trusts. This is because the main reason for considering buying units in a particular trust is its distributions. Obviously, ascertaining stability in a trust is different depending on whether you are buying an existing trust or a brand new one. In the case of an existing trust there are historical data to look at.

A number of websites contain useful information regarding historic yields of trusts. There are also two agencies that have begun to rate income trusts—Standard & Poor's and Dominion Bond Rating Service—and we will discuss these ratings in detail later in the book. One thing you must remember though: Past performance is no guarantee of future results. Things can change, and some changes can affect even the most stable-looking organization.

Buying an IPO can be a little trickier. Because the underlying company has no history as an income trust, there are no historic data regarding distributions. In this case your number one research tool has to be the prospectus. This is the document that should contain all material information about the trust and the underlying business. Historical and pro-forma financial statements are all part of the document, and should give you a financial picture of at least the last three years in the life of this company. It is imperative that you read this document thoroughly. We will discuss the IPO process in more detail in Chapter 8.

As all new trusts that hit the market are based on existing and in most cases well-established businesses, there should be a wealth of material available. If the underlying organization was previously a public company, it will also have published news releases regarding material changes to the organization. Most of this information can be found at www.sedar.ca, the *System for Electronic Document Analysis and Retrieval* website developed for the Canadian Securities Administrators (CSA).

Unfortunately, if the company was *privately* held it is much harder to find information. In this case the prospectus is really your only guide. Have a look at how profitable the organization was in the past several years, and how steady that profitability appeared year after year, and always review its cash flows.

But always remember, and we can't stress this enough: *Past performance does not guarantee future results.* Spend some time there before you commit your money!

Growth Possibilities

Though income may be the number one reason to buy income trust units, the growth potential should not be ignored. Trusts that can demonstrate an increase in their business under this structure may give you a very good return on your money.

Let's take an example in which you invest $10,000 yearly in an income trust in your RRSP. The trust gives you a 10 percent return, and you continue reinvesting these distributions into trusts with similar return. By the end of the 11th year, you would have over $180,000. Now look at the same scenario if the trusts you are investing in can manage to show a 5 percent growth yearly (Figure 4.1). By the end of the 11th year you would have over $240,000 in your RRSP. Quite a difference!

Figure 4.1

YEAR	10% COMPOUNDED RETURN	10% COMPOUNDED RETURN + 5% YEARLY GROWTH
1	10,000.00	10,000.00
2	21,000.00	21,500.00
3	33,100.00	34,725.00
4	46,410.00	49,933.75
5	61,051.00	67,423.81
6	77,156.10	87,537.38
7	94,871.71	110,667.99
8	114,358.88	137,268.19
9	135,794.77	167,858.42
10	159,374.25	203,037.18
11	185,311.67	243,492.76

We cannot ignore growth—if you have the choice of finding trusts with or without good growth potential at the same risk level, always take the one with the growth! We know that no one can foresee the future and be certain about that potential, but we can use our better judgment. Let's look at some of the important factors that affect growth in the four main categories of trust.

Growth: Trademark Royalty Trusts

As we demonstrated earlier, growth in a franchise organization can cost the franchiser relatively little money. Rather, the money it makes comes from the royalties and fees it charges. Corporate-owned stores can cost more to get started, but may be more controllable and transparent, since there is no invisible franchise debt. So as long as there is growing demand for the products and services they provide, it is conceivable that they can grow well. This is much like understanding the underlying business discussed above—carbohydrate-reduced diet fads can affect donut franchises, mad cow disease can hit burger joints, higher interest rates can affect hardware and home renovation outlets, and so on.

Growth: Business Trusts

The main consideration here is to understand what is required to grow the particular business the trust is in. If it is a service-based organization that does not need a lot of capital, chances are it may be able to grow more easily than businesses that require lots of capital. However, if growth is capital intensive, such as in most manufacturing organizations, we have to examine where the capital will be coming from. Will it have money left over after paying distributions to pay for a bank loan or lease on new equipment? Will it be able to issue more units to finance the acquisition of competitors?

Growth: Oil and Gas Trusts

Growth here can be very tricky as we showed in Chapter 2. We believe that for most oil and gas trusts it is increasingly difficult and costly to replace inventory levels as they dwindle—never mind trying to grow them. Oil-sands-based trusts should be stable, but we would generally not suggest that anyone go looking for growth in this sector.

Growth: Real Estate Investment Trusts (REITs)

This category is one where growth may well happen. As we discussed before, your money goes into buying real property. Unless the trust overpays for the assets, there is a good possibility that the property prices will appreciate in the years to come. If we look at real estate prices since the beginning of the industrial revolution, we find that they have generally appreciated in the long run. As long as there is no negative outside influence, such as a factory closing for good in a one-factory town, property values usually keep ahead of inflation. And as long as the three basics of real estate investment—Location!

Location! Location!—are not ignored, your investment could grow very nicely in the years to come.

In conclusion, it is worth investigating the growth potential of any trust, as it can provide you with potentially significant returns, both in the form of higher distributions and in increased market prices.

Management Experience and Reputation

We have seen many great companies become mediocre or even worse after a large-scale management change. On the other hand, the implementation of great management can turn a mediocre organization into a great one. So it is important to pay attention to what is happening within the management of the trust you are investigating.

This can be a crucial issue when you are considering a trust IPO. Review the prospectus to see if there is a management change currently underway or if there has recently been one. This is more likely to happen when a private company is being converted into a trust, as it can be a great way for the original owners to cash out, and bring a professional management team to come in and take over. The question you should be asking is this: Can the new team run the business as successfully as the original owner(s)? To find the answer you must examine the prospectus, which will have bios on all the managers. You may also want to do some research via the Internet to learn about past successes or failures, management style, etc. Read everything carefully and make your judgment call.

If the original owners of a private company are staying on to run the business, it is important to examine whether they have the proper skill sets to manage a public company versus a private one, as considerably different skills are required in each case. Do they still have equity in the company or did they cash out all their shares? You should be cautious when investing in a public company where the original owners stay on to run the business without equity. They may not be motivated because their money is already in the bank. Only by doing your research can you assess if you are comfortable with the situation.

If you are planning to purchase units of an existing trust, chances are that management has been in place for a while. If you are comfortable with the business, distribution, and management history and decide to buy, watch out for any changes. If and when there is a new CFO, CEO, or president, look into *why* they made the change, and then read up on the new candidates to see if you like what they bring to the company. If it does not look good, make your decision accordingly. Management can make or break a company; it is not something that should be taken lightly. Investigate before you buy!

Liquidity

Liquidity is based on the number of trust units traded on an average day on the stock exchange. Does this really matter if all the other aspects are fine? Yes it does. Remember again; trust units behave much like common stocks. If you were to buy 1000 units in a trust that only trades 5000 to 6000 units a day, you will find that the demand your 1000-unit order creates—almost 20 percent of the entire daily trading volume—will drive the price up. This can result in you paying more than the current price. By the same token, when you want to sell the reverse will happen, and your order will drive the price down. This is why we caution people before they get into any thinly traded or relatively illiquid trust. When you decide to sell, you want to be sure there will be a market for your units, and there is nothing that assures this more than good liquidity, or a large number of units traded daily. As "large" is relative, always look at the daily volume in comparison to the number of units you want to buy or sell. One hundred thousand units traded may not be large enough if you want to buy or sell 10,000 units, but it can be plenty to move only 1000 units.

Since daily trading volumes can fluctuate, pay attention to the changes. If you see a trend with the number of units traded declining, you may want to think about selling, as it may hit a level where your order can negatively affect the price.

Funds of Funds—Management and Fees

We have talked about funds of income funds briefly, however, one item is important to discuss here. It has to do with how much money the managers of the fund charge to do their jobs. This is sometimes called the Management Expense Ratio (MER), and it covers the fees and costs associated with running the fund.

As we discussed earlier, when you invest in one of these instruments you should get two things you would not when you invest directly into one or two trusts—diversification and ongoing professional monitoring. The fees you pay are for these services. These fees are usually charged as a percentage of the total assets of the fund, and are not necessarily based on performance. That means that they will come off your monthly distribution even if for some reason that distribution has been reduced. So pay attention to the costs of the fund, including any commission charged, and compare them, as in many cases they can vary considerably.

WHEN TO SELL

So you have done your due diligence and everything came out right. You made the move and purchased your investment, which is hopefully doing well. Now the question is why and when to sell?

Need Some Cash?

One of the bonuses of owning marketable investments is the flexibility they potentially give you in case you need immediate cash. Reasons for selling may vary widely, from buying a home, to starting a business, dealing with a family emergency, or even purchasing engagement rings, cars, and much needed vacations. If you are likely to need cash for any of these expected or unexpected reasons, then you should factor this into the liquidity of your income trust units and purchase a fund that has high liquidity on the exchange.

Selling an income trust is a relatively simple transaction. Call your broker or contact your discount broker (you may also use a discount broker to make these transactions online), and declare that you wish to sell all, or a certain number, of your units, depending on the amount of cash you require. Be sure to factor in the taxes you may have to pay on the funds received from this transaction. Remember, you are not required to tell your broker why you are selling, so don't let him or her make you feel guilty!

Found a Better Investment Vehicle?

Perhaps you have been smart and have continued to look around for investments that are even better than the ones you currently own. Then again, maybe your lifestyle or financial situation has changed, and with it, your risk tolerances and long-term goals. Either way, these can be compelling reasons to sell your units.

But beware: Income trust units are not something you can just convert into a different investment without potential tax liabilities on your profits. It is a very good idea not only to thoroughly research (perform your due diligence) on the new investment, but to factor in the value of that investment against potential gains in the existing fund and potential tax liabilities.

Is the Fund Performing Badly?

Here is where the hard decisions come in, and they need to be assessed very carefully, as they go right to the heart of some fundamental beliefs and behaviours that may or may not need some modification. If a fund is not living up to your expectations, what mechanisms should you have in place to handle the situation? How stringently should you abide by them, no matter what your gut feeling is? There are a number of ugly habits that can come into play here, the two most important being greed and hope.

Greed

Staying in too long and losing is almost human nature, and it takes an almost Herculean effort to resist, yet resisting it is the key to prudent investment—and financial success. Greed isn't necessarily bad; after all, it is a form of greed that has made you decide to invest so you can improve your material and social well-being. But it's important to remember that greed has the ability to take over and cloud your judgment.

Hope

Another uniquely human trait, hope can be as disastrous as greed, and they often go hand in hand. When things go wrong, the tendency is to hope they will get better. While this is a nice sentiment, hoping will do nothing to change the situation either way. It takes courage and discipline to jump off a sinking ship early, but it is something that every investor should learn to do.

SETTING YOUR OWN RISK CONTROLS

It is vital, along with ongoing diligence, that you create and strictly adhere to rules regarding a certain level of loss below which you will not hold on to your units. This is your own version of a risk control mechanism. Let's illustrate with a chart showing performances of an income trust over a year.

Figure 4.2

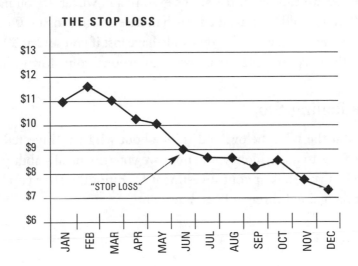

THE STOP LOSS

Stop Loss

Using the above chart, assume that you bought units in this trust on January 1, which were trading at $11. Obviously this was not a wise choice in hindsight, as the trust went up by 50 cents and then started a steady downward slide. In this case, what should your risk control mechanism be?

You should have had a stop loss in place. A stop loss is just what it sounds like: a strategy that says when to stop your losses. In this case, you bought in at $11. Let's say you decide that the most you can afford to lose on this investment is $2 per unit. This means that when the price hits $9, you will sell, no matter what. This is where the discipline comes in—selling at a loss is one of the hardest things to do. As we can see in the above example, however, if you had sold at $9, you would have avoided much more extensive losses. Of course, if the price bounced back, you would have lost if you sold at $9. However, the purpose of the stop loss is to protect your downside.

The Rolling Stop

Look at the table below, and think about why you invested in the first place: to make money, and improve your financial stability, right? So when you look at your investment four months after you bought it, it has gained three dollars. Excellent!

Figure 4.3

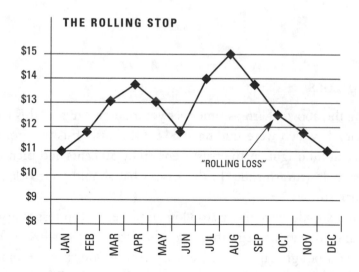

In May, however, it comes down to $13—still $2 more than you paid for it. But the next month, it's down to just below $12. Should you sell? You have lost $1, but you're still up $1. Thankfully, while you are contemplating this, it goes back up to $14. Relax.

Suddenly the unit value jumps to over $14, and you're on a roll again. We're sure you can see where this is going by now. By August, your $11 investment is now worth $15, and life is grand. However, over the next few months, sadly, the price begins to drop steadily. When do you sell? You could sell when the price hits $11 and break even, or end up actually losing money due to hoping it would eventually come back.

Sometimes a trust will go up and down in small fits and starts, like the one depicted above. This can be a hair-raising ride—hopefully the fund you have chosen is more stable than this—but you can smooth it out by putting in place a rolling stop. This is a mechanism stating that there is a certain amount below the most recent high at which point you will sell. It's not as complicated as it sounds.

In the above case, let's say you set a rolling stop at $2.50; rolling stop levels are usually higher than stop losses, as you are in a winning situation. This means that at any point, if the fund is $2.50 below its most recent high, you will sell your units—no matter what. So here, you would have sold it in October, when it dipped to $12.50 from its previous August high of $15.00, eight months into the investment. You would have made a little money, and could sit back and begin looking for a new venture.

Discipline, Discipline, Discipline

We've given you an example where your rolling stop was absolutely the right decision, and you sold while you still had a profit, and before you started losing. The thing to remember is that no matter what, you should stick to your rules. Even if the above fund had continued to rise through the roof after your rolling stop happened and you sold, you made a good decision, and lived to invest another day.

And believe us, this will happen. You will set your risk management, stick rigidly to it, and get out when your own rules tell you to, only to sadly watch the fund start to gain, and gain, and gain. These are the stories you hear about—not the ones where it continued to lose. The "one that got away" is a major fear of investors. How many times have you heard someone whining about how they could have bought Microsoft in 1985, or IBM in 1960?

But know this: If you choose to ignore your risk controls, over the long run, you will probably lose. If, however, you stick to your guns, the payoff can be great.

CASE IN POINT: SPECIALTY FOODS GROUP

Just to give you an idea of how volatile some of these instruments can be, let's look at a specific example. Specialty Foods Group (SFG) became an income trust following the completion of its IPO in April of 2003. SFG is a leading independent U.S. producer and marketer of processed meats. They make bacon, ham, hot dogs, luncheon meats, and more for a host of leading national and regional brands.

You can probably see where this is heading, but neither SFG's management nor investors could have predicted the bovine spongi-form encephalopathy (BSE, or mad cow disease) scare that devastated the Canadian industry and closed the U.S. border to imports of Canadian beef, driving costs—beef is used in almost 50 percent of the company's products—in the United States through the roof.

Things went from bad to worse when private label product customers pulled out, notably McDonald's Japanese operations. The discovery of BSE in the United States did not increase the availability of beef within the country as was hoped, because of export bans. Also, the fund's auditor withdrew, apparently uncomfortable with the U.S. tax risks. What happened after the dust settled? By December, the stock price was trading as low as $5.27, about half of the issuing price. Ouch.

While this kind of disaster is not only rare but impossible to predict, there is much research you can do and effective questions you can ask to increase your chances of avoiding major setbacks. This is the topic of the next chapter.

Measuring Risks:

The Underlying Business

Some investors like to believe that income trusts are just as safe as Canadian government bonds, but pay much higher distributions. Nothing could be further from the truth! As with any investment, with higher rewards come higher risks. Just as you can't defeat the laws of gravity forever, the risk–reward ratio is a fundamental law of the marketplace that should never be forgotten. If you are relying on a 20 percent yield from an income trust to fund your retirement, then you will likely be disappointed! In addition to their tax advantages, one of the reasons that certain income trusts are paying out so well right now is because of their increased risk.

We have talked about some of the risks involved in investing in income funds already. You must remember that, just like any investment, there are inherent pitfalls in income trusts as well. The main problems with them are risks related to the underlying business, any of which can lead to a potential reduction in distributions. This chapter will examine the specifics of some of those risks.

THE NATURE OF THE PARTICULAR INDUSTRY

A unit holder will likely face risks that are inherent in the nature of the specific industry in which the business operates. In the Vincent Income Trust example in Chapter 1, the amount of cash that the trust receives and the amount of cash that can be distributed to its unit holders will depend on the ability to rent the property, the amount of rent received, and the cost of taxes and property repairs, among other things. The Vincent Income Trust therefore faces the risk of receiving either more or less than the projected $22,800 per year.

If, for instance, the business underlying an income trust is an airline, unit holders of the fund will be subject to many industry-specific risks such as the fluctuating price of fuel, prevailing weather conditions and the resulting effect on travel, terrorist acts, labour disruptions, travel industry conditions, air traffic control and airport landing fee cost increases, and so forth. All of these factors would ultimately affect the profitability of the business in any given time period and consequently the amount of cash that could be paid out to the unit holders of the trust. This is the simple nature of the business, and every business has its own challenges. Understanding the risks inherent in a specific business is key in understanding the risks of a trust that engages in that business. Sometimes businesses will hedge their interest rate exposure by in effect locking in a fixed rate for a period of time, much like a homeowner switches to a fixed rate from a floating rate mortgage. That may have a short-term steadying impact, but only until the hedge expires.

VULNERABILITY TO GENERAL ECONOMIC CONDITIONS

The amount of cash that can be distributed to unit holders of an income trust is also affected by the overall condition of the economy, and a company's financial condition and future business may be significantly affected by external factors and events. For example, the demand for a company's products and/or services can be reduced if the overall economy is in a state of recession or depression. Similarly, if the industry in which the company operates is experiencing hard economic times, such as when sales in the auto industry were significantly down in the early 1980s, the whole industry may suffer (including all related businesses). In such a case, unit holders face the same overall economic risks as the company and suffer similar economic losses.

INTEREST RATE FLUCTUATIONS

Fluctuations in interest rates may pose risks to a business as well, and may ultimately affect the amount of cash that can be distributed to unit holders of an income fund that holds that business. If the company has a variable rate bank loan or mortgage, a fluctuating interest rate will either raise or lower the amount of money that has to be paid to the bank. Changing interest rates may also affect the customers of a business. For example, auto sales may decline in periods of high interest rates, since buyers may be less willing to pay the higher financing costs. Fluctuating interest rates, therefore, are a factor that unit holders have to consider when making investments in income trusts, particularly ones with a substantial amount of outstanding external floating rate debt.

COMPETITION

It is the nature of business to be competitive, and the company underlying the income trust will likely compete with other companies in the same industry for customers, suppliers, locations, and sales. The risk here is that these competitors may engage in competitive practices such as cutting prices to increase their market share. For example, they may offer their services at a lower cost than the trust. Competitive pressures such as these may force the company to alter its practices to better compete. For example, if the underlying business is a retail business or a supplier, it may be forced to also reduce its prices (and perhaps its profitability) in order to remain competitive. An additional risk is that if a company fails to compete effectively and hold its ground with its current or any future competitors, the company's financial condition may be in serious jeopardy.

LABOUR AND EMPLOYEE RELATIONS

Especially if the underlying company of the income fund is unionized, there are increased risks related to the labour relations between the union, the employees, and the company that could potentially impact the amount of cash distributed by the income fund at any given time. For example, if an existing collective agreement is up for renewal, and the company is unable to renew the agreement in a reasonable period of time, there is a greater risk that work stoppages or other labour disturbances may occur that could have a negative effect on the company and the amount of cash it can generate. In both union and non-union situations, companies should ensure that they keep valuable employees content and productive. The unique labour and employee relations of an underlying company are therefore another possible risk that a unit holder should consider.

REGULATORY OR ENVIRONMENTAL RISKS

The business underlying an income fund or its products or services may be subject to governmental or industry regulation as well. If the business does not comply with these requirements, it could be shut down, temporarily or permanently, or fined (among other things), and may receive bad publicity and/or even lawsuits, which can obviously affect the bottom line. There is also a risk that the regulatory requirements that apply to the business may change in either a positive or negative way. For example, take an income trust that owns a restaurant that serves alcohol and derives a significant portion of its revenue through alcohol sales. If the liquor control board were to implement a regulatory change that prohibited restaurants from serving alcohol past 10 p.m., that change could significantly reduce the amount of revenue generated (through the sale of alcohol), which could ultimately reduce the amount of cash distributed by the income trust. Alternatively, opening up "happy hours" might increase revenues.

For a trust in heavy industry, accidents, spills, polluting equipment, and the like could need cleaning up under environmental laws—at substantial cost and once again potentially affecting distributions.

FOREIGN EXCHANGE RISK

As we mentioned earlier with our fictitious widget factory in Chapter 4, income trusts can be affected by changes in foreign exchange rates (the value of the Canadian dollar compared to a foreign currency, usually the U.S. dollar). For example, if a company underlying an income fund has operations, or buys or sells products, in the United States (or another foreign country), there is a risk that the foreign exchange rate will fluctuate, causing the Canadian dollar amount of revenue or expenses to increase or decrease at any given time based on changes in the exchange rate and the company's exposure to such changes. In addition, a substantial increase in the value of the Canadian dollar relative to the U.S. dollar may make it difficult for a company that makes products in Canada and sells them to customers in the U.S. to compete with U.S. and other suppliers outside Canada (and vice versa). For a company that imports products from the United States (paying the purchase price in U.S. dollars) and then resells them in Canada in Canadian dollars, an increase in the value of the Canadian dollar may increase its profits. The very volatile Canadian versus U.S. dollar exchange rate during 2003 and 2004 has had a substantial effect on a number of Canadian income funds. While some funds have hedged or locked in their foreign exchange exposure, these hedges will eventually expire, at which time the fund could be exposed.

LITIGATION RISKS

Depending on the type of business underlying the income trust, there is a risk of legal proceedings being brought by third parties for any number of alleged wrongs. For example, take a company that is in shipping and transportation. If a customer were to obtain a significant judgment against the company for a delayed delivery, then the company's financial condition, as well as business and future prospects, could suffer significantly, resulting in lower cash distributions to unit holders of the income fund that owns the company. Many companies are at frequent risk of legal problems, and investors should be aware of any past or pending issues, as well as the potential risk from the underlying business in the future.

THE QUALITY OF CORPORATE GOVERNANCE

With the new corporate governance requirements recently introduced by the Canadian securities regulatory authorities, there is more pressure on public companies (including public income funds) to ensure proper governance. Scandals have been the flavour of the day recently, and the less likely an income fund is willing to comply with these new corporate governance requirements, the more likely the risk that, among other things, (i) errors could be made in accounting for revenue and expenses that could go unnoticed, (ii) unauthorized transactions could take place without proper approval, resulting in potential losses to the company, (iii) management decisions could be made that are not in the best interests of the fund and its unit holders, and so forth. Unit holders should therefore be aware of the risks associated with investing in an income fund with poor corporate governance practices.

THE EXTENT OF INSURANCE COVERAGE

Another factor to be aware of is the insurance coverage in place at the business underlying the income trust. It is important to determine the extent to which the insurance policies in place would cover possible claims. If a company does not have enough insurance to cover the replacement cost of its assets, or does not have insurance to cover a specific type of loss (arson, for example, or possibly fraud-related losses), it may not be in a position to come up with enough money to cover the cost of replacing assets not covered in the policy. In such a case, the company may not be able to operate after the loss of its assets without additional financing. This result could ultimately reduce or diminish the amount of cash that could be generated for distribution purposes, and perhaps even lead to bankruptcy. General information about insurance policies is usually available in the prospectus.

SEASONALITY AND WEATHER

Unit holders should also be aware of risks associated with the seasonal nature of a product or service offered by the underlying business. Take, for example, a business that sells leather coats. Generally, this company is bound to make most of its sales during the fall and winter seasons, when the weather is cold, and is likely to make significantly fewer sales in the summer season when the weather is very warm. While it may manage its cash to smooth out expected fluctuations, there is always the risk that the weather in a given season is not what it is expected to be. If a particular winter happens to be very mild, this could reduce the number of leather coats sold in that season. The construction industry, as well, can be adversely affected by weather—an abnormally cold winter can slow building practices and delay construction deadlines, for instance. Unit holders, therefore, have to be aware of the risks associated with seasonality and weather.

Some income trusts are very exposed to seasonality, such as the Hot House Growers Income Fund, which produces tomatoes. They may use bank loans to pay distributions during certain periods of the year, which could expose them to substantial additional risks. Indeed, the Hot House Growers Income Fund, in response to an unprecedented drop in tomato prices in August of 2004, was forced to suspend its monthly distribution completely.

SUPPLIER-RELATED RISKS

The business owned by an income fund may face supplier-related risks that could affect the amount of cash that is available to be paid out to unit holders. If, for example, the business is a specialty food product manufacturer and it orders all of its ingredients to make its products from one or two main suppliers, then any event that would lead to the bankruptcy of a supplier's business (or the loss of the supplier for other reasons) could significantly impact the business of the manufacturer. This is especially the case if that supplier happens to be one of the very few companies, or even the only one, that produces a specific ingredient for the products. For instance, because the Ivory Coast is a major supplier for the North American chocolate business, the recent uprising there threatened the chocolate business here. Unit holders should, therefore, inform themselves about the main suppliers of a business and become aware of how replaceable they may be, and at what cost.

THE NATURE OF CUSTOMERS AND CUSTOMER RELATIONSHIPS

The flip side of the situation involving the suppliers described above is the risk involved when a particular company is reliant on one or a few large customers for the success of its business. If a company underlying an income trust is a steel producing company, for example, and it sells its steel to two or three big auto parts manufacturing companies, then those customers are crucial to the well-being of the company. Changes in the customer relationship such as bankruptcy or closure of one of those companies, or the loss of one or more of them as a customer for other reasons, or simply reduced volumes or prices, could be highly detrimental to the business. The loss of such an important customer, unless it could be quickly replaced (or associated costs could be reduced very quickly) in order to maintain overall profitability, could greatly reduce the amount of revenue generated by the company, which, in turn, could reduce the amount of cash generated for distribution through the income fund.

COMMODITY PRICE RISKS

If an income fund owns a business that relies heavily on the sale of commodities (such as gasoline refineries that purchase large quantities of petroleum), then the varying price of that commodity and the resulting effect on the company's ability to generate cash for a given period should be carefully considered. Any large jump or drop in the price of the commodity may, unless it is able to be passed through to customers quickly, translate into significantly more or less cash generated by the underlying business of the income fund for distributions.

Some businesses may also attempt to reduce or hedge their commodity price risks in various ways. These structures can be very complex, and we won't go into them in detail here. The upshot is, however, that, just as they may reduce losses, hedges may also reduce gains. In addition, they can sometimes backfire, especially if used for speculative rather than hedging purposes (looking for big gains rather than protecting one's downside) or if the hedge was badly designed and didn't offset the risk as it was supposed to.

THE IMPACT OF TECHNOLOGY

Another important risk to consider is the impact of technology on the business underlying an income trust. Certain changes in technology can often have significant effects on the ability of the company to generate revenue. If the company happens to manufacture CDs and DVDs, for instance, then increased access to and use of the Internet to download music and movies (whether legally or illegally) could reduce the demand for CDs and DVDs, and reduced demand could ultimately reduce the company's long-term ability to generate revenue. The impact of technology on a particular business should thus be considered carefully when investing in an income fund whose underlying business might be negatively affected by advances or changes in technology.

OTHER RISKS

The above is only a sampling of possible areas of risk related to the underlying business of an income fund. Other risks may well exist, and investors must be extremely diligent in assessing any particular income fund. As we have demonstrated, it is imperative to examine the risks associated with the underlying business in a trust. The next chapter will discuss another risk factor associated with income trusts: their structure.

Measuring Risks:
The Trust Structure

In addition to the risks related to the business underlying the income fund and the industry in which it operates, there are a number of risks to unit holders associated with the actual structure of the income fund. The following is a general discussion of some of these risks.

STRUCTURAL COMPLEXITY

The Vincent Income Trust model in Chapter 1 represents a simple version of the basic structure, consisting of a trust that owns shares and debt of a wholly owned subsidiary company. There are many such simple structures around.

There are also a number of substantially more complex structures, with, instead of underlying corporations, second-tier trusts and limited partnerships. The Cineplex Galaxy Income Fund (TSX: CGX_u.TO) is a good example of one of these more complex structures.

Figure 6.1

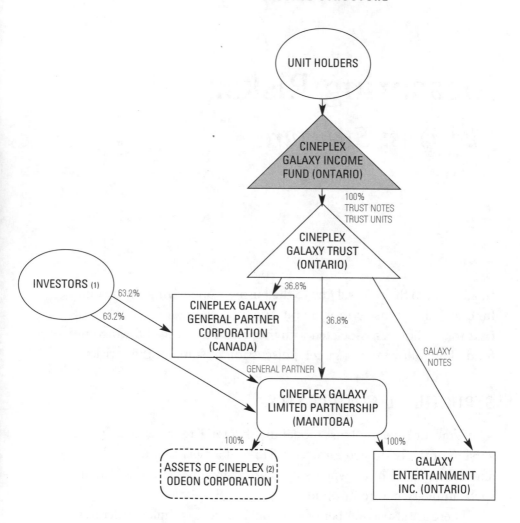

**CINEPLEX GALAXY INCOME FUND
CLOSING STRUCTURE**

(1) Only Investors who are members of the LCE Group will hold shares of Cineplex Galaxy General Partnership.

(2) Excludes certain assets and associated liabilities of CGG which are not integral to its film exhibition operations as well as six Cineplex Odeon Theatres in Canada which do not meet the strategic financial criteria for acquistion by Cineplex Galaxy Limited Partnership.

These are more complex arrangements that seek to achieve more advantageous tax results than are available with a company. While these structures are not uncommon (and are on the increase), all things being equal, most investors would still probably prefer the simple to the complex. Just like with a car or piece of machinery, the more complicated the structure, the more things there are to potentially go wrong. One disadvantage with these structures is that a limited partnership generally does not offer limited liability protection that is as robust as that of a corporation.

POSSIBLE UNLIMITED LIABILITY TO UNIT HOLDERS

This was the problem in Chapter 2 with Mr. Jones and his rental property. Since an income trust is not a corporation, unit holders of most income trusts do not currently benefit from the same statutory limited liability status that shareholders of corporations enjoy. The declaration of trust, the document that creates the income trust, typically attempts to offer some protection to unit holders, by providing that they "will not be subject to personal liability in connection with holding units of the trust" or some similar statement. Despite the protection offered in the declaration of trust, however, there remains a small risk that a unit holder could be held personally liable for the obligations of the income fund to others. This means that sometimes claims against the fund cannot be satisfied out of the assets of the income fund alone. If unsuccessful, unit holders could be potentially liable for the cost of an environmental cleanup, for example. Generally, however, income funds attempt to structure the affairs of the fund in such a way that minimizes this risk to unit holders whenever possible. In addition, statutory limited liability protection now exists for Quebec and Alberta income trusts, and is expected to arrive for Ontario income trusts shortly.

DEPENDENCE ON THE UNDERLYING BUSINESS

Most income funds do not actually carry on an active business, but rather are "limited purpose trusts" which hold some or all of the securities, assets, and/or debt of an underlying limited partnership or company (much like you might invest in a stock). The trustee (or board of trustees) of this type of fund is responsible for making sure that cash payments are distributed from the fund to the unit holders, among other things. The cash is generated through the operations and/or the use of assets of the underlying business. This means that the fund is often entirely dependent on the operations and/or assets of the underlying business to make distribution payments. In this case, the dependency means that any loss of profit to the business will directly translate into a loss to the unit holders.

CASH DISTRIBUTIONS ARE NOT GUARANTEED AND FLUCTUATE WITH PERFORMANCE

Although income trusts endeavour to make cash distributions to unit holders regularly, as we've seen from earlier examples, there are a number of factors that affect the amount of cash that is generated. These include the underlying business's profitability for the time period, its ability to maintain and increase its customer base and sustain its profit margins, and fluctuations in the company's working capital and expenditures. Each of these factors is susceptible to a number of risks, both internal and external. As a result of these variable factors and risks, the actual amount of cash generated cannot be guaranteed and may fluctuate with the performance of the business over time.

RESTRICTIONS ON THE POTENTIAL GROWTH OF THE UNDERLYING BUSINESS

As the underlying business generally pays out almost all of its cash flow in distributions, and this amount is then paid by the income fund to its unit holders, the amount of cash remaining in the underlying business is often very limited. This means that any future acquisitions or expenditures by the business will have to depend on an increased cash flow, or on obtaining additional financing. If a business can't gain access to additional funds through generating more cash flow or obtaining additional financing, then it is possible that the future growth of the business could be limited.

NATURE OF THE TRUST UNITS

Securities such as income trust units are hybrid in nature, meaning that they have attributes that are common to both equity securities (stocks) and high-yield debt instruments such as "junk bonds," which are high-risk bonds issued by companies with high debt. As the units do not represent a direct investment in the underlying business, but rather a fractional interest in the fund, they should not be viewed by investors as direct shares or debt of the underlying company. And as unit holders are not the same as shareholders of a company, they are not entitled to certain statutory rights associated with share ownership in a corporation. These rights include, for example, the right to bring "oppression" or "derivative" actions and to be entitled to legal remedies when a successful claim is made, or the right to bring a direct claim for non-payment of the principal or interest on indebtedness held by the income trust. The trustees, and not unit holders, will have these rights, and may well choose not to exercise them. As well, unit holders would not be entitled to dissent rights under corporate statutes that could enable unhappy shareholders to get paid in cash the fair value of the shares they hold where the company is planning a significant change and the shareholders do not agree with the change.

Since they are not given the protection of these statutory rights, unit holders in an income fund seeking to redress a legal wrong may only be able to do so (i) under the declaration of trust (the extent of legal protection for unit holders may vary from trust to trust), or (ii) under the common law (judge-made laws) applicable to trusts. In a worst case, they may have little or no remedies for certain wrongs.

DISTRIBUTIONS IN KIND ON REDEEMING UNITS, OR ON TERMINATION OF THE INCOME FUND

Under certain conditions, unit holders have the right to demand that the income fund buy back their units (called a redemption of the units). When a cash payment is not required to be made for the units (as in some cases), or where there is not enough cash in the fund to buy back the units, the trustees of the fund may be entitled to distribute the assets of the trust directly to the unit holders attempting to redeem their units. For example, when the trust assets are made up of the securities of the underlying company—the actual stock and debt—the trustees may distribute these securities directly to unit holders upon redemption.

One of the main risks associated with exercising redemption rights and receiving securities instead of cash is the possibility that there is no market through which to trade those securities. Basically, if the securities are not listed on any stock exchange, they may not be freely or readily tradeable—you can't call a broker and sell them. There is also a possibility that the securities may not be eligible investments for RRSPs and the like, making it very difficult to realize any value in them.

The trustees may also distribute the assets of an income trust if and when the income fund is terminated or matures. The same risks apply as above in this situation, and unit holders may possibly get stuck with highly illiquid, or hard to get rid of, exchange securities.

ABSENCE OF A PRIOR PUBLIC MARKET

On a related note, if the trust units of an income fund are being offered to the public for the first time by way of an IPO, there would not have been a market for the trust units prior to the offering—they have never been bought or sold before. Rather than the market determining it, the price of the units offered through the IPO will have been set by negotiations between the trustees of the income fund, the underwriters, and the people who represent the interests of the underlying company (such as certain executive officers or major shareholders). The determination of the price per unit will likely be based on several factors, potentially including negotiations with major institutional investors, and may bear no relationship to the price at which the units ultimately trade at on the public market after the IPO. There is absolutely no guarantee that the units will retain their value. This can be dangerous, as once the units begin to trade freely on any stock exchange(s) on which they are listed, they are subject to the same ups and downs as any security on the market.

ISSUE OF ADDITIONAL TRUST UNITS DILUTING EXISTING UNIT HOLDERS' INTEREST

If the declaration of trust authorizes the trustees of the fund to issue additional trust units without the approval of unit holders, as is usually the case, then there is a risk that each existing unit holder's proportion of the overall number of units outstanding may be reduced. Much like simply printing more money or issuing more stock, the unit price and distributions could be diluted by the influx if it is done at a lower value.

INVESTMENT ELIGIBILITY AND FOREIGN PROPERTY

If, at the time units of an income fund are purchased, the units are considered qualified investments for RRSPs, registered education savings plans, and such, there is a risk that the units of the fund may lose their status and not qualify for these plans in the future. If a unit holder happens to be an investor who must follow certain investment criteria (invest only in eligible securities prescribed by some statute), and if the units held by the investor suddenly become unqualified investments, then the investor risks facing penalties under the *Canadian Income Tax Act*. They may become "unqualified" if they have oversold to non-resident investors or to fewer than 150 unit holders. In this case, the investments may have to be sold at a loss, and tax penalties may be payable.

INCOME TAX MATTERS

As we have seen, an income fund's declaration of trust usually states that a sufficient amount of a fund's net income (and any net realized capital gains) may be distributed each year to unit holders, so that the fund won't be liable to pay tax under the *Canadian Income Tax Act*. This is the basic structure. But if the amount of income and capital gains of the fund in a taxation year exceeds the cash available for distribution in the year, that excess income and capital gains will usually be distributed to unit holders in the form of additional trust units, rather than cash. However, for tax purposes, unit holders receiving those additional units are generally required to claim the fair market value of them in their taxable income, even though they are not directly receiving cash. This, of course, can adversely affect your income tax statement and bank balance.

As we have also seen, income fund structures often involve a significant amount of inter-company or similar debt, which generates a substantial interest expense. This interest expense is used to reduce a company's earnings and, therefore, the amount of income tax payable. There is a risk, however, that tax authorities may challenge the amount of interest expense that is being deducted. If such a challenge were to succeed, it could seriously affect the amount of cash available for distribution by the company and income trust.

RESTRICTIONS ON NON-RESIDENT UNIT HOLDERS

A declaration of trust will likely impose a number of restrictions on unit holders of an income fund. For example, under the *Income Tax Act*, non-residents cannot own more than 49 percent of the units of most income trusts; otherwise, the income trust will lose some of its tax advantages. These restrictions may lead to the forced sale of units held by non-residents of Canada, among other adverse effects. Forced sales, because of the laws of supply and demand, generally cause market prices to suffer.

LEVERAGE

If the business underlying the income fund were to borrow money from a bank, then the degree to which the business is leveraged (how much debt it has, and how much interest it must pay on that debt) could have significant consequences for unit holders. For example:

1. The business's ability to obtain additional financing will likely be affected.

2. Future capital expenditures or acquisition may be limited.

3. A substantial portion of the business's cash flow may need to be dedicated to the payment of the principal and interest on its indebtedness, making less funds available for future operations or distributions.

4. Certain borrowings may be at variable interest rates, or denominated in a foreign currency, which may expose the business to the risk of increased interest rates or exchange rate fluctuations.

5. The business may be more vulnerable to economic downturns and be more limited in its ability to withstand pressure from the competition.

As well, if competitors operate on a less leveraged basis than the income trust, they may have greater operating and financing flexibility. The risk in leverage, then, is that economic conditions, interest rate levels, competition, and business factors beyond the control of the business may have a greater negative impact if it has more debt. And of course, if the business is in fact negatively impacted by these factors, its ability to make cash distributions and to repay its debt (as well as its future performance) may be in trouble.

CONCLUSION

These are just some of the risks that may affect income trusts. Depending upon the circumstances, some risks may not apply while others may apply to any particular income fund. Information about risk factors should be available in a trust's prospectus. The next chapter looks at risks associated with who is managing the income trust and on what terms.

CHAPTER SEVEN

Measuring Risks:

Management, Sponsors, and Other Issues

MANAGEMENT ARRANGEMENTS

Another important area of risk assessment lies in the management arrangements of an income trust. There are two major categories of management: internal and external management. There are also a host of other issues. In this chapter we will examine these issues in detail.

Internal Management and LTIPs

In an internally managed income trust, the management of the underlying business is carried out by executives who are employed, and paid, by the income fund itself. This is increasingly the case, and is similar to the situation at most public companies, which have presidents, CEOs, and CFOs who are paid to operate the business. The issue at these income trusts is the age-old question of whether the executive compensation structure is appropriate. How much are we paying these people anyway? And for what? In this regard, while stock option plans, which received substantial criticism for misaligning incentives and creating "inappropriate" financial reporting during the dot-com era, are relatively rare at income trusts, long-term incentive plans (or LTIPs) are frequent.

LTIPs generally use a portion of any increases in distributable cash over what was originally contemplated at the time of the IPO to purchase trust units for the benefit of the senior management team. They will often have graduated percentages, such as 10 percent of the first five cents per unit annual increase, 15 percent of the second five cents per unit annual increase, and 20 percent of further annual increases. On occasion they will be subject to caps, or adjusted for inflation so as not to compensate managers for increases that are really just the result of inflation. They also tend to have requirements that are designed to encourage managers to stay with the business. While LTIPs may seem to be a substantial improvement to ordinary stock options, their overall relationship to investor interests and success remains to be determined. Because they are relatively new, they are still evolving, as a result of institutional investor preferences and experience.

External Management and "Internalization" Costs

There are income trusts with external management arrangements in place, particularly in the oil and gas sector. In these structures, a management company that is not owned by the income trust agrees to provide services to the business in return for agreed fees.

External management was quite common several years ago, but is less so today. This is because many of these arrangements have been seen to give unfair or improper incentives to the external managers. These arrangements often paid fees based on acquisitions or dispositions of properties for the trust, whether profitable or not. Very large

fees were paid out in situations that were difficult to justify from the perspective of the unit holders. Even worse, when it was decided that these agreements should be terminated to "internalize" the management, huge fees were paid to unwind these external management arrangements. As a result, these arrangements are not very popular. However, they are making a bit of a comeback, although it remains to be seen if they are better designed.

Management Equity Ownership

Like in any public company, management equity ownership in trusts, where managers have an equity interest such as shares in the company, is used to align the interests of management with those of investors so that they're all in the same boat, so to speak. Therefore, both at the time of the IPO and on an ongoing basis, significant levels of management and trustee equity ownership are generally viewed as a good thing.

Overall Management Arrangement Assessment

The nature of management equity ownership, as well as the management arrangements in place—in particular whether the incentives and overall level of compensation are appropriate—are most certainly factors to assess in analyzing the risks associated with a particular income trust investment. Details on management arrangements can be found in a trust's prospectus, and should be properly scrutinized.

SPONSOR-RELATED RISKS

The arrangements with the sponsors—the people (or person) that sell a business to an income trust and then help the income trust set up and operate—are very important, and can have adverse effects.

Frequently, the business is sold completely (100 percent), and the sponsors retain no interest in the ongoing business or in the income trust at all. This is generally not considered as desirable as having sponsors with an ongoing stake in the trust, as it shows that they have some faith (and stake) in future success. In larger IPOs, it is difficult for the sponsors to sell their entire interest at the outset because there is only a limited universe of buyers; consequently, they often keep a "retained interest."

The Nature of Retained Interests

The retained interest may be in the form of trust units, or, more frequently, in the form of an equity interest in the underlying business. This interest is usually equivalent to trust units in dollar value, and is known as an "exchangeable equity interest," because it is exchangeable for units. The reason for this is often tax-related, because the sponsor may not incur tax on the retained piece at the time of the IPO. This means that the tax on the sale of the retained portion can be deferred until it is ultimately exchanged for trust units, which can then be sold.

Non-Competition Agreements

Sometimes, sponsors will agree at the time of an IPO to enter into non-competition agreements. These are designed to limit the ability to carry on a business that competes with the business of the income trust. For obvious reasons, these are very welcome. Such an agreement means that the sponsor cannot sell its business to the trust, and then open up a similar one down the street, so to speak.

Governance Issues—Voting and Veto Rights

The retained interest held by the sponsor may also be accompanied by security holder agreements that give the sponsor a disproportionate say in major decisions and/or the running of the business even though the sponsor may hold well under 50 percent of the interests. The "Security Holders Agreement" section of the prospectus for the Cineplex Galaxy Income Fund, for instance, discloses that the sponsors will continue to have a right to appoint a majority of the board of directors of the business until their interest falls below 30 percent, and even then they will have substantial influence. In addition, they have pre-emptive rights for as long as they hold an effective equity interest of 20 percent or more, and they are given veto power in a number of decision-making areas such as:

• mergers

• material asset sales

• board size changes

• CEO changes

• material agreements or obligations

To sum up, retained interests and the rights associated with them can affect the ability of the income fund to engage in mergers or other value-enhancing transactions, should the sponsors disagree with them. We should note, however, that the Canadian Coalition for Good Governance is apparently currently in the process of adapting its governance framework for corporations for use in the income fund sector, which may lead to a trend towards reduced powers for sponsors.

Representations and Warranties

If you buy a new computer, you will usually get a standard warranty that it will work properly; perhaps one year for parts and three years for labour. Often, you can also pay, usually a great deal of money, for longer-term warranty protection. Generally, when companies buy or sell businesses, the vendor is required to "represent" or give "warranties" as to the state of the business at the time of the sale. The theory is that the purchaser is paying based on an assumed state of facts, and if it turns out that the business was in worse shape than had been thought, then the purchaser overpaid and should be compensated by the vendor.

Because the factors surrounding whether a business does well or not are more varied and complex than those that go into whether a computer works properly, the warranties tend to be more complicated as well. For example, a buyer will want to know about taxes owing, lawsuits pending, potential employee relations, product liability issues for defective and dangerous products, and debts. If, after close examination, the situation turns out to be different than was warranted, the buyer will obviously want to recover any related losses.

The precise terms, length, and protection afforded by the representations and warranties in an income trust IPO are often subject to extensive negotiation. For example, problems must often be identified within a specified period of time, say one to two years, or no compensation will be payable. As well, there may be upper and lower limits on the amount of compensation payable by the vendor if a problem is determined to exist.

In an income trust IPO, the purchaser is the income fund, and the vendor is the sponsor. Frequently, they may not negotiate strenuously over the matters associated with the purchase. It is the underwriters, in this case, who should try to make sure that the representations and warranties given by the sponsor are reasonable.

Warranties can vary substantially. In many cases where extensive warranties have been given by the sponsor, they last for several years and they are limited only by the proceeds received by the sponsor. In other cases, the warranties may be much more abbreviated, available for a much shorter period, and capped at only a percentage of the proceeds received.

In at least one case (the deal did not close, however), absolutely no protection was provided by the sponsor at all, as the underlying business gave all the warranties. If there was a problem here, the trust would only be able to sue its own subsidiary, which may be no protection at all, except perhaps where the vendor has a substantial retained interest, in which case there could be some limited protection.

So once again, investors should review the prospectus to assess the level and extent of the warranties and related protection provided by the sponsor. The Canadian Securities Administrators may also be more carefully reviewing the warranties provided by sponsors in the future—which may be a good thing for investors.

Overall Assessment of Sponsor Relationship

As we have shown, the relationship with the sponsor can be multi-faceted, and investors should review it very carefully to assess any sponsor-related risks associated with an income trust investment. Also, don't forget that sponsors can provide expertise, new opportunities, or financial support, among other forms of assistance.

THE SPECTRE OF UNLIMITED LIABILITY OF UNIT HOLDERS

The risk of unit holder unlimited liability has been a well-publicized concern, and has been put forward by a number of institutional investors (pension funds, for instance) as one of the main reasons for not investing in income trusts. Why is this? In a corporation, shareholders usually have what is referred to as statutory "limited liability." In other words, by law, they cannot be held personally liable for obligations of the corporation. In essence, and with certain specified exceptions, their losses are limited to the value of their shares and, once those shares have no further value, because the assets of the corporation have been depleted to satisfy its obligations, they cannot be held personally liable for more. Basically, limited liability means shareholders can only lose the value of the shares they own.

Limited liability is seen as one of the great advantages of the capitalist system, since it enables wealthy individuals to invest in risky businesses without fear of losing their accumulated wealth. Shareholders of most corporations benefit from limited liability provisions that are provided for in federal or provincial corporate legislation.

Trusts, however, are a different story. In all provinces outside Québec and Alberta, they are not creatures of statute, but simply creatures of contract and the common (judge-made) law. As a result, unit holders of trusts do not currently benefit from statutory limited liability (except those created under the laws of Québec or Alberta). In addition, because trusts have not been commonly used as business vehicles in Canada, the judge-made case law is generally old and uncertain. This means that there is a risk that unit holders will not have limited liability. The concern, obviously, is that, without limited liability, unit holders could conceivably be held financially accountable should the underlying business collapse. In that case, they would lose not only the value of their units, but also be liable for the debts and other obligations of the underlying business as well, such as litigation and environmental cleanups.

However, the issue has been somewhat blown out of proportion. In most income trusts, the underlying business is run by a company, so the risks to a unit holder are really no more than those that apply to the shares and debt owned by the trust, which should be minimal.

In more complex structures, there may be a slightly greater risk of unlimited liability. For example, where a limited partnership carries on the business, there are more liability issues, because a limited partnership is considered to be less firm (passing through liability to investors) than a corporation. The laws governing limited partnerships can help, though, as some jurisdictions (Manitoba, for one) currently offer better limited liability protection to limited partners than others such as Ontario.

In real estate investment trusts, where the REIT owns real estate directly, there is the risk of potential liability due to environmental and other risks, which are usually addressed through careful property selection, ongoing property management, appropriate insurance, and environmental audits.

In our view, the risks are overstated in the case of most income funds, and legislative relief is on the horizon for many of these concerns. In Ontario, the provincial government has proposed legislation to specifically create unit holder limited liability for public income trusts governed by the laws of Ontario. In Québec, existing legislation actually provides substantial limited liability protection, and has done for a number of years. Other provinces may follow suit. So the issue of potential unlimited liability of unit holders of income trusts will hopefully soon disappear. It is interesting also to note that even if you are an investor living outside Ontario, you will be able, when the law is passed, to benefit from statutory limited liability protection if you are investing in an income trust governed by Ontario law. Income trusts select their own governing law, and because of the pending legislation, many are governed by the laws of Ontario or Alberta.

Measuring Risks:

Stability Ratings

Now we come to the issue of stability ratings. Only some income trusts have obtained formal stability ratings, from rating agencies such as Standard & Poor's (S&P) and Dominion Bond Rating Service (DBRS). Somewhat like credit ratings, they are designed to measure the stability or sustainability of the distributions of an income trust.

These ratings can be very helpful in assessing a trust, especially when used to compare one against another. And obviously, it is great to have the assessment of a large professional company such as Standard & Poor's in your arsenal when looking at investing.

First developed in 1999, the stability rating is a relatively new concept. In the words of S&P, its stability rating scale "conveys opinions about the relative stability of the cash distribution stream across various income funds." The stability rating is quite distinct from a credit, preferred share, or debt rating, and takes into account a number of important issues to arrive at a rating. It is important to note that these ratings are on a comparative basis, meaning that each fund is rated relative to others. Both Standard & Poor's and Dominion Bond Rating Service offer these ratings, and we will examine them carefully.

SOME THINGS TO CONSIDER ABOUT STABILITY RATINGS

While they can be extremely helpful, and may give you a good understanding of the fundamentals in a fund, there are a few issues to keep in mind with stability ratings.

First of all, they are a new product with a limited history, and therefore their validity is not really certain yet. If the rating agencies' approach to credit ratings is any guide, frequently the horse will have already bolted from the barn before they will be reduced. Often, companies will publicly declare severe financial difficulties before their debt credit ratings are reduced, showing that credit ratings may have a substantial lag time associated with them. Having said that, however, especially at the IPO stage (before any financial issues have arisen), stability ratings can provide an additional independent assessment of the riskiness of an income trust.

Second, as we mentioned, only some trusts have to date obtained stability ratings, and so most Canadian income trusts have no ratings at all. Income trusts are generally unwilling to be the first one on the block to have a lower-than-top rating, as it would make them look bad in comparison to other trusts.

Third, do not allow these ratings to create a false sense of security—an income trust unit is not a fixed income security, and stability ratings are not credit ratings. Furthermore, stability ratings may not consider a number of other associated risks, and should not be compared to either traditional bond ratings or fundamental equity analysis.

Finally, keep in mind that these are simply opinions, albeit relatively expert opinions, and not guarantees. The rating agencies involved are for-profit businesses subject to potential conflicts of interest, since issuers must pay for such ratings, and therefore the ratings are subject to error. They can assist with, but are no substitute for, a full and proper analysis of an income fund.

STANDARD AND POOR'S (S&P)

S&P assigns a rating ranging from SR-1 (representing both the highest level of expected sustainability of, and the lowest degree of expected variability in, distributions) to SR-7 (representing both the lowest degree of expected sustainability of, and the highest level of expected variability in, distributions). These ratings are based on S&P's "assessment of a fund's underlying business model, and the sustainability and variability in distributable cash flow generation in the medium to long term." The various levels are described below:

SR-1 HIGHEST level of cash distribution stability relative to other rated Canadian income trusts

SR-2 VERY HIGH level of cash distribution stability relative to other rated Canadian income trusts

SR-3 HIGH level of cash distribution stability relative to other rated Canadian income trusts

SR-4 MODERATE level of cash distribution stability relative to other rated Canadian income trusts

SR-5 MARGINAL level of cash distribution stability relative to other rated Canadian income trusts

SR-6 LOW level of cash distribution stability relative to other rated Canadian income trusts

SR-7 VERY LOW level of cash distribution stability relative to other rated Canadian income trusts

Funds that have not paid out distributions for a period of time, due to any number of the issues we have discussed, may get an SR-6 or SR-7 rating depending upon S&P's assessment of their future, if and when the distributions start up again.

Again, ratings are influenced by relative considerations—in other words, comparing one income fund to others. S&P states that it employs an exhaustive four-phase analytical process:

1. *Analysis of structure and governance*

   The first phase, the structure and governance analysis, is intended to determine risks arising from ownership, governance, and structural considerations, and how they have been mitigated.

2. *Business profile analysis*

   Factors that go into the business profile risk assessment include market share, cost competitiveness, barriers to entry, capital intensity, diversification, age of assets, operating arrangements, supplier relations, and independent engineering valuations.

3. *Financial profile analysis*

   Factors that affect the financial profile analysis include, among other things, capital structure and cash flow analysis.

4. *Distribution analysis*

   Finally, in the all-important final phase, the distribution analysis, S&P reviews the fund's consistency, both on a historical and projected basis, in light of the risk profile resulting from the first three phases.

S&P has rated income funds in the energy, real estate, telecommunications, services, and phone directories business. Its ratings in the energy sector are among the oldest ratings. Interestingly, its assessment in early 2004 of the oil and gas income trust universe was that they should be at the lower end of the stability ratings scale, because of the inherently volatile nature of the oil and gas industry, the risk of wide price variations, the rapid depletion of oil and gas reserves by these funds, and the inherent need to expend capital—especially given their relatively high pay-out ratios. As we saw earlier, it is expensive to both find and bring new oil reserves on stream, but if an oil and gas income fund doesn't do so, it will use up its reserves eventually. Exchange rates also affect oil and gas income funds, since oil and gas are generally sold in U.S. dollars. Then there is the commodity price risk itself—the volatile ups and downs of commodities such as oil and gas—which can hurt performance.

S&P ratings as of January 12, 2004 included an SR-4 (moderate level of cash distribution) for Canadian Oil Sands Trust, the highest rating in the sector at the time. Given the characteristics of the oil and gas sector however, with its relative volatility and capital constraints, SR-5 and SR-6 ratings predominated among producers, with much fewer SR-4 ratings.

Other S&P ratings in late December 2003 included an SR-2 (very high stability of cash distributions) rating for both the Yellow Pages™ Income Fund and Riocan Real Estate Investment Trust, an SR-1 rating (highest level of stability of distributions) for power funds Gaz Metropolitain and Co LP, TransAlta Power LP and TransCanada Power LP, and SR-1 ratings for a number of diversified funds of funds, including the Brompton Stable Income Fund and the Citadel S-1 Investment Trust.

Many income trusts that might be ranked lower have chosen not to pay for ratings—yes, it costs them to be rated. Because of this, S&P has had to perform analysis on income trusts that have not chosen to be rated, in order to ensure that its ratings remain accurate. The contrast is interesting; most publicly rated income funds (ratings obtained by funds that paid) hold SR-2 ratings, whereas overall the most common rating (both paid and unpaid) is an SR-4. Note that even within the same sector, the ratings can vary substantially, for instance, SR-1 to SR-4 in pipelines and SR-2 to SR-5 in real estate. The reason for this is simple. Would you want your fund rated if it had only moderate, or worse, stability of distributions?

More information regarding the stability rating of various income funds by S&P can be obtained on the Internet at www.standardandpoors.com.

DOMINION BOND RATING SERVICE (DBRS)

Dominion Bond Rating Service (DBRS) is also in the business of rating the stability of income trusts. Its ratings are STA-1 (the highest possible rating) through STA-7 (the lowest). Each category is then sub-divided into three categories—high, middle, and low. This gives us a total of 21 different ratings, from STA-1 in the top category (the highest) to STA-7 in the bottom category (the lowest of the low).

The ratings used by DBRS are as follows:

STA-1/STA-2 The two highest stability categories; rated superior in a majority of classifications, especially operating factors; expected to include some power, pipeline, and gas distribution funds

STA-3 Good distribution stability and sustainability; may be more sensitive to economic factors and have greater cyclical tendencies; may be less diversified

STA-4/STA-5 Likely to be subject to cyclicality, seasonality and price fluctuations; may include conventional oil income funds due to sensitivity to commodity price

STA-6/STA-7 Likely to have volatile and relatively unstable distributions; tend to be "below average" in many or most factors

DBRS's stability ratings consider seven main factors:

1. *Operating characteristics*

   These are considered by DBRS to be "the single most important component of the stability rating," and include such matters as products, the make-up of the revenue stream, cyclicality, seasonality and weather effects, the regulatory environment affecting the business, trade restrictions, technological change issues, environmental matters, and structural changes that could impact operational performance.

2. *Financial flexibility*

   The financial flexibility analysis examines the debt level, sources of liquidity, and alternative ways to finance the business.

3. *Growth*

   Growth is categorized as weak, moderate, or strong. "Stable" earnings and cash distributions are generally considered "moderate," while per-unit income growth is considered "strong" (DBRS also considers it rare). Declining income per unit leads to a "weak" categorization.

4. Asset quality

Asset quality looks at factors such as the remaining life of an asset (which is identified by DBRS as "particularly important"), its age and condition, location, utilization, product differentiation, obsolescence, and inherent asset values (both tangible and intangible).

5. Diversification

The diversification analysis examines the diversity of both the assets and the revenue stream. Asset type and geography can affect this review.

6. Size/market position

Size and market position looks at market clout, pricing power, strategy to deal with competitors, the breadth and scale of operations, etc. DBRS considers income trusts with market capitalizations under $400 million to be small (many would fall into this category). Market capitalizations of $400–$800 million are viewed as medium in size, and $800 million and over are considered large.

7. Sponsorship/governance

In the sponsorship/governance category, the ability to obtain resources is examined. Such resources may include management or technical expertise, financial help, and new business opportunities. Other factors examined include the management fee structure (if applicable) and the fund-manager relationship.

DBRS's ratings are described as being effective "through an economic cycle," meaning that non-structural quarterly or annual fluctuations in cash flow, or non-recurring effects, may not result in a ratings change. We must remember that stability ratings already punish companies with negative recurring characteristics, and so any expected variability may already have been reflected in their ratings.

DBRS uses its own methodology to try to enhance comparability, so that its financial ratios may vary from an income fund's actual reported results. Financial ratios examined include, among others, cash distributions per unit, cash available for distribution per unit (often, not all cash available will in fact be distributed), net income before extras per unit (designed to capture recurring net income), gross debt as a percentage of capital, cash flow divided by debt, EBITDA (earnings before interest, taxes, depreciation, and amortization), interest coverage, and market capitalization.

DBRS also divides income funds into five major categories. These include:

1. *Power income funds*

   Based on electricity-generating companies, these funds are typically quite stable with long-life assets and are often rated in the STA-1 to STA-3 range.

2. *Pipelines and gas distribution funds*

   These funds are also stable and often rated in the STA-1 to STA-3 range unless small or undiversified.

3. *Conventional oil and gas income funds*

   With depleting reserves and volatile product prices, these funds often have stability ratings in the STA-4 or STA-5 range.

4. *REITs*

   These real estate funds can be quite stable, particularly if they have long-term leases or a diversified portfolio, and may well be rated from STA-2 to STA-4.

5. Infrastructure and other funds

These include mainly business trusts and can have a wide range of stability and sustainability ratings based on the underlying business.

Note that there can be wide variations in ratings within a sector, such as in the REIT industry. There are a number of different types of REITs, including office, industrial, hotel, residential, and long-term care, which may have different characteristics and challenges. They are not, unlike other income trusts, required to have redeemable units to avoid adverse tax consequences. As a result, there are both closed-end REITs, which do not have redemption features but instead are more restricted in what they can invest in, and open-ended REITs, which provide a unit redemption mechanism but can be more flexible in their investments. REITs can also either be diversified over a number of products, or can be specifically focused on apartment buildings, office space, hotel rooms, retail space, or retirement homes, among others. Recently, they have been suffering from adverse factors in the real estate sector, including lower occupancy and rental rates and inferior marketing. This has combined with increasing prices for real estate—believed to be caused in part by offshore investor demand, low interest rates, and investor wariness regarding certain financial instruments caused by the dot-com collapse and problems in the mutual fund sector—to make the waters a little rough. As a result, most REITs now have internal management, leverage restrictions, and single property diversification limits.

DBRS has issued a number of reports comparing different income trusts in the same sector, such as pipeline funds, REITs, and power funds. S&P has also issued comparative reports of this nature. These can be very helpful and are available on the Internet. As well, DBRS has also begun to release unsolicited (and presumably unpaid) ratings, based on public information. These are rated with the letter "(p)" on its website. For DBRS reports, visit www.dbrs.com.

A FINAL NOTE ON RISK

Over the past four chapters, we have discussed many of the risks associated with investing in income trusts. The key one, which cannot be stated too often, is that when it comes to risk, income funds should be treated much like equity investments. To view them as guaranteed high-yielding fixed income investments is a serious mistake.

CHAPTER NINE

IPOs and Conversions:

The Recipe for Making Income Trusts

Understanding the way trusts come into being can aid in making investment decisions, so we will spend some time explaining this process.

There are two ways of forming an income trust. In this chapter, we will describe the process and timetable of an income trust initial public offering (IPO) of what was previously a private (or part of a public) business and which will become the underlying business of the income trust itself. This differs from the conversion process, where an already public company converts to being a trust. One of the main differences is that a public company already has a large number of shareholders, instead of a small number of owners. We will also examine how the conversion process works.

THE IPO PROCESS

An IPO is the process by which a new income trust is born, and its pricing or yield is indicative of how risky the underwriters, and often key institutional investors, perceive the new income trust to be. While in retrospect a number of current trusts—the Hot House Growers Income Fund is a good example—may not represent ideal businesses for the income trust structure, nonetheless when the market is hot one often sees products come to market that perhaps should have stayed on the shelf. An IPO of an income trust is not much different from an IPO of common shares of a new public company, with three key differences:

1. The pricing of an income trust is yield-based, meaning that it is dependent substantially on expected distributions.

2. The structure of an income trust may be significantly more complex and tax-efficient than most public companies.

3. All or most of the net proceeds generally go into the sponsors' pockets, or to pay off debt, rather than into the business itself.

While the average investor may or may not choose to become directly involved in an IPO—IPO's can be very volatile, with unit prices fluctuating up and down when they begin trading—it is important to understand the process itself, as it aids in evaluating a trust.

The Preliminary Prospectus

In an IPO process, the key document to be prepared is the prospectus. The law requires that there is first a preliminary prospectus, possibly an amended preliminary prospectus, and later a final prospectus.

The preliminary prospectus is prepared by the sponsor and the management of the business in consultation with the underwriters, the auditors of the trust, and the legal counsel for both the trust and the underwriters. Its preparation typically involves an extensive process of reviewing the underlying business and developing an appropriate marketing strategy to sell the units when they are issued, as well as seeking to disclose all relevant material information.

The preliminary prospectus is usually a lengthy, detailed, and sometimes tedious document that nonetheless contains a wealth of information about the proposed income trust and its underlying business. It will usually contain a shorter, but fairly complex, summary towards the front—a kind of executive summary that is a little easier to digest. It is called preliminary because, until a final prospectus has been examined, reviewed, and receipted (accepted) by the Canadian securities regulators, sales of trust units cannot legally be made. Before the securities regulators approve a final prospectus, underwriters can only solicit non-binding expressions of interest (i.e. they can't get any signed agreements or contract to buy) from prospective purchasers—often together with a copy of the preliminary prospectus. Preliminary prospectus documents can be obtained at www.sedar.com.

It is also called preliminary because it usually does not contain final pricing information. In the case of income trust IPOs, trust units are generally priced at $10 each, but it is the determination of how many will be offered and the effective yield (the expected annual distributions per unit, generally expressed as a percentage) that drive the pricing process and that are not usually known at the preliminary prospectus stage. During the period between the filing of the preliminary and the final prospectus, underwriters (the institution arranging the financing for the deal) will review the trading prices of similar products and, if applicable, negotiate with lead institutional investors to determine unit price and the number of units to be sold to these investors, among other things. The final prospectus should contain all pricing information and enable investors to determine the expected yield.

After the preliminary prospectus has been filed, the Canadian securities regulators will usually review and issue comments on the disclosure, to which the trust will be required to respond. To obtain a receipt for the final prospectus, the responses must be to the satisfaction of the securities regulators. Often two rounds of comments occur, with several different Canadian securities commissions from different provinces providing input, before the final prospectus can be filed. This process is often redundant, and many experts are calling for a single national securities regulation to speed up the process and make it less complicated. Often the comments are highly technical, but on occasion they are substantive and affect, or sometimes prevent, the progress of the transaction.

Sometimes, additional underwriters will be added, and other changes may be made and matters updated, in which case an amended preliminary prospectus will usually be filed with the regulators and distributed to prospective purchasers as well.

Between the filing of the preliminary or amended preliminary prospectus and the final prospectus, the marketing process commences. To build interest in the new income trust, road show presentations, in which representatives of management and the underwriters visit with selected investors and brokerage salespersons (usually in several different cities), are common. After the underwriters have canvassed the market, they will then enter into a formal agreement, called an underwriting agreement, under which they agree to purchase the trust units on their own behalf, for resale to investors. This agreement is usually subject to various terms and conditions, but it sets the formal pricing of the units. Immediately following the signing of the underwriting agreement, the final prospectus containing the pricing details is filed with the Canadian securities commissions. Once a receipt for the final prospectus is obtained— usually a very quick process, as it has already been reviewed—the underwriters can take binding commitments to purchase the securities from investors. Even after the final prospectus has been receipted, amendments may be required if material changes occur after the filing of the final prospectus. These amendments must then be provided to later purchasers.

The prospectus is required to contain full, true, and plain disclosure of all material facts relating to the securities offered. It should contain a comprehensive discussion of the trust and the underlying business, describing the good points as well as the challenges and risks facing the business. It is an excellent resource and is very useful even after the IPO. The prospectus will also include financial statements, summaries of material agreements (the detailed agreements may be filed at www.sedar.com), descriptions of management and executive compensation arrangements, governance arrangements, tax matters, material litigation, and risk factors. These are the most useful parts of the prospectus as they indicate the key risks facing the business.

The prospectus also contains signed certificates of the issuer, the promoter (if any), and the underwriters' certification of its accuracy. Investors should read the prospectus carefully. Additional information may also be available at www.sedar.com.

Stock Exchange Listing and Liquidity

Before filing a final prospectus, the trust will also seek approval for the units to be listed on a Canadian stock exchange, such as the Toronto Stock Exchange. This is designed to provide investors with a market on which, assuming there is sufficient interest, they can resell their units at a later date.

We have spoken about liquidity earlier. The market for any given security may be liquid, meaning that investors should be able to resell their securities fairly easily, or illiquid, in which case it may be very difficult to resell. Just because listing approval has been obtained from the stock exchange in question as described in the final prospectus, it is no assurance that there will in fact be a liquid market to facilitate resale. There is also no guarantee that the trust units will always be listed, since the stock exchange or securities regulator, or even the issuer itself, could suspend trading in the units or de-list them from the stock exchange. As a general guideline the larger and more successful the trust, the more liquid the market for its securities can be expected to be. The same is true of corporations.

Withdrawal Rights

Under the securities laws of most provinces, investors have a time-limited statutory right to change their minds and withdraw from an agreement to purchase securities offered under a prospectus within two business days following their receipt of the final prospectus and any amendments to it. This right is very rarely exercised, but if it is properly exercised, it can allow an investor to get his or her money back without providing any reason at all. It puts the risk of holding the unsold securities on the dealer from whom they were originally purchased.

Dealers generally do not like to hold securities, since their business model is to profit from sales commissions rather than to profit from longer-term potential increases in the value of the securities— or risk potential decreases as well! So you can expect to be discouraged from exercising any withdrawal rights. And be warned, if you do exercise them, you may, among other things, not be given the opportunity to purchase IPOs again. It is a right to be exercised carefully!

Investors' Rights on a Misrepresentation

In addition to the withdrawal rights, which allow a purchaser to simply walk away from a proposed purchase without any reason, investors who purchase an IPO also have certain statutory rights to either reverse the transaction and/or seek monetary compensation if the prospectus contains a misrepresentation, a material misstatement, or omission. Subject to available defences, these rights may be available against the issuer, its trustees, the underwriters, and any others who signed the prospectus, as well as experts such as auditors and legal counsel for expert reports or opinions in the prospectus.

The maximum amount of damages per unit that can be recovered by a purchaser is the price at which the units were offered to the public. So if it is found that anyone involved in the prospectus misrepresented facts or figures that affect the unit price, there are steps the investor may take to recover any potential losses.

IPO Closing Mechanics

The closing usually occurs about one to two weeks after the receipt for the final prospectus has been obtained. This period is designed to allow the underwriters to finalize their sale commitments with prospective buyers and collect the money, and for the withdrawal rights, described above, to expire. These usually expire without having been exercised, but if a lot of investors have exercised their withdrawal rights and they cannot be easily replaced, the closing may not take place.

At the closing of the IPO, the underwriters will present the trust with a cheque in the amount of the gross proceeds raised, less their commission, whereupon the trust will usually use the net proceeds received by it from the underwriters to pay its transaction-related expenses and any outstanding debt, if applicable. The balance is used to purchase some or all of the underlying business from the vendor.

As a result, the vendors usually walk away with the vast majority of the proceeds raised. This, coupled with the very attractive pricing offered by income trusts to vendors and sponsors, and certain other factors, is one of the reasons the income trust market has been so hot lately. Among the other factors driving the income trust market was the credit crunch in the early years of the 21st century, which saw commercial banks tighten up on credit availability, and the general slowdown in the buying and selling of businesses, often referred to as the mergers and acquisition, or M&A, market.

At closing, the trust units are issued to the underwriters, who then distribute them to the purchasers. Typically, income trusts are in book-based form, which means that investors cannot obtain a unit certificate in the same way that they can usually obtain a share certificate registered in their own name for a stock that they purchase.

Instead, all trust units are generally registered in the name of a securities depository such as the Canadian Depository for Securities (CDS). The role of the securities depository is to hold the securities, which are represented by a single global security certificate registered in its name, for the benefit of its members, who include brokers and dealers. In turn, these brokers and dealers are obliged to hold their interest for the benefit of their applicable customers. Investors' holdings are therefore somewhat indirect, but nonetheless, transfers are facilitated this way.

Post–IPO Obligations of Income Trusts

Income trusts that have completed their IPOs will then, as publicly traded issuers, be subject to a number of ongoing obligations. These include, among other things:

- Ongoing annual and quarterly financial reporting obligations. Annual financial statements are required to be audited.

- Ongoing annual and quarterly analysis of their financial results and situation, referred to as "management's discussion and analysis" (MD&A).

- Annual filing known as an annual information form (AIF), which acts as an annual update of material information regarding an issuer.

- Holding an annual meeting of unit holders to carry on usual business such as electing trustees, appointing auditors, and receiving financial statements. If appropriate, special meetings to deal with other matters may be held.

- Issuing press releases and filing what are called material change reports in the event that material changes occur. In certain cases, these reports can be filed on a temporarily confidential basis with the Canadian securities regulators where disclosure would be unduly detrimental to the income trust.

- The obligation under stock exchange rules to disclose other ongoing material information.

- The obligations of insiders to report their trading in the units promptly. These are publicly reported at www.sedi.ca.

Available Information

There should be plenty of available information about an income trust for you to read, starting with the prospectus and continuing with ongoing disclosure information, which should also be available through the Internet at www.sedar.com. In addition, as noted above, reports of insider trades can be accessed at www.sedi.ca.

Many income trusts maintain their own individual websites which may contain investor relations information, press releases, public disclosure documents, and other useful information. However, the importance of the IPO prospectus cannot be overemphasized, especially for recent public income trusts.

THE INCOME TRUST CONVERSION PROCESS

Now we come to the second way to make an income trust. The process of converting an existing public company into an income trust is quite different from the IPO process. As we mentioned earlier, a public company already has a large number of shareholders, rather than one or a small number of owners. As well, there is often no need for financing, and so a prospectus may not be involved at all. In some cases, a new financing will accompany a conversion.

Management Proxy Circular

In an income trust conversion process, the key document is the management proxy circular, also known as the management information circular. It is prepared by management, with the help of the company's lawyers and the auditors, and with the possible assistance of an investment dealer, for the purpose of providing shareholders with the information needed for them to vote to decide whether or not they approve of converting the company into an income trust.

On occasion, any immature businesses, such as oil and gas exploration, that do not generate regular and positive cash flow will be spun off (removed from the equation) at the same time, so that the income trust will only contain a portion of the former business. In this case, shareholders will end up with both an income trust unit and a share of the spun-off business.

As with a prospectus, the management proxy circular will typically contain a wealth of information regarding the proposal; it is required by law to contain the same information as a prospectus. The difference, however, is that it is generally not reviewed and commented on by securities regulators, and there is no preliminary and final management proxy circular. There may also be other information available at www.sedar.com. However, in the past, material agreements have often not been disclosed as thoroughly as in the prospectus process, so be careful.

Since a meeting of shareholders is required, the votes of shareholders are usually solicited for use at the meeting, and shareholders will be entitled to approve or disapprove of the conversion. If they disapprove, they will frequently be provided with dissent rights, which allow them not to participate in the conversion and instead to elect to be paid the fair value of their shares in cash, either in an amount agreed to with the company or in an amount determined by a judge (after potentially lengthy and expensive court proceedings which could potentially affect the fair value). There are no change-your-mind withdrawal rights as there are in an IPO situation.

Arrangement Proceedings

The conversion process is usually accomplished under what is called the arrangement provisions of Canadian corporate law. Under these procedures, a judge is called upon to approve the fairness and reasonableness of the process before it can proceed. Unhappy shareholders have an opportunity to make their feelings known to a judge, through a lawyer at this point.

Rather than an underwriting agreement, there is an arrangement or conversion agreement under which, among other things, the trust agrees to acquire the underlying business in return for its trust units. Often, there will be made available a limited number of exchangeable shares or similar exchangeable securities to reduce the tax impact of the transaction to investors who select the exchangeable securities. In that case, the tax will not be paid until the exchangeable securities are later exchanged for trust units.

Stock Exchange Listing

As with an IPO, the new income trust will want to have its units listed for trading on a stock exchange, and thus will need the approval of that exchange. Again, as with an IPO, the existence of a listing does not guarantee that the market will be liquid, although the pre-conversion liquidity of the public company will likely be a good guide as to the liquidity post-conversion.

Investors' Rights on a Misrepresentation

Unlike in a prospectus, there are currently no statutory rights against the trust, company, or others in the event of a misrepresentation in the management proxy circular.

This may change if Bill 198, as proposed in Ontario, comes into force. The Bill would introduce statutory liability for all types of ongoing misrepresentations, although the rights against the company or trust will likely be more limited than the full recovery of purchase price as it is in cases with a prospectus. Similar changes are also underway in British Columbia.

Post-Conversion Obligations of Income Trusts

Income trusts that have completed a conversion will then, as publicly traded issuers, generally be subject to a number of ongoing obligations, in the same way as if they had completed an IPO. These obligations are described earlier in this chapter.

Pricing on Conversion

Typically, a conversion will lead to a substantial increase in the trading price of the shares after the announcement of the conversion, which is carried through to the units post-conversion. The reason for this is that the market generally prices income trusts at a higher valuation than comparable companies, partly because of their expected higher distributions and increased tax efficiency. As well, due to the recent increased interest in these vehicles, there may be a bubble effect in play. As a result, certain companies have considered converting into an income trust as a response to a hostile or unsolicited tender offer. A prime recent example is Fording Coal. In the Fording case, upon proposing an income trust in the face of a hostile takeover bid, the effect was an increase in share value that was ultimately paid out to shareholders of Fording Inc. It seems, therefore, that one investment strategy might be to invest in public companies that are likely candidates to convert into income trusts, although this, like any investment strategy, may well be risky.

Closing Mechanics

Closing of the conversion transaction usually occurs within a few days after shareholder and court approval has been obtained. There is often no money exchanged at closing. Rather, the trust units are issued in exchange for the shares, and investors must send in their share certificates in order to receive their trust units. The entire process often takes from 60 to 120 days.

Available Information

There is plenty of available information about converted income trusts for you to read. The key document for any specific situation is the management proxy circular, but post-closing there will be also be ongoing disclosure information, which should generally be available through www.sedar.com. Information about insider rights should be available at www.sedi.ca. Converted income trusts may maintain individual websites for you to browse as well.

CHAPTER TEN

The Legal State
of Affairs in Canada
Preventative Medicine for Liability

The increasingly litigious environment—it seems like everyone is suing somebody for something these days—coupled with new regulations is increasing the need to take great care in operating income trusts, as well as other public companies. In this climate investors need to be very diligent in watching out for problems. As we saw before, there are some statutory rights that are held by investors, such as the withdrawal rights discussed in the previous chapter, but many of the rights to remedy any misrepresentations currently rely on common law, requiring the investors to clearly demonstrate that they relied on false or misleading statements in deciding to buy, sell, or hold their units. This is no easy task! Proving that either a written or oral statement encouraged you to act in some manner can be almost impossible.

In this chapter we will briefly review the state of affairs in Canada with regard to liability from both sides of the fence, from both the trust and the investor perspectives.

ONTARIO'S BILL 198

To begin with, various government-appointed committees have called for a simpler way to remedy investors' claims for misleading statements or misrepresentations. As a result, in 2003, the Ontario government adopted, but has not yet implemented, a piece of legislation known as Bill 198. This legislation was designed in part as a confidence-boosting mechanism after the Enron and Worldcom scandals, among others, and in light of the U.S. *Sarbanes-Oxley Act of 2002*, which significantly tightens U.S. governance practices.

The proposed legislation is expected to be implemented shortly by the new Liberal government. By putting in place mechanisms to bring more transparent disclosure of misrepresentations, investors, including unit holders of income trusts, will likely have a simpler way to remedy these situations, and have a much better chance at recouping any losses from false or misleading statements. These actions should also serve to further discourage such statements from being made in the future.

This legislation has also been designed with class actions in mind, providing further assistance to small investors without deep pockets or major investments. Under the proposed bill, misrepresentations in public documents or oral statements, or when changes are made and not disclosed in a timely fashion, investors will have the statutory right to seek to cover their losses. British Columbia is in the process of implementing similar changes, and other provinces can be expected to follow suit.

MAKING THE FACTS CLEAR:
THE DISCLOSURE POLICY

In order that everyone is on the same page, and there can be fewer questions about what, how, when, and to whom disclosures of information should occur, every income trust should have a disclosure policy. The purpose of this document is to give a thorough understanding of all the legal disclosure requirements, and it should be practical and individually tailored to each trust, and include information about:

- Deciding when information is sufficiently relevant to investors that it needs to be publicly disclosed

- Analysts' reports

- Earnings announcements

- Disclosure to only certain investors, such as one or two large institutional investors (this is called selective disclosure, and is generally inappropriate), and dealing with unintentional selective disclosure

- The use of electronic media (including e-mail, chat rooms, and bulletin boards)

- Postings on the corporate website

- The use of forward-looking information (future predictions)

- The involvement of the board and/or board committees

- Reacting to rumours

- Authorized spokespersons

- Quiet periods (periods, usually around quarter and year-ends, during which insiders should not trade in the income trust's units to reduce the risk that they are seen to be participating in insider trading)

- Any other trading restrictions

DISCLOSURE COMPLIANCE SYSTEM

Consistent with the disclosure policy, the disclosure compliance system is a set of procedures that should seek to ensure the correctness of all disclosures, including oral presentations, press releases, and website postings. These procedures may include, for example:

- Questionnaires

- Due diligence sessions

- Internal certification requirements (for example, where divisional managers confirm in writing the absence of material developments in their areas)

- Debriefings

- Involvement of or review by experienced legal counsel

- The involvement of a board-level disclosure committee

- Circulation to directors of all disclosures

- The investigation of allegations made by whistle-blowers

As well, other compliance procedures should include:

- Developing a process for enabling officers and trustees or directors to notify the board promptly in order to facilitate quick corrective action to rectify any incorrect disclosure as soon as possible, so as to minimize both personal and trust liability

- Instituting a process for dealing with forward-looking information (forecasting) of all types, so as to seek to ensure that it is reasonably based and contains appropriate cautionary language and key assumptions

- Formalizing procedures to improve management's discussion and analysis (MD&A) in response to recent regulatory and other developments

- Defining the roles and responsibilities of directors and committees by setting out charters or mandates, which should be carefully designed to satisfy required obligations while seeking to avoid increasing personal liability

- Developing a process to review expert reports that are to be relied upon

In the face of a misrepresentation or incorrect disclosure, all procedures should be complied with, or else the income trust and its trustees and officers may be even worse off. Proper compliance with disclosure obligations will not necessarily prevent lawsuits, but can certainly go a long way towards being able to establish a defence.

INSIDER TRADING POLICIES

An insider is defined as a director, officer, or 10 percent shareholder (or unit holder). And, as Martha Stewart found out, it may also include a person that has non-public information about a public company or trust that could affect the value or market price of the securities of that company or trust. In an income fund, insiders would generally include the trustee(s) and the directors and officers of the underlying business. Once insiders have become aware of undisclosed material information, it is generally illegal for them to buy or sell the units of an income fund while that information has not been generally released to the public. It is also generally illegal to tip (or pass on) this information to other people, whether or not these other people choose to act on it, except strictly in the necessary course of business.

Insider trading is dealt with under both corporate law and securities law. As well, a bill has just been passed by the federal Parliament which introduces penalties for insider trading under Canadian criminal law.

The penalties for breach of insider trading rules are severe. Under the Ontario *Securities Act*, for instance, breaking insider trading rules could result in (i) a prison term of up to five years less a day, and/or (ii) a fine that is the greater of $5 million and three times the amount of profit made (or loss avoided) by the person as a result of engaging in insider trading. Penalties under the federal *Criminal Code* amendments would provide that those people convicted of insider trading could face a prison sentence of up to 10 years, while those people convicted of tipping could face a prison sentence of up to five years.

Determining what sort of information is important enough to affect the price of units of an income fund (and therefore be considered inside information) is not always a clear-cut task. Events that have a significant effect on one income fund may not have any noticeable impact on another. Insiders with access to confidential information should therefore err on the side of caution when deciding on the appropriate time to buy or sell the units or securities of an income fund. Even after the fund has publicly disclosed material information, an insider should probably wait at least one trading day before buying or selling the securities of that fund.

Income funds should therefore review their policies to seek to ensure compliance with trading restrictions and proper reporting of insider transactions, especially in light of the new Internet-based System for Electronic Disclosure by Insiders (SEDI) procedures. SEDI is an electronic system operated by the Canadian Depository for Securities on behalf of the securities commissions. The system allows for the filing and public dissemination of reports by insiders of public companies, including public income funds. Filings are made via the Internet through SEDI's website at www.sedi.ca.

CORPORATE GOVERNANCE MATTERS

With recent corporate governance scandals in Canada and the United States involving companies such as Worldcom, Enron, Livent, Bre-X, YBM, Magnex, and Hollinger, among others, there have been moves by securities regulatory authorities and other organizations in Canada and the United States, as well as other countries, to restore investor confidence in the public markets. Canadian securities regulatory authorities have passed and are introducing mandatory rules and guidelines to improve the corporate governance practices of companies whose securities trade in the public market. These rules and guidelines are fairly broad in scope, and generally apply to both corporations and non-corporate entities such as income trusts.

Rules of the Canadian Securities Regulatory Authorities

The securities regulatory authorities of all Canadian jurisdictions, except British Columbia in certain cases, published three final rules that came into force on March 30, 2004, all designed to keep a tighter reign on corporate governance.

The first rule (*Multilateral Instrument 52-109*) requires that the chief executive officer and the chief financial officer of a public company, or of the underlying business in the case of most income trusts, personally certify the correctness of certain financial information and controls. This of course helps put pressure on senior officers to make sure things are being done properly, to avoid personal liability in case of an infraction or misstatement.

The second rule (*Multilateral Instrument 52-110*) sets out rules to regulate the role and composition of audit committees (a committee of the board of directors of a public company or of the board of trustees of a public income trust). The committee members must be both independent and financially literate. This rule serves to make sure that the committee involved in any audits of financial statements is unrelated to the business or trust, and therefore theoretically unbiased.

The third rule (*Multilateral Instrument 52-108)* sets out rules that support the work of the new Canadian Public Accountability Board (CPAB) in its responsibility to oversee the work of auditors of public companies and income trusts. Audit firms must be members of the CPAB, and will be regulated by it.

The Canadian regulators have said they believe these three final rules, which along with other OSC initiatives are available at www.osc.gov.on.ca, will be as robust as similar rules that are in force in the United States. However, Canadian rules have been designed to reflect the differences in Canadian markets, especially the significant number of controlled companies and the generally smaller size and resources of Canadian public companies.

The regulators are serious. The penalty for making a false certification contrary to this rule could result in a quasi-criminal sanction, an administrative sanction or, if and when Bill 198 or similar laws come on board, civil proceedings under securities laws.

Corporate Governance Disclosure: The Proposed Policy and Rule

In addition to the three rules discussed above, on January 16, 2004, the securities regulatory authorities of all Canadian jurisdictions (except Québec and British Columbia) introduced a proposed policy called Effective Corporate Governance and a proposed rule entitled Disclosure of Corporate Governance Practices.

Recognizing that corporate governance is in a constant state of evolution and that different companies may need to have different governance mechanisms, the Canadian regulators have maintained the guideline approach that was initially adopted several years ago by the Toronto Stock Exchange. This approach proposes to recommend best practices of corporate governance to public companies—including income funds—while requiring Canadian public companies and income funds to disclose in their AIFs a comparison of their actual corporate governance practices against the recommended best practices.

The participating provinces have said that they intend to review the proposed policy and rule during the two years following their implementation, to make sure that the recommendations and disclosure requirements set out in the proposals continue to be appropriate for issuers in the Canadian marketplace.

Objectives

It is hoped that the stronger emphasis by securities regulatory authorities on improving corporate governance practices will result in more transparency, including in income funds. This improved transparency should ultimately create a positive market perception and improved market integrity. The question remains, though, whether increased disclosure will cure the deficiencies that lead to corporate governance problems, as it is often the actions and motives of particular individuals who lead a company that matter most. The theory is that if competent directors or trustees of income funds are combined with proper processes and procedures, there is a higher chance that problems will be identified, and that those people who make the decisions will be accountable for them and may as a result be more likely to make better decisions.

So, overall, the future seems bright for both trusts and investors with regard to misinformation and corruption. As an investor, you can dig as far as you like into the actual rules and regulations being introduced and proposed—they are public—and as regulations become tighter, and disclosures more transparent, we may well see more large—even institutional—investors getting into income trusts, which will serve to strengthen the industry and keep practices on the level.

CHAPTER ELEVEN

Selling a Business to an Income Trust–Issues for Business Owners

In Chapter 9 we explained the IPO and conversion process. Now we feel it important to explore the ins and outs of an income trust IPO from the perspective of a business owner who wishes to sell for cash all or a portion of his or her investment in a private company. With the continued, relatively low interest rate environment we are currently experiencing, among other things, there can be any number of reasons a business owner would consider this an attractive option.

WHY SELL YOUR BUSINESS TO AN INCOME TRUST?

Of course, remembering all you have read thus far, you first need to have a sizeable and mature business (with a minimum EBITDA— earnings before interest, taxes, depreciation, and amortization— after required capital expenditures of the order of C$6 million per annum, and ideally more) that has good, stable cash flows and a predictable and preferably low need for ongoing capital expenditures. Growth prospects are desirable, but not necessarily essential.

So let's say that your business fulfills these essential requirements. Why would you consider selling to an income trust? Among the benefits of an income trust IPO, in addition to the cash received from the sale of a business owner's stake in the business that is purchased, are the following:

- Greater access to capital. In the future, you can raise money by issuing more units.

- Improved liquidity for any remaining investors. They should be able to sell their units on a stock exchange after the IPO closes.

- The ability to use equity (in the form of trust units) to complete mergers and acquisitions. The trust may be able to buy another business and pay for it with units instead of cash.

- Improved opportunities for management and employee compensation. You can use units as currency, such as long-term incentive plans based on trust units and/or unit option plans.

- A higher profile in the business community with potential improvements from a branding and corporate image perspective. However, adverse events could turn this into a detriment.

- Simplified ongoing credit evaluations for creditors and suppliers. However, this is subject to the fact that the income trust will be distributing much of its cash flows, which could potentially transform this into a negative.

When contemplating these benefits, do not forget to take into account the deal-related costs, portions of which might be owed in cash even if an IPO isn't ultimately completed. There are also many ongoing costs, as well as the headaches of being publicly traded.

Out-of-pocket costs will include:

- Legal and accounting fees, which may well exceed $1 million

- Trustee, director, and officer liability insurance fees. D&O insurance has been getting much more expensive of late, and you should expect to pay six figures each year.

- Printing and investor relations fees—likely a few hundred thousand dollars

- Stock exchange and securities commission fees. The regulators and stock exchange take their pound of flesh!

- Trustees' and directors' compensation

In addition to these, there are the indirect costs (on the order of $20,000 or more per person per year in Canada and increasing):

- Increased disclosure to your competitors, employees, customers, suppliers, and others, both initially and on an ongoing basis. As a result, you may see increased competition and potentially less flexibility in negotiating with customers, suppliers, and employees.

- Increased demands on management and board time, including board meetings and investor meetings.

- Increased short-term performance pressures. The stock market reacts quickly to bad news.

- The adverse branding impact of poor public company performance, or other adverse circumstances. As a public company, you are in the public eye and the media will quickly broadcast any bad news.

- Reduced cash in the business. Profits are being distributed through the trust and can't be reinvested in the business; this in turn leads to reduced flexibility in making capital expenditures or reacting to changing circumstances or competitive pressures.

- The loss of control that comes with both selling your business and going public. Even if you were to retain a substantial or even majority interest, the board, including independent directors, will be the chief decision-maker, not the former owner.

- The sharing of future upside profits with unit holders—and downside losses, of course!

- The potential loss of flexibility as a public company, especially in relation to future transactions between you and the new public income trust. Non-arm's-length transactions tend to be vigorously reviewed by boards.

- Securities laws and market pressures will restrict the sale of the part of the company that you did not sell initially. As a significant unit holder, you may not need to sell via a prospectus which takes time and costs money.

- Potential impact of stock market fluctuations and market perceptions can result in perceived lower valuations that could lead to negative credit-related decisions by creditors, customers, and suppliers.

- Not to be dismissed, the increasing possibility of civil, regulatory, and even criminal liability in an apparently ever more litigious world.

Obviously, you should weigh the benefits against the costs and be very comfortable before embarking on the process of an income trust IPO.

FIRST STEPS

Even before you decide to proceed with an income trust, one of your first steps should be to retain knowledgeable and experienced legal, tax, and financial advisors who are familiar with the world of income trusts. A small number of major Canadian law firms are very experienced in this area, including Stikeman Elliott LLP (Simon Romano's law firm), Goodmans LLP, and Torys LLP, among others. You must ensure that the lawyers you are dealing with have, or have ready access to, income trust, securities, M&A, and tax expertise, and that you are comfortable with the individuals involved, since you will be spending a lot of time together.

Major accounting firms, among others, all have substantial income trust expertise on staff, and can advise you from both a financial and tax perspective. They will often also express interest in being the auditor of the public income trust. If you have other pre-existing legal or accounting relationships, but those firms are not experienced with income trusts, it can be useful to include these trusted advisors as well, although this may increase your overall fees.

You should also contact investment dealers to determine their level of interest in leading the underwriting of the IPO and to assess their abilities in your particular circumstances. A list of such dealers is available through www.ida.ca; your banker, lawyer, or accountant should also be able to help. Usually, there will be one or two (or perhaps three, usually in very large cases) lead or co-lead underwriters who will spearhead the underwriting process. Other underwriters may be added to purchase and resell portions of the offering, but will not be as involved in the process as the lead underwriting group. The major Canadian investment dealers include, in alphabetical order, BMO Nesbitt Burns, CIBC World Markets, National Bank Financial, RBC Dominion Securities, Scotia Capital, and TD Securities. They all have income trust experience. It may be particularly beneficial to speak with dealers who have substantial experience with income trust IPOs of businesses similar to yours. Demonstrated income trust research capability on the part of the investment dealer is also highly desirable, since even though you can't influence the analysis, it is beneficial. If an investment dealer is interested, it will ask you to sign an agreement letter (among other things) that indicates its fees.

Another extremely useful way to get information is to contact CEOs or other executives of income trusts who have gone through the IPO process. Check out www.sedar.com for contact details, and the prospectus for key managers.

PRICING

The first, and perhaps most important, issue in an IPO is pricing. As has been discussed above, the pricing on an IPO of income trust units is usually higher than the pricing of shares in the underlying company would be. In addition, at least in the past few years, the pricing on an IPO has often been more attractive than could be obtained by a sale in the private mergers and acquisitions market, whether to financial or industry players.

As a result of this recent boom, Kohlberg Kravis Roberts & Co. and the Ontario Teachers Pension Plan Board were able to do very well by acquiring the Yellow Pages™ business from BCE Inc. in 2002. BCE Inc. wished to raise cash quickly, and so sold a portion of its acquisition a short time later into an income trust at a substantial increase.   Similarly, other financial investors have made substantial gains by buying businesses privately and then selling them via an income trust IPO at a higher price. With the help of your financial advisor, you should review the likely pricing under an income trust scenario and compare it with available alternatives.

EXCHANGEABLE SECURITIES, RETAINED INTERESTS, AND SUBORDINATION

It's quite a mouthful, but important to understand. While the sale of your business will usually be taxable, the use of exchangeable securities (those that can be exchanged for trust units at a later date) can defer part of the tax owing to the government on the sale to the income trust until the ultimate exchange into trust units, which can, at that time, hopefully be funded by selling the trust units.

You will probably be encouraged to sell less than 100 percent of your business, particularly in larger transactions. It may prove beneficial from a tax perspective to keep some or all of this retained interest in the form of exchangeable securities, and the overall proceeds to you may also be improved if you agree to subordinate your right to distributions to those of the public investors for a period of time. This can help assure greater comfort that the expected level of distributions can be obtained, and create a greater willingness to accept a higher price.

By creating expectations of higher ongoing distributions, you can probably get paid more today, but at the cost of higher performance expectations in the future, of course. Planning to keep a reserve behind, rather than distributing 100 percent of cash flow, will likely produce less by way of purchase price, but give the business more room for error— and more flexibility in the future. Adding some additional bank debt may in certain cases increase your overall proceeds as well.

AUDITED FINANCIAL STATEMENTS

You will usually be required to have three years worth of unqualified (clean) audited financial statements on your business in order to prepare the prospectus. The underwriters and some investors may want to see even longer-term stability of revenues, EBITDA, or positive-cash-generating ability as well. You may also need to have audited financial statements on significant recent acquisitions.

Being prepared for an income trust IPO, and the many transactions involved, may mean getting your accounting house into shape well ahead of time.

REPORTING SYSTEMS AND INTERNAL CONTROLS

Your business may need to develop the reporting systems and internal controls, such as two signatures on cheques, different people to receive cash and issue invoices, etc., needed for acceptance as a public company. Your accountants and lawyers will be able to assist here. Again, these procedures are appropriately implemented at least partly ahead of time.

BUSINESS AND STRATEGIC PLAN

You should have a realistic and credible business and strategic plan to present to prospective underwriters, investors, the financial media, and others. This is much like a regular business plan, but it should reflect the post-IPO situation.

PRE-IPO RESTRUCTURING OR CHANGES

It may be necessary to make changes to your corporate structure or business in conjunction with the IPO. In that case to function effectively, the ability of the parts of the business that are going public will need to be assured. The earlier in the process these sorts of issues are grappled with, the better.

Contracts may need to be put in place or adjusted in areas of the business that were previously undocumented, such as:

- Agreements that ensure confidentiality and company ownership of, or rights to, key technology will need to be put into place.

- Appropriate arrangements with related parties, leases, etc. may need to be entered into.

- Shareholders' agreements may need to be terminated or amended substantially.

• Management or employee compensation arrangements may need to be put into place, as well as employment agreements to assure that key personnel remain with the business.

OUTSIDE DIRECTORS AND TRUSTEES

You will need to have independent outside trustees and directors. If you do not have ready candidates, your lawyers, accountants, and underwriters may be able to assist you in recruiting appropriate people. Given the increasing liabilities of directors and trustees of income trusts, as much time as possible should be allocated to this part of the process.

THE PROSPECTUS

The preparation of the prospectus will be an intense, and at times tedious and time-consuming, process of meetings, drafting, reviewing, and revising by the working group. Its preparation will also likely involve a very demanding due diligence review of your business by the underwriters and their counsel as well as by your counsel. You will have to answer many questions.

The prospectus will require disclosure of all material facts related to your business, including:

• Deal structure. Are you using a company or limited partnership; how much are you selling versus retaining?

• Financial statements and financial performance discussion and analysis

• The business, as well as the industry generally (forecasts for both stability and growth)

• Your strategy for the future

- Risk factors. What can go wrong?

- Recent material acquisitions and/or dispositions of other businesses

- Principal properties of the business, e.g., owned or leased real estate

- Promoters, if any. Likely you and other vendors, if any, may be seen as the promoters

- Litigation. Is the business embroiled in any lawsuits?

- Trustees, directors, officers, and other key employees. Name them and describe their backgrounds

- Compensation and executive indebtedness. How much do the executives earn in total, and do they own the business?

- Recent non-arm's-length transactions

THE UNDERWRITING AND SALE AGREEMENTS

The underwriting and sale agreements will likely require you to stand behind the disclosure in the prospectus, as well as make some representations and warranties to the trust and the underwriters. Be careful; if these agreements turn out to be incorrect, you could face liability as a result. Refer to our previous discussions about warranties in Chapter 7.

THE MARKETING PROCESS

You had better enjoy—or at least be prepared for—a lot of public speaking, because you are likely to have to make endless presentations to key prospective investors, brokerage house sales representatives, and others as part of the marketing process for the IPO. This will also likely involve a substantial amount of time on the road. And don't think it will end once you close the IPO. After that, you will be expected to meet with key investors periodically, speak at conferences and to the financial press, and otherwise be accessible and communicative.

A public relations or investor relations firm may be retained to assist with the road show, but there are serious legal impediments to advertising or marketing the offering other than through the prospectus process, so legal advice should be obtained prior to engaging in any marketing activities related to the IPO.

Of course, there are plenty of marketing and communications firms out there that can give you media coaching and public speaking lessons if you are not confident in your abilities.

POST-IPO OBLIGATIONS

As outlined in Chapter 9, after the closing of the IPO, the income trust will be faced with ongoing obligations as a public company, including:

- Ongoing annual audited and quarterly financial reporting obligations

- Ongoing annual and quarterly discussion of financial results and performance, referred to as management's discussion and analysis (MD&A)

- An annual filing known as an annual information form (AIF), which is supposed to act as an annual update of material information regarding the trust

- Holding an annual meeting of unit holders to elect trustees, appoint auditors, and receive financial statements. Special meetings to deal with other matters may also be required from time to time.

- Disclosing ongoing material information by press release and other reports

INSIDER TRADING

Also, the trustees, officers, and significant—over 10 percent—unit holders, among others, of the income fund will be considered insiders, and will therefore be required to promptly report all of their personal trading in the trust units. These will be publicly disseminated at www.sedi.ca. In addition to reporting trades, remember that it is illegal to buy or sell securities with knowledge of undisclosed material information.

CONCLUSION

As you can see, an income trust IPO is not for everyone. But if you have a mature, cash-generating business of sufficient size, you may find that the advantages—including the substantial cash you may receive upon the completion or closing of the IPO—can outweigh the disadvantages.

CHAPTER TWELVE

The Canadian Income Trust Market Today

By now you have a solid understanding of income funds, how they work, how they're structured, and how they might be of benefit to an investment portfolio. So let's summarize some of those benefits and take a look at possible future developments.

THE TWO MAIN BENEFITS

As we have discussed before, there are two main benefits to the income trust structure that make income trusts very attractive to investors: tax effectiveness and generally higher distributions.

Tax Effectiveness

One of the leading attributes of income trusts is their tax effectiveness. Because of the reduction in taxes on the corporate side (the underlying business), or by use of a limited partnership, through the trust model, distributions are higher overall than dividends would be if a public company distributed all of its after-tax income. As well, we have seen that some income trusts can also provide a substantial return of capital, and when held in an RRSP or RRIF, can provide advantageous tax treatment.

Higher Distributions

Income trusts generally make higher distributions than other public companies, which often declare no or very modest dividends. This means that for investors seeking income they can be attractive investments, particularly in low-interest rate environments. Government bonds, guaranteed investment certificates, and the like are currently distributing small amounts of interest when compared to income trusts. Thus, for investors looking for higher cash distributions, income trusts, if carefully selected, may be a good investment to add to your portfolio. They should not replace all of your other investments since they are not risk-free, but they may well have a place in your overall investments. Keep in mind, however, that with these higher returns come increased risks.

LOOKING TO THE FUTURE OF INCOME TRUSTS

There has been much press and speculation regarding income trusts in the recent past, with many people regarding them with a leery eye. In our opinion, however, the future of this investment vehicle looks bright, for a number of reasons.

Increasing Size and Quality

The Fording Coal and Yellow Pages funds demonstrate that bigger and better companies are joining the income trust field. As larger and more stable companies shift to this model, interest and confidence in the income trust model have been steadily growing, and income trusts have now graduated to become an accepted investment vehicle. This can be expected to continue, although the federal government may well seek to restrict this movement by pension funds.

Unit Holder Limited Liability Protection Is On the Way!

The Ontario government has confirmed that it plans to pass legislation providing statutory limited liability for unit holders of publicly traded income trusts governed by Ontario law. Alberta has already passed similar legislation, Québec has its own version, and other provincial governments may well follow suit. This should serve to assist in opening up the market to higher levels of institutional investment, thus creating bigger transactions and greater liquidity. Again, this will be affected by any move by the federal government to impose restrictions on pension fund ownership of business trusts, as they represent a potentially large investment community.

More Institutional Involvement

Even without limited liability protection, institutional investment is slowly increasing. Since institutional investors are generally better at monitoring problems than retail investors with fewer dollars at stake, and given their current corporate governance focus, this should lead to improved governance of income trusts. This focus on improved governance is exemplified in Canada by the efforts of the Canadian Coalition for Good Governance. For more information, see www.ccgg.ca The federal government pension fund restrictions will adversely affect this trend, however.

Institutions are also often better than retail investors at stock-pricing and valuing securities, because they spend more time and money on these issues. This should increase the overall quality of the income trust market through increased investment by institutions.

More Choices

New income trusts are emerging steadily, whether via an initial public offering or a conversion transaction. Although merger activity has to date been very limited, it can be expected to pick up over time, and insolvencies are expected to be limited due to the relatively low external leverage of the businesses underlying income trusts. As a result, the investor is able to select from a greater variety of income trusts and is thus better able to diversify.

Conversion activity, namely turning existing public companies into income trusts, is also increasing, with several high-profile companies allegedly considering their options, and activist investors proposing conversions—as was the case with Manitoba Tel.

More Funds of Income Funds

The proliferation of income trusts makes building and maintaining an appropriate portfolio of income trusts increasingly difficult. There are so many to choose from! As we described earlier, an alternative is to invest in a fund of funds product, in which professional managers select the underlying investments—for a fee, of course. Funds of funds have seen an increase in investors, in part because of the low yields of other investments and the less than spectacular performance of some mutual funds. Another factor in income trust funds' popularity is the recent negative publicity surrounding some equity and mutual funds. The benefits of professional income trust selection and other portfolio management services and diversification are an attractive aspect as well for some investors.

Don't Forget the Risks!

As noted previously, income trusts, despite their high yields, are not fixed income investments. They carry all the risks of their underlying businesses and are more like equities than bonds from a risk perspective. We cannot stress this enough!

A KEY QUESTION: IS THIS A BUBBLE?

There has been some media commentary in newspapers and elsewhere to the effect that the income trust phenomenon is a bubble, much like the dot-com craze turned out to be. However, there is a major difference. Dot-com companies had little or no revenues or earnings, whereas income trusts tend to own mature, cash-generating businesses. Having said that, however, the trading prices for income trust units in the market are considered by some observers to be on the high side. For example, in August, 2004, preferred shares of most of the big banks were yielding about 5 percent, for an equivalent after-tax return of about 6.16 percent. In comparison, yields on a number of even the lowest-yielding income funds were in the 7.5 percent range, and many REITs were in the 7 percent range. This suggests that investors are paying almost as much for units of a modestly sized but well-regarded income fund or REIT as they are for bank preferred shares.

To look at it another way, for an IPO with a promised yield of 10 percent (on the original $10 per unit issue price), investors are paying 10 times estimated distributable cash. At 8 percent, the figure is 12.5 times. These are high prices. Often, strategic purchasers, such as those in the same or related industries, will pay perhaps 6 to 8 times EBITDA—earnings before interest, taxes, depreciation, and amortization—for control of a business, whereas income trust buyers are paying more for a minority stake. No wonder the vendors are pleased to sell via an IPO!

In addition, as has been made clear by example, income trusts are not government bonds. They do have to cut distributions in certain cases, and it may be that income funds are being priced for—or beyond—perfection, and that the risks have not been fully reflected in the marketplace.

As a result, it may well be that we are due for a broad-based reduction in income trust prices. The increasing entry of institutional investors—if they are not halted by the federal government's pension fund initiatives—along with increased research may also lead to a reduction in the price of income trust units if they are perceived to be too expensive.

Increases in general interest rates may also reduce the overall demand, and thus the valuations, of income trust units. In 2003 and 2004, trusts have been benefiting from the overall very low interest rate environment, and the dearth of other products providing similar income streams. Yield-hungry retail investors, including retirees, have therefore flocked to them.

THE LONG-TERM UNDER-INVESTMENT RISK FACING CANADA

Income trusts tend to distribute much more of their cash flow than companies. As a result, they have less to reinvest in their businesses, and face the risk of being less competitive than their corporate competitors (including those in other countries) over the mid to long term. This means that there is a risk that the increasing attractiveness of income trusts could have adverse long-term impacts on the competitiveness of the Canadian economy and Canadian business. However, this remains to be seen.

CONCLUSION

Without fundamental governmental tax changes, income trusts seem here to stay; they are a valuable addition to the universe of investment products available to Canadian investors.

Good luck with your income fund investments—but be careful!

Canadian Income Fund Profiles

A&W Revenue Royalties Income Fund

Original Unit Price
$10.00

Symbol:	TSX: AW.UN
Address:	#300, 171 West Esplanade
	North Vancouver, British Columbia
	Canada V7M 3K9
O/S Units:	Approx. 8,340,000
Phone:	(604) 988-2141
Fax:	(604) 988-7271
Email:	investorrelations@aw.ca
Contact:	Paul Hollands, President
	Don Leslie, VP, Finance

Business: A&W Revenue Royalties Income Fund owns the A&W trade-marks, which include some of the strongest brand names in the Canadian food service industry. It licenses these trade-marks to A&W Food Services of Canada Inc. in exchange for a royalty of 3 percent of the gross sales of 620 A&W restaurants in Canada. A&W is the second largest quick-service hamburger restaurant in Canada by number of restaurants. Operating coast-to-coast, A&W restaurants feature famous trademarked menu items such as The Burger Family, Chubby Chicken, and A&W Root Beer.

Distribution History

2004 YTD (Yield)
$0.72 (5.98%)

2003 (Yield)
$1.08000 (9.54%)

2002 (Yield)
$0.93800 (8.62%)

2001 (Yield)
$0.00000 (N/A)

2000 (Yield)
$0.00000 (N/A)

Acclaim Energy Trust

Original Unit Price
$4.00

Symbol:	TSX: AE.UN
Address:	#1900, 255 – 5th Avenue S.W.
	Calgary, Alberta
	Canada T2P 3G6
O/S Units:	Approx. 74,000,000
Phone:	(403) 539-6300 / 1(877) 539-6300
Fax:	(403) 539-6499
Email:	info@acclaimtrust.com
Contact:	Paul Charron, President / Kerk Hilton, IR

Business: Acclaim Energy Trust is an open-ended, actively managed Canadian energy trust, engaged in the development and acquisition of long-life, high-quality oil and natural gas reserves in western Canada. With an enterprise value exceeding $1 billion, in 2004, Acclaim expects to produce approximately 25,000 barrels of oil equivalent per day (boe/d), weighted 52 percent to natural gas, and 48 percent to oil and natural gas liquids. Since inception, the trust's monthly distributions have been classified as 100 percent return of capital, which is expected to be maintained throughout 2004. Acclaim has a history of making accretive acquisitions on a per-unit basis and in providing stable, consistent monthly distributions to its unitholders.

Distribution History

2004 YTD (Yield)
$1.46250 (10.09%)

2003 (Yield)
$1.95000 (16.25%)

2002 (Yield)
$1.73750 (17.64%)

2001 (Yield)
$0.65000 (7.88%)

2000 (Yield)
$0.00000 (N/A)

ACS Media Income Fund

Original Unit Price
$10.00

Symbol:	TSX: AYP.UN
Address:	#3000, 79 Wellington Street West
	Toronto, Ontario
	Canada M5K 1N2
O/S Units:	Approx. 20,000,000
Phone:	(416) 865-7500
Fax:	(416) 865-7380
Email:	investors@acsmedia.net
Contact:	Wesley E. Carson

Business: ACS Media Income Fund is an open-ended, limited purpose trust established under the laws of the province of Ontario, which indirectly holds an 87.4 percent interest of ACS Media LLC. ACS Media is the largest provider of yellow pages advertising directories in Alaska. The company produces directories which serve substantially all of the Alaskan market, representing approximately 95 percent of the state's population. ACS Media is the exclusive directory publisher for Alaska Communications Systems, the largest local exchange carrier and leading diversified telecommunications provider in Alaska. ACS Media and its predecessors have been publishing advertising print directories for over 80 years.

Distribution History

2004 YTD (Yield)
$0.82440 (7.60%)

2003 (Yield)
$0.71220 (6.59%)

2002 (Yield)
$0.00000 (N/A)

2001 (Yield)
$0.00000 (N/A)

2000 (Yield)
$0.00000 (N/A)

Advanced Fiber Technologies (AFT) Income Fund

Original Unit Price
$10.00

Symbol:	TSX: AFT.UN
Address:	72 Queen Street
	Lennoxville, Québec
	Canada J1M 2C3
O/S Units:	Approx. 13,100,000
Phone:	(819) 821-4930
Fax:	(819) 562-6849
Email:	normand.potvin@aft-global.com
Contact:	Roch Leblanc

Business: AFT is the worlds leading producer of customized screening solutions to pulp and paper producers based on its advanced screening component technology and its in-depth knowledge of pulp screening processes. Pulp screens are used to remove contaminants from pulp and are critical in ensuring the quality of the pulp, which in turn impacts the quality of resulting paper products.

Distribution History

2004 YTD (Yield)
$0.80000 (8.15%)

2003 (Yield)
$1.20000 (9.72%)

2002 (Yield)
$0.91300 (10.35%)

2001 (Yield)
$0.00000 (N/A)

2000 (Yield)
$0.00000 (N/A)

Advantage Energy Income Fund

Original Unit Price
$12.50

Symbol:	TSX: AVN.UN
Address:	Petro-Canada Centre, West Tower, Suite 3100,
	150 – 6 Avenue S.W. Calgary, Alberta
	Canada T2P 3Y7
O/S Units:	Approx. 31,400,000
Phone:	(403) 261-8810 / 1(866) 393-0393
Fax:	(403) 262-0723
Email:	advantage@advantageincome.com
Contact:	Kelly I. Drader

Business: Advantage Energy Income Fund is an oil and gas producer with operations in Alberta and British Columbia. The fund's primary objective is to provide investors with a low-risk investment in the oil and gas industry, while generating returns comparable to other investment alternatives.

Distribution History

2004 YTD (Yield)
$2.07000 (10.14%)

2003 (Yield)
$2.71000 (15.11%)

2002 (Yield)
$1.73000 (13.31%)

2001 (Yield)
$1.45000 (17.86%)

2000 (Yield)
$0.00000 (N/A)

Ag Growth Income Fund

Original Unit Price
$10.00

Symbol:	TSX: AFN.UN
Address:	P.O. Box 39, #74, Highway 205 East
	Rosenort, Manitoba
	Canada R0G 1W0
O/S Units:	Approx. 6,900,000
Phone:	(204) 746-2396
Fax:	(204) 746-2241
Email:	steve@aggrowth.com
Contact:	Rob Stenson

Business: Ag Growth Income Fund indirectly holds approximately 72 percent of Ag Growth Industries Inc. through its ownership of the partnership units of AGX Holding Limited Partnership. Ag Growth is a leading manufacturer of portable grain-handling equipment including grain augers, belt conveyors, and numerous other grain-handling accessories. Ag Growth has three operating divisions: Westfield Industries, Wheatheart Manufacturing, and Batco Manufacturing.

Distribution History

2004 YTD (Yield)
$0.48300 (4.47%)

2003 (Yield)
$0.00000 (N/A)

2002 (Yield)
$0.00000 (N/A)

2001 (Yield)
$0.00000 (N/A)

2000 (Yield)
$0.00000 (N/A)

Alexis Nihon Real Estate Investment Trust

Original Unit Price
$10.00

Symbol:	TSX: AN.UN
Address:	6380 CÜte-de-Liesse Road
	Saint-Laurent, Québec
	Canada H4T 1E3
O/S Units:	Approx. 16,900,000
Phone:	(514) 737-3344
Fax:	(514) 341-5712
Email:	info@alexisnihon.com
Contact:	Paul J. Massicotte, President and CEO

Business: Alexis Nihon Real Estate Investment Trust owns interests in 33 office, retail, industrial, and mixed-use properties, including a 426-unit multi-family residential property, all located in the greater Montreal area. The REIT 's portfolio has an aggregate of over 4.9 million square feet of leasable area.

Distribution History

2004 YTD (Yield)
$0.82530 (6.65%)

2003 (Yield)
$1.10040 (8.16%)

2002 (Yield)
$0.03548 (0.36%)

2001 (Yield)
$0.00000 (N/A)

2000 (Yield)
$0.00000 (N/A)

Algonquin Power Income Fund

Original Unit Price
$10.00

Symbol:	TSX: APF.UN
Address:	2845 Bristol Circle
	Oakville, Ontario
	Canada L6H 7H7
O/S Units:	Approx. 69,700,000
Phone:	(905) 465-4500
Fax:	(905) 465-4540
Email:	apif@algonquinpower.com
Contact:	John Huxley

Business: Algonquin Power is an open-ended investment trust. The Fund owns direct interest or equity in hydroelectric, co-generating and alternative fuels facilities. The Hydroelectric Division holds direct and indirect equity interests in 47 hydroelectric generating facilities; The Cogeneration Division is composed of three natural gas fired generating stations and minority term investments in a further three gas fired generating facilities; The Alternative Fuels Division is comprised of one energy-from-waste facility, one landfill gas powered generating station, and partnership, share and debt interests in three bio-mass fired facilities.

In addition,the Fund's Algonquin Water owns six water reclamation and distribution facilities.

Distribution History

2004 YTD (Yield)
$0.68940 (7.23%)

2003 (Yield)
$0.91920 (8.59%)

2002 (Yield)
$0.91980 (9.91%)

2001 (Yield)
$0.92000 (8.85%)

2000 (Yield)
$0.97000 (9.60%)

Allied Properties REIT

Original Unit Price
$10.00

Symbol:	TSX: AP.UN
Address:	469 King Street West, 4th Floor
	Toronto, Ontario
	Canada M5V 1K4
O/S Units:	Approx. 6,200,000
Phone:	(416) 977-9002
Fax:	(416) 977-9053
Email:	info@alliedpropertiesreit.com
Contact:	Michael R. Emory, President

Business: Allied Properties REIT is a leading owner of Class I (brick-and-beam) office properties in downtown Toronto. With 872,000 square feet of space concentrated strategically to the east and west of Toronto's downtown core, the REIT's portfolio of 15 buildings accommodates a diversified base of business tenants. The objectives of the REIT are to provide stable cash distributions to its unitholders and to maximize unitholder value through the effective management and accretive growth of its portfolio. In addition to competitive advantages within its target market, the REIT has access to a substantial pipeline of development properties currently at various stages of development or redevelopment.

Distribution History

2004 YTD (Yield)
$0.84832 (6.63%)

2003 (Yield)
$0.94604 (7.36%)

2002 (Yield)
$0.00000 (N/A)

2001 (Yield)
$0.00000 (N/A)

2000 (Yield)
$0.00000 (N/A)

AltaGas Income Trust

Original Unit Price
N/A

Symbol:	TSX: ALA.UN
Address:	#1700, 355 — 4th Avenue S.W.
	Calgary, Alberta
	Canada T2P 0J17
O/S Units:	Approx. 33,700,000
Phone:	(403) 691-7575
Fax:	(403) 691-7576
Email:	david_cornhill@altagas.ca
Contact:	David Cornhill

Business: AltaGas distributes natural gas to Alberta customers through AltaGas Utilities Inc., to customers in the Northwest Territories through the Ikhil Gas Project and is distributing natural gas in Nova Scotia through its interest in Heritage Gas Limited. AltaGas provides energy services to customers, including marketing of natural gas and natural gas liquids and sale of power from its power purchase arrangements.

Distribution History

2004 YTD (Yield)
$0.75000 (3.63%)

2003 (Yield)
$0.00000 (N/A)

2002 (Yield)
$0.00000 (N/A)

2001 (Yield)
$0.00000 (N/A)

2000 (Yield)
$0.00000 (N/A)

Amtelecom Income Fund

Original Unit Price
$10.00

Symbol:	TSX: AMT.UN
Address:	18 Sydenham Street East
	Aylmer, Ontario
	Canada N5H 3E7
O/S Units:	Approx. 6,000,000
Phone:	(519) 773-1420
Fax:	(519) 773- 3296
Email:	investorrelations@amtelecom.ca
Contact:	Michael J. Andrews, *President*

Business: Amtelecom Income Fund is an unincorporated, open-ended, limited purpose trust established under the laws of the Province of Ontario created to hold all of the common shares and notes of Amtelecom Communications Inc. and its operating subsidiaries. Amtelecom Communications is the local telephone service provider to several communities in southwestern and central Ontario, currently providing services through approximately 21,600 residential and business-access lines. Amtelecom Communications also provides cable television service to approximately 9200 subscribers and Internet services to approximately 4000 subscribers in certain of its territories.

Distribution History

2004 YTD (Yield)
$0.89160 (7.20%)

2003 (Yield)
$0.96320 (7.96%)

2002 (Yield)
$0.00000 (N/A)

2001 (Yield)
$0.00000 (N/A)

2000 (Yield)
$0.00000 (N/A)

APF Energy Trust

Original Unit Price
$10.00

Symbol:	TSX: AY.UN
Address:	#2100, 144 – 4th Avenue S.W.
	Calgary, Alberta
	Canada T2P 3N4
O/S Units:	Approx. 33,900,000
Phone:	(403) 294-1000 / 1(800) 838-9206
Fax:	(403) 294-1074
Email:	invest@apfenergy.com
Contact:	Steve Cloutier, President

Business: APF Energy Trust is a conventional oil and gas income fund that makes monthly distributions to unitholders based on a royalty it receives from cash flow on oil and gas wells in western Canada. It is owned by APF Energy.

Distribution History

2004 YTD (Yield)
$1.51500 (12.95%)

2003 (Yield)
$2.19500 (17.50%)

2002 (Yield)
$1.81000 (18.49%)

2001 (Yield)
$2.97500 (30.20%)

2000 (Yield)
$1.99500 (20.46%)

ARC Energy Trust

Original Unit Price
$10.00

Symbol:	TSX: AET.UN
Address:	#2100, 440 – 2nd Avenue S.W.
	Calagary, Alberta
	Canada T2P 5E9
O/S Units:	Approx. 175,800,000
Phone:	(403) 503.8600 / 1(888) 272-4900
Fax:	(403) 503-8609
Email:	ir@arcresources.com
Contact:	Mac Van Wielingen
	John Dielwart

Business: ARC Energy Trust is one of Canada's largest conventional oil and gas royalty trusts with an enterprise value of approximately $3.2 billion. The trust's production volumes for 2004 are expected to average approximately 55,000 barrels of oil equivalent per day (boe/d). The royalty trust structure allows net cash flow to be distributed to unitholders in a tax efficient manner.

Distribution History

2004 YTD (Yield)
$1.35000 (8.02%)

2003 (Yield)
$1.80000 (12.21%)

2002 (Yield)
$1.56000 (13.11%)

2001 (Yield)
$2.31000 (19.09%)

2000 (Yield)
$2.01000 (17.79%)

Arctic Glacier Income Fund

Original Unit Price
$9.50

Symbol:	TSX: AG.UN
Address:	625 Henry Avenue
	Winnipeg, Manitoba
	Canada R3A 0V1
O/S Shares:	Approx. 23,300,000
Phone:	(204) 772-2473 / 1(888) 573-9237
Fax:	(204) 783-9857
Email:	info@arcticglacierinc.com
Contact:	Robert Nagy, President and CEO

Business: Arctic Glacier Income Fund, through its operating company Arctic Glacier Inc., is a leading producer, marketer, and distributor of high-quality packaged ice in North America under the brand name of Arctic Glacier Premium Ice. Arctic Glacier operates 21 production plants and 35 distribution facilities across Canada and the central and northeastern United States servicing approximately 40,000 retail accounts. Arctic Glacier also licenses its trade names and proprietary technology to independently owned companies in Canada and the United States under franchise and licence agreements.

Distribution History

2004 YTD (Yield)
$0.80280 (6.83%)

2003 (Yield)
$1.07040 (10.19%)

2002 (Yield)
$0.81500 (9.37%)

2001 (Yield)
$0.00000 (N/A)

2000 (Yield)
$0.00000 (N/A)

Armtec Infrastructure Income Fund

Original Unit Price $10.00

Symbol: TSX: ARF.UN
Address: 15 Campbell Road
Guelph, Ontario
Canada N1H 6P2
O/S Units: Approx. 9,015,000
Phone: (519) 822-0210
Fax: (519) 822-1160
Email: armtecincomefund@armtec.com
Contact: Charles M. Phillips, President

Business: Armtec Infrastructure Income Fund is an unincorporated, open-ended, limited purpose trust established under the laws of the Province of Ontario. Armtec is a manufacturer and marketer of drainage products and engineered solutions for infrastructure applications for a broad cross-section of industries, including the public infrastructure market and private sector markets such as natural resources, residential drainage, and agricultural drainage. Armtec has approximately 8300 industrial, residential, and commercial customers. It has 28 manufacturing plants and sales distribution centers across Canada.

Distribution History

2004 YTD (Yield)
$0.21300 (1.81%)

2003 (Yield)
$0.00000 (N/A)

2002 (Yield)
$0.00000 (N/A)

2001 (Yield)
$0.00000 (N/A)

2000 (Yield)
$0.00000 (N/A)

Art In Motion Income Fund

Original Unit Price $10.00

Symbol: TSX: AIM.UN
Address: 2000 Brigantine Drive
Coquitlam, British Columbia
Canada V3K 7B5
O/S Units: Approx. 7,500,000
Phone: (604) 523-2627
Fax: N/A
Email: N/A
Contact: Paul Wagler

Business: Art In Motion Income Fund is an unincorporated open-ended trust that holds approximately 70 percent of the partnership units of Art In Motion Limited Partnership. Art In Motion is a global publisher, framer, and licensor of images and fine-art reproductions. The company designs, manufactures, and markets fine-art reproductions based on proprietary artwork produced by over 80 artists who are under contract.

The company sells its products through a variety of distribution channels, which then resell them to consumers around the world.

Distribution History

2004 YTD (Yield)
$0.09745 (0.90%)

2003 (Yield)
$0.00000 (N/A)

2002 (Yield)
$0.00000 (N/A)

2001 (Yield)
$0.00000 (N/A)

2000 (Yield)
$0.00000 (N/A)

Associated Brands Income Fund

Original Unit Price
$10.00

Symbol:	TSX: ABF.UN
Address:	335 Judson Street
	Toronto, Ontario
	Canada M8Z 1B2
O/S Units:	Approx. 11,800,000
Phone:	(416) 503-7023
Fax:	(416) 259-4317
Email:	info@associatedbrands.com
Contact:	Robert Dougans, President

Business: Associated Brands Income Fund, through its operating subsidiaries, is a leading North American manufacturer and supplier of private-label dry blend food products and household products. Associated Brands has grown to become one of the three largest suppliers of a diverse range of private-label, dry-blend food products in North America, producing over 10 million cases annually across multiple product categories currently sold to 43 of the 50 largest North American food retailers. Associated Brands plans to build unitholder value by leveraging its solid presence in the fast-growing U.S. private-label market, expanding its product offerings to current and new customers, and through accretive acquisitions that meet its strict operating and strategic criteria.

Distribution History

2004 YTD (Yield)
$0.80640 (7.40%)

2003 (Yield)
$1.07520 (9.46%)

2002 (Yield)
$0.13440 (1.24%)

2001 (Yield)
$0.00000 (N/A)

2000 (Yield)
$0.00000 (N/A)

Atlas Cold Storage Income Trust

Original Unit Price
$10.00

Symbol:	TSX: FZR.UN
Address:	#900, 5255 Yonge Street
	Toronto, Ontario
	Canada M2N 5P8
O/S Units:	Approx. 53,100,000
Phone:	(416) 512-2352 / 1(888) 642-3333
Fax:	(416) 512-2353
Email:	inquiries@atlascold.com
Contact:	Peter Day

Business: Atlas Cold Storage Income Trust, through its operating arm Atlas Cold Storage, is an integral part of the supply chain for the frozen and chilled food industry. Through a network of 54 facilities with over 270 million cubic feet of space, Atlas Cold Storage provides temperature-controlled storage and logistics services to processors, distributors, food service providers, and retailers across North America. Atlas Cold Storage is Canada's largest and North America's second largest integrated temperature-controlled distribution network.

Distribution History

2004 YTD (Yield)
$0.00000 (0.00%)

2003 (Yield)
$0.49000 (7.72%)

2002 (Yield)
$0.94000 (8.36%)

2001 (Yield)
$0.90000 (8.26%)

2000 (Yield)
$0.92000 (11.72%)

Avenir Diversified Income Trust

Original Unit Price
$0.55

Symbol: TSX: AVF.UN
Address: #300, 808 – 1st Street S.W.
Calgary, Alberta
Canada T2P 1M9
O/S Units: Approx. 7,200,000
Phone: (403) 237-9949
Fax: (403) 237-0903
Email: info@avenirtrust.com
Contact: William Gallacher, President

Business: Avenir Diversified Income Trust has three
business units. It is engaged in oil and gas
operations, through Avenir Operating Corp. in
financial services through Avenir Financial
Services Limited Partnership and real estate
acquisition and in development through its
recently formed Avenir Real Estate Acquistiion
Corp. Avenir Operating Corp. is the Manager of
the trust. Approximately 70 percent of the
Trustís revenues are derived from oil and gas
assets, with real estate revenues contributing
approximately 22 percent and the remaining
8% contribution coming from financial services.

Distribution History

2004 YTD (Yield)
$0.80475 (8.99%)

2003 (Yield)
$0.94095 (10.82%)

2002 (Yield)
$0.00000 (N/A)

2001 (Yield)
$0.00000 (N/A)

2000 (Yield)
$0.00000 (N/A)

Badger Income Fund

Original Unit Price
(N/A)

Symbol: TSX: BAD.UN
Address: #815, 715 – 5th Avenue S.W.
Calgary, Alberta
Canada T2P 2X6
O/S Units: Approx. 10,400,000
Phone: (403) 264-8500 / 1(800) 465-4273
Fax: (403) 228-9773
Email: tor@badgerinc.com
Contact: Tor Wilson, President

Business: Badger is North America's largest provider of
non-destructive excavating services. Badger
traditionally works for contractors and facility
owners in the utility and petroleum industries.
Its key technology is the Badger Hydrovac,
which is used primarily for safe digging in
congested grounds and challenging conditions.
The Badger Hydrovac utilizes a pressurized
water stream to liquefy the soil cover, which is
then removed by using a powerful vacuum
system and deposited into a storage tank.

Distribution History

2004 YTD (Yield)
$0.40800 (3.40%)

2003 (Yield)
$0.00000 (N/A)

2002 (Yield)
$0.00000 (N/A)

2001 (Yield)
$0.00000 (N/A)

2000 (Yield)
$0.00000 (N/A)

Baytex Energy Trust

Original Unit Price (N/A)

Symbol: TSX: BTE.UN
Address: #2200, 205 – 5th Avenue S.W.
Calgary, Alberta
Canada T2P 2V7
O/S Units: Approx. 54,000,000
Phone: (403) 269-4282 / 1(800) 524-5521
Fax: (403) 267-0777
Email: investor@baytex.ab.ca
Contact: Ray Chan, President and CEO

Business: Baytex Energy Trust is an oil and gas producer with properties located primarily in central Alberta with production at approximately 37,000 barrels of oil equivalent per day (boe/d), consisting of 27,000 barrels per day (bbl/d) of oil and 60 million cubic feet per day (mmcf/d) of natural gas.

Distribution History

2004 YTD (Yield)
$1.35000 (10.71%)

2003 (Yield)
$0.60000 (5.53%)

2002 (Yield)
$0.00000 (N/A)

2001 (Yield)
$0.00000 (N/A)

2000 (Yield)
$0.00000 (N/A)

Bell Nordiq Income Fund

Original Unit Price $10.00

Symbol: TSX: BNQ.UN
Address: 8th floor, 1050, cÙte du Beaver Hall
Montreal, Québec
Canada H2Z 1S4
O/S Shares: Approx. 32,600,000
Phone: (514) 493-5531
Fax: (514) 493-5516
Email: Investor.relations@bellnordiq.ca
Contact: Isabelle Courville

Business: Bell Nordiq Income Fund is an unincorporated limited purpose trust created to indirectly acquire and hold the outstanding partnership units of NorthernTel, Limited Partnership, and Télèbec, Limited Partnership. Currently, the Fund indirectly holds a 36.6 percent interest in both partnerships, while Bell Canada indirectly holds the remaining 63.4 percent interest. Télèbec and its subsidiaries provide innovative integrated telecommunications solutions to customers in 300 municipalities across Québec. Northern Telephone and its wireless communication subsidiary offer telecommunications services in northeastern Ontario communities.

Distribution History

2004 YTD (Yield)
$0.74720 (5.34%)

2003 (Yield)
$0.95500 (6.83%)

2002 (Yield)
$0.62120 (5.78%)

2001 (Yield)
$0.00000 (N/A)

2000 (Yield)
$0.00000 (N/A)

BFI Canada Income Fund

Original Unit Price
$10.00

Symbol: TSX: BFC.UN
Address: #300, 135 Queen's Plate Drive
Toronto, Ontario
Canada M9W 6V1
O/S Shares: Approx. 26,500,000
Phone: (416) 741-5221
Fax: (416) 741-4565
Email: investorrelations@bficanada.com
Contact: Keith A. Carrigan, President
Anne MacMicken, IR

Business: BFI Canada Income Fund, through its
subsidiaries, is one of Canada's largest
full-service waste management companies,
providing non-hazardous solid waste collection
and landfill disposal services for commercial,
industrial, and residential customers in the
provinces of British Columbia, Alberta,
Manitoba, Ontario, and Québec. Through its
wholly owned subsidiaries, the fund operates
one landfill site, owns and operates three
others, and carries on collection operations in
19 markets. As well, the trust operates three
transfer collection stations, seven material
recovery collection facilities and one landfill
gas-to-energy facility.

Distribution History

2004 YTD (Yield)
$0.97750 (4.55%)

2003 (Yield)
$1.23125 (7.46%)

2002 (Yield)
$0.81667 (6.89%)

2001 (Yield)
$0.00000 (N/A)

2000 (Yield)
$0.00000 (N/A)

Big Rock Brewery Income Trust

Original Unit Price
$6.50

Symbol: TSX: BR.UN
Address: 5555, 76th Avenue S.E.
Calgary, Alberta
Canada T2C 4L8
O/S Units: Approx. 5,300,000
Phone: (403) 720-3239 / 1(800) 242-3107
Fax: (403) 236-7523
Email: ale@bigrockbeer.com
Contact: Bob King

Business: Big Rock Brewery Income Trust is an
open-ended limited purpose trust. The trust
owns all of the securities of Big Rock Brewery
Ltd., which entitles the trust to receive all cash
flow available for distribution from the business
of Big Rock, after debt service payments,
maintenance capital expenditures, and other
cash requirements. Big Rock is a
regional producer and marketer of premium
quality beers that is headquartered in Calgary,
Alberta, Canada. Big Rock's products are
available in draught, bottles, and cans. Big
Rock also produces or distributes cider and
cooler products.

Distribution History

2004 YTD (Yield)
$0.70000 (4.84%)

2003 (Yield)
$0.70000 (6.48%)

2002 (Yield)
$0.00000 (N/A)

2001 (Yield)
$0.00000 (N/A)

2000 (Yield)
$0.00000 (N/A)

Boardwalk Real Estate Investment Trust

Original Unit Price (N/A)

Symbol:	TSX: BEI.UN
Address:	#200, 1501 – 1st Street S.W.
	Calgary, Alberta
	Canada T2R 0W1
O/S Units:	Approx. 53,000,000
Phone:	(403) 531-9255
Fax:	(403) 531-9565
Email:	investor@bwalk.com
Contact:	Sam Kolias, President

Business: Boardwalk REIT is an open-ended real estate investment trust formed to acquire all of the assets and undertakings of Boardwalk Equities Incorporated. Boardwalk REIT currently owns and operates in excess of 250 properties with over 31,700 units totalling approximately 27 million net rentable square feet, and is Canada's largest owner/operator of multi-family rental communities. The company's portfolio is concentrated in the provinces of Alberta, Saskatchewan, Ontario, and Québec.

Distribution History

2004 YTD (Yield)
$0.51500 (3.01%)

2003 (Yield)
$0.00000 (N/A)

2002 (Yield)
$0.00000 (N/A)

2001 (Yield)
$0.00000 (N/A)

2000 (Yield)
$0.00000 (N/A)

Bonavista Energy Trust

Original Unit Price (N/A)

Symbol:	TSX: BNP.UN
Address:	#1100, 321 – 6th Avenue S.W.
	Calgary, Alberta
	Canada T2P 3H3
O/S Units:	Approx. 50,900,000
Phone:	(403) 213-4300
Fax:	(403) 262-5184
Email:	inv_rel@bonavistapete.com
Contact:	Keith A. MacPhail, President and CEO

Business: Bonavista Petroleum is an investment trust that owns oil- and gas-producing properties primarily in western Canada.

Distribution History

2004 YTD (Yield)
$2.25000 (8.79%)

2003 (Yield)
$1.50000 (7.15%)

2002 (Yield)
$0.00000 (N/A)

2001 (Yield)
$0.00000 (N/A)

2000 (Yield)
$0.00000 (N/A)

Bonterra Energy Income Trust

Original Unit Price (N/A)

Symbol:	TSX: BNE.UN
Address:	#901, 1015 – 4th Street
	Calgary, Alberta
	Canada T2R 1J4
O/S Shares:	Approx. 13,500,000
Phone:	(403) 750-2565
Fax:	(403) 265-7488
Email:	info@bonterraenergy.com
Contact:	George F. Fink, President and CEO

Business: Bonterra Energy Income Trust is a conventional oil and gas royalty trust with operations in Alberta and Saskatchewan. The trust engaged the services of an independent engineering firm to prepare a reserve evaluation with an effective date of January 1, 2002. The majority of the trust's production is comprised of light, sweet crude, which results in higher oil prices, and better marketing opportunities.

Distribution History

2004 YTD (Yield)
$1.15000 (4.54%)

2003 (Yield)
$1.55000 (10.00%)

2002 (Yield)
$1.43000 (14.90%)

2001 (Yield)
$0.65000 (9.15%)

2000 (Yield)
$0.00000 (N/A)

Boralex Power Income Fund

Original Unit Price $10.00

Symbol:	TSX: BPT.UN
Address:	36 Lajeunesse St.
	Kingsey Falls, Québec
	Canada J0A 1B0
O/S Units:	Approx. 45,300,000
Phone:	(514) 985-1353
Fax:	(514) 985-1355
Email:	jgauthier@cascades.com
Contact:	Jacques Gauthier, President and CEO

Business: Boralex Power Income Fund is an unincorporated open-ended trust that indirectly owns 10 power-generating stations located in the province of Québec and the United States that produces energy from different sources, including wood-residue or natural-gas-fired thermal and cogenerating facilities as well as hydroelectric power stations. In total, these power stations have an installed capacity of close to 191.0 megawatts (MW).

Distribution History

2004 YTD (Yield)
$0.67500 (6.37%)

2003 (Yield)
$0.88110 (8.64%)

2002 (Yield)
$0.75240 (7.34%)

2001 (Yield)
$0.00000 (N/A)

2000 (Yield)
$0.00000 (N/A)

Borealis Retail Real Estate Investment Trust

Original Unit Price
$10.00

Symbol: TSX: BRE.UN
Address: #2800, One Financial Place
1 Adelaide Street East
Toronto, Ontario, Canada M5C 2V9
O/S Units: Approx. 30,500,000
Phone: (416) 361-1012
Fax: (416) 361-6062
Email: N/A
Contact: R. Michael Latimer, President and CEO

Business: Borealis Retail Real Estate Investment Trust holds a
portfolio consisting of 9 shopping centres. The
investment strategy of the REIT is to invest primarily
in Canadian properties that are mid-market retail
centres in major cities or major retail centres in
secondary cities. The objectives of the REIT are: (i)
to generate stable and growing cash distributions on
a tax efficient basis; (ii) to enhance the value of the
REIT's assets and maximize long-term unit value
through the active management of its assets: and (iii)
to expand the asset base of the REIT and increase
distributable income through an accretive acquisition
program by accessing the network of relationships
and depth of commercial property and financing
experience offered by Borealis Capital Corporation.

Distribution History

2004 YTD (Yield)
$0.78240 (6.11%)

2003 (Yield)
$0.46830 (4.01%)

2002 (Yield)
$0.00000 (N/A)

2001 (Yield)
$0.00000 (N/A)

2000 (Yield)
$0.00000 (N/A)

Boston Pizza Royalties Income Fund

Original Unit Price
$10.00

Symbol: TSX: BPF.UN
Address: #200, 5500 Parkwood Way
Vancouver, B.C.
Canada V6V 2M4
O/S Units: Approx. 8,000,000
Phone: (604) 270-1108
Fax: (604) 270-4168
Email: investorrelations@bostonpizza.com
Contact: Michael Cordoba
Robert Groom

Business: Boston Pizza Royalties Income Fund is an
open-ended trust created to acquire the Canadian
trademarks owned by Boston Pizza International Inc.
Boston Pizza franchises both the "Boston Pizza" and
"Boston Pizza Quick Express" concepts. Boston
Pizza is a full service restaurant and sports bar
concept competing in the casual dining segment
of the restaurant industry. Boston Pizza Quick
Express serves a limited menu and is targeted to
"captured traffic" locations such as arenas, food
courts and airports.

Distribution History

2004 YTD (Yield)
$0.72840 (5.29%)

2003 (Yield)
$1.02000 (8.51%)

2002 (Yield)
$0.45850 (4.53%)

2001 (Yield)
$0.00000 (N/A)

2000 (Yield)
$0.00000 (N/A)

Boyd Group Income Fund

Original Unit Price $8.60

Symbol:	TSX: BYD.UN
Address:	3570 Portage Avenue
	Winnipeg, Manitoba
	Canada R3K 0Z8
O/S Units:	Approx. 3,700,000
Phone:	(204) 895-1244 / 1(877) 522-1222
Fax:	(204) 895-1283
Email:	info@boydgroup.com
Contact:	Terry Smith, President
	Mike Graham, IR

Business: Boyd Group Income Fund is an unincorporated, open-ended mutual fund trust created for the purposes of acquiring and holding certain investments, including an interest in The Boyd Group Inc. and its subsidiaries. The Boyd Group Inc. is the largest operator of collision repair facilities in Canada and among the largest such operators in North America.

The Boyd Group is involved in the operation of collision repair centres in western Canada and in the states of Oklahoma, Washington, Kansas, Nevada, Arizona, Illinois, Indiana, and Georgia in the United States. The company has 84 company-owned locations abd 11 third-partly owned licensed locations operating under its trade names.

Distribution History

2004 YTD (Yield)
$0.85500 (11.22%)

2003 (Yield)
$0.95000 (10.05%)

2002 (Yield)
$0.00000 (N/A)

2001 (Yield)
$0.00000 (N/A)

2000 (Yield)
$0.00000 (N/A)

Calloway Real Estate Investment Trust

Original Unit Price $10.00

Symbol:	TSX: CWT.UN
Address:	#310, 855 – 8th Avenue S.W.
	Calgary, Alberta
	Canada T2P 3P1
O/S Units:	Approx. 11,300,000
Phone:	(403) 266-6442
Fax:	(403) 266-6522
Email:	investorrelations@callowayreit.com
Contact:	J. Michael Storey, President and CEO

Business: Calloway is a real estate investment trust established to invest in income-producing rental properties located in Canada through the acquisition of a portfolio of mid-market retail, office, and industrial properties. Calloway's assets now consist of properties located in Nova Scotia, Ontario, Manitoba, Alberta, and British Columbia. The combined property portfolio continues to be divided into three segments of the real estate market: (i) retail properties; (ii) office properties; and (iii) industrial properties, although with a significantly higher retail component.

Distribution History

2004 YTD (Yield)
$0.90270 (5.37%)

2003 (Yield)
$1.15080 (8.37%)

2002 (Yield)
$0.19180 (1.82%)

2001 (Yield)
$0.00000 (N/A)

2000 (Yield)
$0.00000 (N/A)

Calpine Natural Gas Trust

Original Unit Price
$10.00

Symbol:	TSX: CXT.UN
Address:	#2900, 240 – 4th Avenue S.W.
	Calgary, Alberta
	Canada T2P 4H4
O/S Units:	Approx. 27,100,000
Phone:	(403) 750-3300 / 1(800) 750-1013
Fax:	(403) 303-1653
Email:	ir@cngtrust.com
Contact:	Gary S. Guidry, President

Business: Calpine Natural Gas Trust owns interests in several major natural gas and oil fields throughout Alberta, including interests in the Markerville, Sylvan Lake, Innisfail, Whitecourt, Provost and Bellshill Lake areas.

The fund seeks to grow distributions through active, strategic acquisitions and management, a continuous program of attracting risk investment capital, controlling costs, proactive environmental and safety programs, and actively hedging a portion of the trust's production to enhance long-term returns.

Distribution History

2004 YTD (Yield)
$01.35000 (10.67%)

2003 (Yield)
$0.37500 (3.07%)

2002 (Yield)
$0.00000 (N/A)

2001 (Yield)
$0.00000 (N/A)

2000 (Yield)
$0.00000 (N/A)

Calpine Power Income Fund

Original Unit Price
$10.00

Symbol:	TSX: CF.UN
Address:	#2900, 240 – 4th Avenue S.W.
	Calgary, Alberta
	Canada T2P 4H4
O/S Shares:	Approx. 49,300,000
Phone:	(403) 781-6205
Fax:	(403) 266-3896
Email:	ir@calpinecanada.com
Contact:	Toby Austin

Business: Calpine Power Income Fund is an unincorporated open-ended trust that invests in electrical power assets. The fund indirectly owns interests in two power plants in British Columbia and Alberta and has a loan interest in a power plant in Ontario. These interests consist of a 225 megawatt (MW) power generating facility in British Columbia, a 300 MW power generating facility presently under construction in Alberta with an expected completion date of March 31, 2003, and an investment in a loan to Calpine Canada Whitby Holdings Ltd., the owner of a 50 percent interest in a power generating facility located in Ontario.

Distribution History

2004 YTD (Yield)
$0.71900 (6.95%)

2003 (Yield)
$0.97850 (8.47%)

2002 (Yield)
$0.32000 (3.39%)

2001 (Yield)
$0.00000 (N/A)

2000 (Yield)
$0.00000 (N/A)

Canadian Apartment Properties REIT

Original Unit Price $10.00

Symbol:	TSX: CAR.UN
Address:	#401, 11 Church Street
	Toronto, Ontario
	Canada M5E 1W1
O/S Units:	Approx. 51,000,000
Phone:	(416) 861-8282
Fax:	(416) 861-9330
Email:	ir@capreit.net
Contact:	Thomas Schwartz, President and CEO

Business: Canadian Apartment Properties REIT is a growth-oriented investment trust owning a freehold interest in multi-unit residential properties, including apartment buildings and townhouses located in major urban centres across Canada. CAP REIT's objectives are to provide unitholders with long-term, stable and predictable monthly cash distributions, while growing distributable income and unit value through the active management of the properties, accretive acquisitions and strong financial management. The investment trust owning freehold interests in 13,438 residential suites, including apartments and townhouses located in major urban centres across the country.

Distribution History

2004 YTD (Yield)
$0.81000 (5.89%)

2003 (Yield)
$1.07250 (6.98%)

2002 (Yield)
$1.05000 (8.11%)

2001 (Yield)
$1.05000 (7.39%)

2000 (Yield)
$1.04500 (8.64%)

Canadian Hotel Income Properties REIT

Original Unit Price $10.00

Symbol:	TSX: HOT.UN
Address:	#1600, 1030 West Georgia Street
	Vancouver, British Columbia
	Canada V6E 2Y3
O/S Shares:	Approx. 39,000,000
Phone:	(604) 646-2447
Fax:	(604) 646-2404
Email:	investor@chipreit.com
Contact:	Edward Pitoniak, President

Business: CHIP REIT is an integrated hotel real estate investment trust focused on mid-market and upscale full-service hotels. Through its large, diversified portfolio, CHIP REIT provides investors with stable, tax-advantaged income as well as growth potential through acquisitions, repositioning, and franchising. CHIP REIT currently owns or manages 33 hotels with over 7700 rooms.

Distribution History

2004 YTD (Yield)
$0.67500 (6.73%)

2003 (Yield)
$0.90000 (9.23%)

2002 (Yield)
$0.90000 (10.00%)

2001 (Yield)
$1.12500 (13.20%)

2000 (Yield)
$1.20000 (13.71%)

Canadian Oil Sands Trust Units

Original Unit Price (N/A)

Symbol:	TSX: COS.UN
Address:	#2500, 350 – 7th Avenue S.W.
	Calgary, Alberta
	Canada T2P 3N9
O/S Units:	Approx. 86,700,000
Phone:	(403) 218-6200
Fax:	(403) 218-6210
Email:	investor_relations@cos-trust.com
Contact:	Marcel Coutu

Business: Canadian Oil Sands Trust is an open-ended investment trust that generates income from its 35.49 percent working interest in the Syncrude Joint Venture. Located near Fort McMurray, Alberta, Syncrude operates large oil sands mines, a utilities plant, bitumen extraction plants and an upgrading complex that processes bitumen into a light sweet crude oil. Syncrude is the world's largest producer of crude oil from oil sands and the largest single source producer in Canada.

Distribution History

2004 YTD (Yield)
$1.00000 (1.95%)

2003 (Yield)
$2.00000 (5.26%)

2002 (Yield)
$2.00000 (5.26%)

2001 (Yield)
$1.25000 (3.25%)

2000 (Yield)
$0.00000 (N/A)

Canadian Real Estate Investment Trust

Original Unit Price $9.00

Symbol:	TSX: REF.UN
Address:	#1001, 130 Bloor Street West
	Toronto, Ontario
	Canada M5S 1N5
O/S Units:	Approx. 51,900,000
Phone:	(416) 628-7771 / 1(800) 962-7348
Fax:	(416) 628-7777
Email:	info@creit.ca
Contact:	Stephen Johnson
	Tim McSorley

Business: Canadian Real Estate Investment Trust (CREIT) is dedicated to building wealth for its unitholders through reliable and, over time, growing monthly income as well as long-term value enhancement. CREIT owns a quality portfolio of more than 110 retail, office, and industrial properties. Its disciplined approach minimizes risk while delivering exceptional long-term returns.

Distribution History

2004 YTD (Yield)
$0.93000 (5.66%)

2003 (Yield)
$1.23000 (7.70%)

2002 (Yield)
$1.19500 (9.10%)

2001 (Yield)
$1.17000 (9.55%)

2000 (Yield)
$1.17000 (10.22%)

Cathedral Energy Services Income Trust

Original Unit Price (N/A)

Symbol: TSX:CET.UN
Address: #2800, 715 – 5th Avenue S.W.
Calgary, Alberta
Canada T2P 2X6
O/S Units: Approx. 21,800,000
Phone: (604) 265-2560
Fax: (604) 262-4682
Email: smacfarlane@directionalplus.com
Contact: Mark L. Bentsen, President and CEO
P. Scott MacFarlane, CFO
Business: Cathedral Energy Services Income Trust is a limited purpose trust that owns the securities of Cathedral Energy Services Ltd., representing the right to receive cash flow available for distribution from Cathedral. Cathedral is engaged in the business of providing drilling services and related equipment rentals to oil and natural gas companies in western Canada and the Rocky Mountain region of the United States. Cathedral markets its services under three brand names: Directional Plus and The Directional Company, which provide horizontal and directional drilling services; and CAT Downhole Tools, which provides downhole equipment including drilling jars, shock subs, and high-performance drilling motors on a rental basis.

Distribution History

2004 YTD (Yield)
$0.18000(7.09%)

2003 (Yield)
$0.22000 (11.64%)

2002 (Yield)
$0.09380 (7.82%)

2001 (Yield)
$0.00000 (N/A)

2000 (Yield)
$0.00000 (N/A)

CCS Income Trust

Original Unit Price (N/A)

Symbol: TSX:CCR.UN
Address: #2400, 530 – 8th Avenue S.W.
Calgary, Alberta
Canada T2P 3S8
O/S Units: Approx. 19,700,000
Phone: (403) 233-7565
Fax: (403) 261-5612
Email: dwerklund@ccsincometrust.com
Contact: David Werklund

Business: CCS is a dynamic, rapidly expanding Calgary-based energy service company, that had been operating since 1984. Through its CCS Energy Services division, the trust offers crude oil treatment, terminaling, and storage in western Canada. CCS also provides treatment, recovery, and disposal solutions for oilfield by-products at 27 Canadian facilities. CCS offers drilling-fluid technology and drilling services through its division ProDrill. Through its Concord Well Servicing division, which employs 53 service rigs, the trust provides well completions, workovers, and abandonments in western Canada.

Distribution History

2004 YTD (Yield)
$1.54500 (4.73%)

2003 (Yield)
$1.81000 (5.93%)

2002 (Yield)
$1.02000 (6.07%)

2001 (Yield)
$0.00000 (N/A)

2000 (Yield)
$0.00000 (N/A)

Central Gold-Trust

Original Unit Price
$20.00

Symbol:	TSX:GTU.UN
Address:	55 Broadleaf Crescent
	Ancaster, Ontario
	Canada L9G 3P2
O/S Units:	Approx. 2,300,000
Phone:	(905) 304-4653
Fax:	(905) 648-4196
Email:	info@gold-trust.com
Contact:	J.C. Spicer

Business: Gold-Trust has been created to substantially invest all of its assets in gold bullion, with the primary investment objective of achieving long-term appreciation in the value of its gold holdings. The strategy of the Gold-Trust is primarily to invest in long-term holdings of unencumbered gold bullion, in 400 troy ounce international sizes, and not to actively speculate with regard to short-term changes in gold prices. Sprott Asset Management Inc. has been retained to act as an advisor.

Distribution History

2004 YTD (Yield)
$0.00000 (N/A)

2003 (Yield)
$0.00000 (N/A)

2002 (Yield)
$0.00000 (N/A)

2001 (Yield)
$0.00000 (N/A)

2000 (Yield)
$0.00000 (N/A)

Chartwell Seniors Housing REIT

Original Unit Price
$10.00

Symbol:	TSX:CSH.UN
Address:	2829 Sherwood Heights Drive, Suite 101
	Oakville, Ontario
	Canada L6S 7R7
O/S Units:	Approx. 25,200,000
Phone:	(905) 829-1665
Fax:	(905) 829-0943
Email:	ssuske@chartwellreit.ca
Contact:	Stephen A. Suske, President

Business: Chartwell Seniors Housing Real Estate Investment Trust is an internally managed, unincorporated, open-ended real estate investment trust formed to own and manage seniors housing facilities and projects throughout Canada. The REIT owns or manages a portfolio of income-producing, independent-living seniors housing facilities, retirement homes and long-term care facilities, and a seniors housing operations and development management business, all of which are located in Canada.

Distribution History

2004 YTD (Yield)
$0.76860 (6.44%)

2003 (Yield)
$0.13310 (1.05%)

2002 (Yield)
$0.00000 (N/A)

2001 (Yield)
$0.00000 (N/A)

2000 (Yield)
$0.00000 (N/A)

Chemtrade Logistics Income Fund

Original Unit Price $10.00

Symbol: TSX:CHE.UN
Address: #301, 111 Gordon Baker Road
North York, Ontario,
Canada M2H 3R1
O/S Units: Approx. 22,100,000
Phone: (416) 496-5856
Fax: (416) 496-9942
Email: investor-relations@chemtradelogistics.com
Contact: Mark Davis, President and CEO

Business: Chemtrade Logistics Income Fund is a limited
purpose trust created to hold the securities of
Chemtrade Logistics Inc. Chemtrade Logistics is one
of the world's largest independent providers of
chemical by-product removal services and a leading
distributor of these by-products. Chemtrade Logistics
removes or produces four major products: sulphuric
acid, liquid sulphur dioxide, and elemental sulphur
(collectively, "Commercial By-Products"), and sodium
hydrosulphite ("SHS"). Chemtrade is the largest
North American producer and marketer of SHS, a
high value sulphur-based product, and is the largest
North American independent provider of removal and
marketing services for Commercial By-Products.

Distribution History

2004 YTD (Yield)
$1.11000 (5.81%)

2003 (Yield)
$1.64000 (9.09%)

2002 (Yield)
$1.59000 (11.36%)

2001 (Yield)
$0.58000 (4.94%)

2000 (Yield)
$0.00000 (N/A)

Cineplex Galaxy Income Fund

Original Unit Price $10.00

Symbol: TSX:CGX.UN
Address: 1303 Yonge Street, 2nd Floor
Toronto, Ontario
Canada M4T 2Y9
O/S Units: Approx. 17,500,000
Phone: (416) 323-6600
Fax: (416) 323-6623
Email: N/A
Contact: Anthony Munk, Chairman

Business: Cineplex Galaxy Income Fund is an unincorporated,
open-ended, limited purpose trust established under
the laws of the province of Ontario to hold, directly or
indirectly, investments in entities engaged in the
business of film exhibition. The income trust fund
holds interests in 83 theatres in Canada under the
Cineplex Odeon and Galaxy brand names, with 750
screens.

Distribution History

2004 YTD (Yield)
$0.86220 (6.76%)

2003 (Yield)
$0.11180 (1.11%)

2002 (Yield)
$0.00000 (N/A)

2001 (Yield)
$0.00000 (N/A)

2000 (Yield)
$0.00000 (N/A)

Clean Power Income Fund

Original Unit Price
$10.00

Symbol: TSX:CLE.UN
Address: #1600, 67 Yonge Street
Toronto, Ontario
Canada M5E 1J8
O/S Units: Approx. 35,800,000
Phone: (416) 777-2800
Fax: (416) 777-1190
Email: info@cleanpowerincomefund.com
Contact: A. Stephen Probyn

Business: Clean Power Income Fund is an open-ended income
trust that invests in environmentally preferred power
generating assets and distributes the resulting cash
to unitholders. Clean Power Income Fund provides
stable, long-term cash flow to investors from the
environmentally preferred generation of electricity.
The fund invests only in power-generating assets that
use renewable energy sources such as water, wind,
wood waste, and landfill gas. Clean Power is the first
income fund to be certified under Canada's
Environmental ChoiceM Program.

Distribution History

2004 YTD (Yield)
$0.71253 (7.62%)

2003 (Yield)
$0.95002 (9.50%)

2002 (Yield)
$0.93125 (9.80%)

2001 (Yield)
$0.11815 (1.15%)

2000 (Yield)
$0.00000 (N/A)

Clearwater Seafoods Income Fund

Original Unit Price
$10.00

Symbol: TSX:CLR.UN
Address: 757 Bedford Highway
Bedford, Nova Scotia
Canada B4A 3Z7
O/S Units: Approx. 29,400,000
Phone: (902) 443-0550 / 1(888) 722-5567
Fax: (902) 443-7797
Email: tcotie@clearwater.ca
Contact: Colin E. MacDonald
Tyrone Cotie

Business: Clearwater is a leader in the global seafood industry
and the largest integrated shellfish company in North
America, delivering sea scallops, lobster, Arctic surf
clams, cold water shrimp, Argentine scallops, and
Jonah crab. It currently has operations in Canada,
the United States, Europe, Asia, and Argentina.
Clearwater is the largest holder of rights to harvest
each of these products in Canada. It harvests,
processes and sells more than 80 million pounds of
seafood annually.

Distribution History

2004 YTD (Yield)
$0.86220 (8.60%)

2003 (Yield)
$1.14960 (9.58%)

2002 (Yield)
$0.47900 (4.65%)

2001 (Yield)
$0.00000 (N/A)

2000 (Yield)
$0.00000 (N/A)

CML Healthcare Income Fund

Original Unit Price (N/A)

Symbol:	TSX:CLC.UN
Address:	6560 Kennedy Road
	Mississauga, Ontario
	Canada L5T 2X4
O/S Units:	Approx. 78,100,000
Phone:	(905) 656-0043 / 1(888) 265-5227
Fax:	(905) 565-1776
Email:	bhildred@equicomgroup.com
Contact:	John D. Mull, President
IR Counsel:	Equicom Group Inc.
Business:	CML Healthcare Income Fund operates licensed medical diagnostic laboratories in Ontario and has a central reference laboratory in Mississauga through which it conducts a wide range of medical tests to assist physicians diagnose and treat patients.

Distribution History

2004 YTD (Yield)
$0.47340 (4.14%)

2003 (Yield)
$0.00000 (N/A)

2002 (Yield)
$0.00000 (N/A)

2001 (Yield)
$0.00000 (N/A)

2000 (Yield)
$0.00000 (N/A)

Cominar REIT

Original Unit Price $10.00

Symbol:	TSX:CUF.UN
Address:	455 Marais Street
	Vanier, Québec
	Canada G1M 3A2
O/S Units:	Approx. 31,000,000
Phone:	(418) 681-8151
Fax:	(418) 681-2946
Email:	info@cominar.com
Contact:	Jules Dallaire, Chairman and CEO
	Michel Berthelot, CFO
Business:	Cominar REIT is a closed-ended real estate investment trust to provide unitholders with stable and growing cash distributions, payable monthly and, to the extent practicable, tax-deferred, from investments in a diversified portfolio of income-producing properties, primarily located in the Greater Québec city area. The REIT currently owns a diversified portfolio of 111 properties consisting of 12 office buildings, 25 retail buildings, and 74 industrial and mixed-use buildings which cover about 7.9 million square feet of leasable space.

Distribution History

2004 YTD (Yield)
$0.87000 (5.54%)

2003 (Yield)
$1.15200 (7.79%)

2002 (Yield)
$1.10700 (9.17%)

2001 (Yield)
$1.08600 (9.05%)

2000 (Yield)
$1.06100 (10.45%)

Connors Bros. Income Fund

Original Unit Price
$10.00

Symbol:	TSX:CBF.UN
Address:	669 Main Street
	Blacks Harbour, New Brunswick
	Canada E5H 1K1
O/S Units:	Approx. 30,800,000
Phone:	(506) 456-1625
Fax:	(506) 456-1266
Email:	investors@connors.ca
Contact:	Christopher Lischewski, CEO

Business: Connors Bros. Income Fund is an unincorporated, open-ended, limited purpose trust established under the laws of Ontario, created to indirectly acquire and hold, through its subsidiaries approximately 68 percent in Clover Leaf Seafoods, L.P., and Bumble Bee Seafoods, LLC, North America's largest branded seafood company. The company offers a full line of canned tuna, salmon, sardine, and specialty seafood products, marketed under leading brands including Clover Leaf, Bumble Bee, Brunswick, and Beech Cliff.

Distribution History

2004 YTD (Yield)
$0.96667 (5.69%)

2003 (Yield)
$1.20000 (8.26%)

2002 (Yield)
$1.20000 (8.76%)

2001 (Yield)
$0.17700 (1.48%)

2000 (Yield)
$1.06100 (10.45%)

Contrans Income Fund

Original Unit Price
$9.50

Symbol:	TSX:CSS.UN
Address:	P.O. Box 1210, 1179 Ridgeway Road
	Woodstock, Ontario
	Canada N4S 8P6
O/S Units:	Approx. 16,900,000
Phone:	(519) 421-4600
Fax:	(519) 539-9220
Email:	info@contrans.ca
Contact:	Stan G. Dunford, Chairman
	Gregory W. Rumble, President

Business: Contrans, through its various subsidiaries, is one of Canada's leading regional providers of freight transportation services. It offers a wide range of services to the flatbed, van, tank, and dump trailer areas of the truckload transportation market. This gives customers with a need for various modes of transportation a single-source provider. The company operates predominantly throughout Ontario, Québec, Atlantic Canada, and the eastern, midwestern and southern United States.

Distribution History

2004 YTD (Yield)
$0.93780 (7.00%)

2003 (Yield)
$1.25040 (12.26%)

2002 (Yield)
$0.52100 (5.99%)

2001 (Yield)
$0.00000 (N/A)

2000 (Yield)
$0.00000 (N/A)

Countryside Power Income Fund

Original Unit Price
$10.00

Symbol:	TSX:COU.UN
Address:	495 Richmond Street, 9th Floor
	London, Ontario
	Canada N6A 5A9
O/S Units:	Approx. 14,900,000
Phone:	(519) 435-0298
Fax:	(519) 435-0396
Email:	info@countrysidepowerfund.com
Contact:	Gˆran Mˆrnhed

Business: Countryside Power Income Fund is an unincorporated, open-ended, limited purpose trust formed under the laws of the Province of Ontario. The fund owns indirect investments in 22 biogas projects and two district energy systems. The biogas projects, located in the United States, currently have approximately 51 megawatts of electric generation capacity and sold approximately 700,000 million BTUs (MMBtus) of boiler fuel in 2003. The district energy systems are located in Charlottetown, Prince Edward Island and London, Ontario, and together have approximately 122 megawatts of thermal and electric generation capacity. The fund's indirect investments consist of loans to, and a convertible royalty interest in, U.S. Energy Biogas Corporation and the ownership of the district energy systems.

Distribution History

2004 YTD (Yield)
$0.49250 (5.42%)

2003 (Yield)
$0.00000 (N/A)

2002 (Yield)
$0.00000 (N/A)

2001 (Yield)
$0.00000 (N/A)

2000 (Yield)
$0.00000 (N/A)

Crescent Point Energy Trust

Original Unit Price
(N/A)

Symbol:	TSX:CPG.UN
Address:	#1800, 500 – 4th Avenue S.W.
	Calgary, Alberta
	Canada T2P 2V6
O/S Units:	Approx. 16,400,000
Phone:	(403) 693-0020
Fax:	(403) 693-0070
Email:	N/A
Contact:	Scott Saxberg, President

Business: Crescent Point Energy Trust is an energy trust with oil and gas production in western Canada. The assets of the trust are strategically focused in five properties located in southeast Saskatchewan and south/central Alberta, and are comprised of four crude oil properties and one natural gas property.

Distribution History

2004 YTD (Yield)
$1.53000 (9.45%)

2003 (Yield)
$0.68000 (5.13%)

2002 (Yield)
$0.00000 (N/A)

2001 (Yield)
$0.00000 (N/A)

2000 (Yield)
$0.00000 (N/A)

Custom Direct Income Fund

Original Unit Price
$10.00

Symbol:	TSX:CDI.UN
Address:	79 Wellington St. W., Box 270, TD Centre
	Toronto, Ontario
	Canada M5K 1N2
O/S Units:	Approx. 15,600,000
Phone:	(410) 670-3300
Fax:	(410) 676-0950
Email:	investorrelations@cdifund.com
Contact:	John C. Browning

Business: Custom Direct Income Fund indirectly holds an 80 precent interest in the Custom Direct business. Custom Direct has been selling cheques and cheque-related accessories across the United States since 1992 and offers the industry's widest selection of product designs.

The company is the second largest participant in the U.S. direct-to-consumer segment of the cheque market and had sales of $102.9 million for the year ended December 31, 2002. The company provides customers with the broadest product offering in the industry through several marketing channels, including free-standing newspaper inserts, package enclosures, magazines, coupon co-ops, and the Internet.

Distribution History

2004 YTD (Yield)
$1.01250 (9.05%)

2003 (Yield)
$0.79840 (7.71%)

2002 (Yield)
$0.00000 (N/A)

2001 (Yield)
$0.00000 (N/A)

2000 (Yield)
$0.00000 (N/A)

Davis + Henderson Income Fund

Original Unit Price
$10.00

Symbol:	TSX:DHF.UN
Address:	#201, 939 Eglinton Avenue East
	Toronto, Ontario
	Canada M4G 4H7
O/S Units:	Approx. 37,900,000
Phone:	(416) 696-7700
Fax:	(416) 696-7700
Email:	investorrelations@dhif.com
Contact:	Stephen Pusti

Business: Davis + Henderson Income Fund is a limited purpose trust formed to indirectly hold a 49.99 percent interest in the Davis + Henderson business. Davis + Henderson and its predecessors have been serving Canadian financial institutions and their account holders since 1875. Through an integrated service offering, Davis + Henderson has become the market-leading company in Canada, assisting financial institutions with the operation of their cheque supply programs.

Distribution History

2004 YTD (Yield)
$1.04760 (5.43%)

2003 (Yield)
$1.35990 (7.79%)

2002 (Yield)
$1.32000 (10.26%)

2001 (Yield)
$0.04270 (0.40%)

2000 (Yield)
$0.00000 (N/A)

Dundee REIT

Original Unit Price (N/A)

Symbol:	TSX:D.UN
Address:	State Street Financial Centre, Suite 1600
	30 Adelaide Street East
	Toronto, Ontario
	Canada M5C 3H1
O/S Shares:	Approx. 12,000,000
Phone:	(416) 365-3535
Fax:	(416) 365-6565
Email:	mcooper@dundeerealty.com
Contact:	Michael J. Cooper, President and CEO
	R. Bruce Traversy

Business: Dundee REIT is an unincorporated, open-ended, limited purpose real estate investment trust that owns a portfolio of revenue properties totalling over 13.1 million square feet. Dundee REIT offers an opportunity to invest, through a tax-efficient Canadian real estate investment trust structure, in a diversified portfolio of high-quality and affordable office, industrial, and retail properties situated across Canada. Dundee REIT's properties are located in selected markets in major Canadian cities and select U.S. cities that offer growth opportunities and diversification.

Distribution History

2004 YTD (Yield)
$1.64700 (6.69%)

2003 (Yield)
$1.09800 (4.69%)

2002 (Yield)
$0.00000 (N/A)

2001 (Yield)
$0.00000 (N/A)

2000 (Yield)
$0.00000 (N/A)

Enbridge Income Fund

Original Unit Price $10.00

Symbol:	TSX:ENF.UN
Address:	#3000, 425 – 1st Street S.W.
	Calgary, Alberta
	Canada T2P 2L8
O/S Units:	Approx. 17,500,000
Phone:	(403) 231-3938
Fax:	(403) 231-5929
Email:	colin.gruending@enbridge.com
Contact:	J. Richard Bird

Business: Enbridge Income Fund is an unincorporated, open-ended trust. Its assets include a 50 percent interest in the Canadian segment of the Alliance Pipeline and a 100 percent interest in Enbridge Pipelines (Saskatchewan) Inc., both acquired from Enbridge Inc. In addition, the Alliance Canada Pipeline includes the Alliance System's lateral pipelines which connect the mainline to 43 receipt locations, primarily at natural gas processing facilities. Enbridge Saskatchewan owns and operates crude oil and liquids pipeline systems comprised of four principal assets: the Saskatchewan System; the Westspur System; the Weyburn System; and the Virden System.

Distribution History

2004 YTD (Yield)
$0.63754 (5.16%)

2003 (Yield)
$0.41250 (3.20%)

2002 (Yield)
$0.00000 (N/A)

2001 (Yield)
$0.00000 (N/A)

2000 (Yield)
$0.00000 (N/A)

Energy Savings Income Fund

Original Unit Price
$10.00

Symbol:	TSX:SIF.UN
Address:	#400, 6345 Dixie Road
	Mississauga, Ontario
	Canada L5T 2E6
O/S Units:	Approx. 89,000,000
Phone:	(905) 670-4440
Fax:	(905) 670-9462
Email:	info@energysavingsincomefund.ca
Contact:	Rebecca MacDonald, CEO

Business: Energy Savings Income Fund is an open-ended, limited purpose trust. Ontario Energy Savings Corp. carries on the operating business involving the marketing and sale of fixed-price, fixed-term natural gas contracts to users of natural gas in the province of Ontario. The fund distributes its cash flow by way of (i) interest payments on notes and (ii) dividends on common shares that are owned by the fund and enable the fund to make monthly distributions to unitholders.

Distribution History

2004 YTD (Yield)
$0.66980 (4.34%)

2003 (Yield)
$1.41260 (5.02%)

2002 (Yield)
$1.44468 (10.78%)

2001 (Yield)
$0.76240 (4.13%)

2000 (Yield)
$0.00000 (N/A)

Enerplus Resources Fund

Original Unit Price
N/A

Symbol:	TSX:ERF.UN
Address:	#3000, 333 – 7th Avenue S.W.
	Calgary, Alberta
	Canada T2P 2Z1
O/S Units:	Approx. 89,500,000
Phone:	(403) 298-2200 / 1(800) 319-6462
Fax:	(403) 298-2211
Email:	investorrelations@enerplus.com
Contact:	Gordon J. Kerr / Jo-Anne Caza

Business: Enerplus Resources Fund is North America's largest conventional oil and natural gas income fund. Enerplus offers investors the benefits of owning a large, diversified portfolio of income-generating crude oil and natural gas properties without the exploration risks commonly associated with traditional exploration and production companies. Enerplus invests in mature crude oil and natural gas producing properties located primarily in western Canada with predictable production profiles, long reserve life indices, high-cash netbacks and opportunities for low-risk development.

Distribution History

2004 YTD (Yield)
$2.80000 (6.95%)

2003 (Yield)
$4.28980 (10.90%)

2002 (Yield)
$3.25000 (11.59%)

2001 (Yield)
$6.25000 (25.25%)

2000 (Yield)
$4.58000 (20.00%)

Enterra Energy Trust

Original Unit Price (N/A)

Symbol: TSX:ENT.UN   Nasdaq Canada: EENC
Address: #2600, 500 - 4th Avenue S.W.
Calgary, Alberta
Canada T2P 2V6
O/S Units: Approx. 18,900,000
Phone: (403) 263-0262
Fax: (403) 294-1197
Email: rgreenslade@enterraenergy.com
Contact: Reg Greenslade, President

Business: Enterra Energy Trust is an operating oil and gas company that drills, acquires, operates, and exploits crude oil and natural gas wells in its core areas in western Canada. The Company's core areas include the Peace River Arch area of Alberta, central Alberta and east central Alberta. The Trust acquires, operates, drills, and exploits crude oil and natural gas wells, focusing on low-risk and low-cost development.

Distribution History

2004 YTD (Yield)
$1.02000 (5.67%)

2003 (Yield)
$0.10000 (0.69%)

2002 (Yield)
$0.00000 (N/A)

2001 (Yield)
$0.00000 (N/A)

2000 (Yield)
$0.00000 (N/A)

Exchange Industrial Income Fund

Original Unit Price N/A

Symbol: TSX:EIF.UN
Address: #665, 167 Lombard Avenue
Winnipeg, Manitoba
Canada R3B 0V3
O/S Units: Approx. 1,000,000
Phone: (204) 227-2660
Fax: (204) 957-4224
Email: N/A
Contact: Michael Pyle

Business: Exchange Industrial Income Fund (EIIF) is an unincorporated, open-ended mutual fund trust. EIIF invests in a portfolio of industrial and manufacturing operations located across North America with the objectives of (i) providing unitholders with stable and growing cash distributions, payable quarterly, and (ii) tmaximizing unit value through ongoing monitoring of the assets of EIIF, the acquisition of additional companies, and the financing of expansion opportunities. EIIF will focus on investing in quality businesses with proven track records of profitability in markets across North America.

Distribution History

2004 YTD (Yield)
$0.17000 (1.89%)

2003 (Yield)
$0.00000 (N/A)

2002 (Yield)
$0.00000 (N/A)

2001 (Yield)
$0.00000 (N/A)

2000 (Yield)
$0.00000 (N/A)

Firm Capital Mortgage Investment Trust

Original Unit Price
$10.00

Symbol:	TSX:FC.UN
Address:	#1244 Caledonia Road
	Toronto, Ontario
	Canada M6A 2X5
O/S Units:	Approx. 8,000,000
Phone:	(416) 635-0221
Fax:	(416) 635-1713
Email:	trust@firmcapital.com
Contact:	Eli Dadouch

Business: Firm Capital Mortgage Investment Trust, through its Mortgage Banker, Firm Capital Corporation, is a non-bank lender that provides residential and commercial real estate finance. The trust achieves its investment objectives by pursuing a strategy of growth through investments in selected niche markets that are underserviced by large lending institutions. Firm Capital Corporation, as the trust's Mortgage Banker, provides loan origination, underwriting, loan servicing and syndication services to the trust. Firm Capital Corporation is a specialized lender, that provides bridge financing, construction lending, short-term first and second mortgages, performing and non-performing debt acquisitions, and mezzanine financing.

Distribution History

2004 YTD (Yield)
$0.52500 (4.92%)

2003 (Yield)
$0.92500 (8.56%)

2002 (Yield)
$0.97200 (9.72%)

2001 (Yield)
$0.96500 (10.16%)

2000 (Yield)
$0.95180 (11.20%)

Focus Energy Trust

Original Unit Price
(N/A)

Symbol:	TSX:FET.UN
Address:	#3250, 205 – 5th Avenue S.W.
	Calgary, Alberta
	Canada T2P 2V7
O/S Units:	Approx. 26,900,000
Phone:	(403) 781-8409
Fax:	(403) 781-8408
Email:	billo@focusenergytrust.com
Contact:	Derek W. Evans, President and CEO

Business: Focus Energy Trust is an open-end unincorporated investment trust created in August 2002 from the harvest assets of a junior oil and gas exploration and production company, Storm Energy Inc. These assets represent approximately 8,800 BOE per day of long reserve life, light oil and natural gas production in the Western Canadian Sedimentary Basin. Cash distributions are announced quarterly and paid monthly. Distributions are subject to monthly review. The distribution policy incorporates the withholding of 15-20% of cash flow to fund a significant portion of development expenditures. The distributions are generally 100% taxable as ordinary income.

Distribution History

2004 YTD (Yield)
$1.32000 (7.33%)

2003 (Yield)
$1.66500 (11.10%)

2002 (Yield)
$0.44000 (4.33%)

2001 (Yield)
$0.00000 (N/A)

2000 (Yield)
$0.00000 (N/A)

Fording Canadian Coal Trust

Original Unit Price (N/A)

Symbol: TSX:FDG.UN
Address: #1000, 205 Ninth Avenue S.E.
Calgary, Alberta
Canada T2G 0R4
O/S Units: Approx. 48,900,000
Phone: (403) 260-9800
Fax: (403) 264-7339
Email: investors@fording.ca
Contact: J.G. Gardiner

Business: Fording Canadian Coal Trust is an open-ended investment trust. Through investments in metallurgical coal and industrial minerals mining and processing operations, the trust makes quarterly cash distributions to unitholders. The trust, through its wholly-owned subsidiary, Fording Inc., holds a 65 percent ownership of the Elk Valley Coal Corporation and is the world's largest producer of the industrial mineral wollastonite. The Elk Valley Coal Corporation, comprised of Canada's senior metallurgical coal mining properties, is the world's second largest exporter of metallurgical coal, and is capable of supplying approximately 25 million tonnes of high-quality coal products annually to the international steel industry.

Distribution History

2004 YTD (Yield)
$3.10000 (4.34%)

2003 (Yield)
$4.49000 (9.76%)

2002 (Yield)
$0.00000 (N/A)

2001 (Yield)
$0.00000 (N/A)

2000 (Yield)
$0.00000 (N/A)

Foremost Industries Income Fund

Original Unit Price $4.00

Symbol: TSX:FMO.UN
Address: 1225 – 64th Avenue N.E.
Calgary, Alberta
Canada T2E 8P9
O/S Units: Approx. 6,200,000
Phone: (403) 295-5800 / 1(800) 661-9190
Fax: (403) 295-5810
Email: investorrelations@foremost.ca
Contact: Pat Breen, President

Business: Foremost Industries Income Fund is an income trust that holds complementary manufacturing businesses that are recognized leaders in their fields. Through its separate business models, the fund's operating entities design, manufacture, and sell: drilling equipment, off-road vehicles, oil treating systems, pressure vessels, petroleum storage tanks, gas separation, and steam generator equipment.

Distribution History

2004 YTD (Yield)
$0.97500 (4.55%)

2003 (Yield)
$0.80000 (8.00%)

2002 (Yield)
$1.20000 (?%)

2001 (Yield)
$0.00000 (N/A)

2000 (Yield)
$0.00000 (N/A)

Fort Chicago Energy Partners L.P.

Original Unit Price
$5.95

Symbol: TSX:FCE.UN
Address: #2150, 300 – 5th Avenue S.W.
Calgary, Alberta
Canada T2P 3C4
O/S Units: Approx. 104,200,000
Phone: (403) 296-0140
Fax: (403) 213-3648
Email: hkyle@fortchicago.com
Contact: Stephen H. White

Business: Fort Chicago is a limited partnership which, together with its affiliates, presently owns an approximate 50.0 percent interest in the Alliance Canada Pipeline, an approximate 48.9 percent interest in the Alliance U.S. Pipeline and an approximate 42.7 percent interest in Aux Sable and Alliance Canada Marketing. The Alliance Pipeline is a 3000 kilometre mainline natural gas pipeline from northeastern British Columbia to delivery points near Chicago, Illinois. Aux Sable operates natural gas liquids extraction, fractionation, and delivery facilities near Chicago.

Distribution History

2004 YTD (Yield)
$0.48125 (4.65%)

2003 (Yield)
$0.75000 (7.35%)

2002 (Yield)
$0.66000 (8.00%)

2001 (Yield)
$0.67000 (7.24%)

2000 (Yield)
$0.07500 (0.88%)

FP Newspapers Income Fund

Original Unit Price
$10.00

Symbol: TSX:FP.UN
Address: 1355 Mountain Avenue
Winnipeg, Manitoba
Canada R2X 3B6
O/S Units: Approx. 6,900,000
Phone: (204) 697-7364
Fax: (204) 697-7344
Email: kkarr@estrellagroup.com
Contact: Hans Rudolph Redekop

Business: FP Newspapers Income Fund owns securities entitling it to 49 percent of the distributable cash of FP Canadian Newspapers Limited Partnership. FP Canadian Newspapers Limited Partnership owns the *Winnipeg Free Press*, the *Brandon Sun*, and their related businesses. The *Winnipeg Free Press* newspaper publishes seven days a week, serving Winnipeg and Manitoba with an average seven-day circulation of approximately of 129,000. The *Brandon Sun* also publishes seven days a week, serving the region with an average circulation of approximately 15,000.

Distribution History

2004 YTD (Yield)
$0.37800 (2.82%)

2003 (Yield)
$1.21000 (10.13%)

2002 (Yield)
$0.76450 (8.31%)

2001 (Yield)
$0.00000 (N/A)

2000 (Yield)
$0.00000 (N/A)

Freehold Royalty Trust

Original Unit Price $10.00

Symbol: TSX:FRU.UN
Address: #400, 144 – 4th Avenue S.W.
Calgary, Alberta
Canada T2P 3N4
O/S Units: Approx. 31,400,000
Phone: (403) 221-0802 / 1(888) 257-1873
Fax: (403) 221-0888
Email: ir@freeholdtrust.com
Contact: David J. Sandmeyer / Karen Taylor

Business: Freehold Royalty Trust is an oil and gas royalty trust with more than 85 percent of distributable income coming from mineral title and gross overriding royalties, the majority of which Freehold owns in perpetuity. Freehold currently receives royalty income from over 16,000 producing wells in western Canada.

Approximately 10 percent of the mineral rights in the provinces of Alberta, Saskatchewan, and British Columbia are privately owned, while the majority, about 90 percent, is held by the provincial and federal governments. Freehold owns primarily royalty-generating properties that provide income from crude oil, natural gas, natural gas liquids, and potash.

Distribution History

2004 YTD (Yield)
$1.24000 (7.61%)

2003 (Yield)
$1.70000 (10.40%)

2002 (Yield)
$1.31000 (12.04%)

2001 (Yield)
$1.56000 (16.96%)

2000 (Yield)
$1.32000 (15.17%)

Gamehost Income Fund

Original Unit Price (N/A)

Symbol: TSX: GH.UN
Address: 6204 – 46th Avenue
Red Deer, Alberta
Canada T4N 7A2
O/S Units: Approx. 3,200,000
Phone: (403) 346-4545
Fax: (403) 340-0683
Email: N/A
Contact: Darcy Will

Business: Gamehost Income Fund is involved in hospitality, hotels, and gaming services.

Distribution History

2004 YTD (Yield)
$0.96000 (4.36%)

2003 (Yield)
$0.80500 (4.73%)

2002 (Yield)
$0.00000 (N/A)

2001 (Yield)
$0.00000 (N/A)

2000 (Yield)
$0.00000 (N/A)

Gateway Casinos Income Fund

Original Unit Price
$10.00

Symbol:	TSX: GCI.UN
Address:	#210, 4240 Manor Street
	Burnaby, British Columbia
	Canada V5G 1B2
O/S Units:	Approx. 26,400,000
Phone:	(604) 412-0166
Fax:	(604) 412-0169
Email:	investorrelations@gatewaycasinos.com
Contact:	Dave Gadhia
	Bradley D. Bardua

Business: Gateway Casinos Income Fund is one of the largest casino operators in western Canada. The fund operates six casino in British Columbia, and Alberta, and also provides management services to Gateway Casinos Inc., a privately held casino operator that operates four casinos in British Columbia and Alberta. The fund operates the Burnaby Casino in Greater Vancouver, British Columbia, the Palace Casino in Edmonton, Alberta, and the Lake City Casinos in Kamloops, Kelowna, Penticton and Vernon, British Columbia.

Distribution History

2004 YTD (Yield)
$0.84000 (4.88%)

2003 (Yield)
$1.27600 (8.18%)

2002 (Yield)
$0.11000 (1.07%)

2001 (Yield)
$0.00000 (N/A)

2000 (Yield)
$0.00000 (N/A)

Gaz Metro Limited Partnership

Original Unit Price
$10.00

Symbol:	TSX:GZM.UN
Address:	1717 du Harve Street
	Montreal, Québec
	Canada H2K 2X3
O/S Units:	Approx. 114,400,000
Phone:	(514) 598-3444
Fax:	(514) 598-3725
Email:	investors@gazmet.com
Contact:	Robert Tessier

Business: Gaz Metro Limited Partnership is a major energy player in Québec, the third largest natural gas distributor in Canada, and the sole gas distributor in Vermont. While the distribution of natural gas is Gaz Mètropolitain's core business, the partnership also owns significant financial interests in two natural gas transmission companies, in addition to selling goods and services through various companies in the energy and fibre optics fields, and in drinking water and wastewater infrastructures diagnosis and rehabilitation.

Distribution History

2004 YTD (Yield)
$0.68000 (3.24%)

2003 (Yield)
$1.36000 (6.13%)

2002 (Yield)
$1.30000 (6.86%)

2001 (Yield)
$1.28000 (7.27%)

2000 (Yield)
$1.25000 (7.91%)

General Donlee Income Fund

Original Unit Price
$10.00

Symbol:	TSX:GDI.UN
Address:	9 Fenmar Drive
	Toronto, Ontario
	Canada M9L 1L5
O/S Units:	Approx. 8,900,000
Phone:	(416) 743-4417
Fax:	(416) 947-0866
Email:	rbarnes@generaldonlee.com
Contact:	Thomas Faucette

Business: General Donlee Income Fund is a trust established to hold the securities of General Donlee Limited, which is a leading diversified manufacturer of precision-machined products for the military, commercial, and general aviation industries. It is also a specialist in the manufacture of precision-machined products for the industrial products and power-generation industries.

Distribution History

2004 YTD (Yield)
$0.34139 (12.46%)

2003 (Yield)
$1.05431 (17.69%)

2002 (Yield)
$0.96259 (10.94%)

2001 (Yield)
$0.00000 (0.00%)

2000 (Yield)
$0.00000 (0.00%)

Great Lakes Carbon Income Fund

Original Unit Price
$10.00

Symbol:	TSX:GLC.UN
Address:	#3000, 79 Wellington St. W., Box 270,
	TD Centre
	Toronto, Ontario
	Canada M5K 1N2
O/S Units:	Approx. 20,300,000
Phone:	(416) 865-7500
Fax:	(416) 865-7380
Email:	N/A
Contact:	James D. McKenzie

Business: Great Lakes Carbon Income Fund has been established to indirectly acquire a 35.05 percent economic interest in GLC Carbon USA Inc., which indirectly owns a 100 percent equity interest in the Great Lakes Carbon LLC Business GLC). GLC is the world's largest producer of both anode and industrial grade calcined petroleum coke ("CPC"), used to produce carbon anodes for use in aluminum smelting, in the production of titanium dioxide, and a variety of other industrial applications.

Distribution History

2004 YTD (Yield)
$0.95625 (9.56%)

2003 (Yield)
$0.49355 (4.49%)

2002 (Yield)
$0.00000 (N/A)

2001 (Yield)
$0.00000 (N/A)

2000 (Yield)
$0.00000 (N/A)

Great Lakes Hydro Income Trust Fund

Original Unit Price
$10.00

Symbol:	TSX:GLH.UN
Address:	#200, 480 de la Citè Blvd
	Gatineau, Québec
	Canada J8T 8R3
O/S Units:	Approx. 48,300,000
Phone:	(819) 561-2722
Fax:	(819) 561-7188
Email:	richard.legault@greatlakeshydro.com
Contact:	Richard Legault

Business: Great Lakes Hydro Income Fund produces electricity exclusively from environmentally friendly hydroelectric resources. The fund owns, operates, and manages five integrated hydroelectric generation systems located in Québec, Ontario, British Columbia, Maine, and New Hampshire with 24 hydroelectric generating stations, with installed capacity of 982 megawatts (MW) and significant water storage. The facilities generate, on average, 3,700 gigawatts per hour (GWh) of electricity annually, with interconnections to the Québec, Ontario, British Columbia, and New England power grids.

Distribution History

2004 YTD (Yield)
$0.90000 (5.42%)

2003 (Yield)
$1.20000 (6.92%)

2002 (Yield)
$1.18500 (7.78%)

2001 (Yield)
$1.10000 (8.21%)

2000 (Yield)
$1.05000 (8.82%)

H&R Real Estate Investment Trust

Original Unit Price
$10.00

Symbol:	TSX:HR.UN
Address:	#500, 3625 Dufferin Street
	North York, Ontario
	Canada M3K 1N4
O/S Units:	Approx. 88,300,000
Phone:	(416) 635-7520
Fax:	(416) 398-0040
Email:	info@hr-reit.com
Contact:	Thomas J. Hofstedter, President

Business: H&R Real Estate Investment Trust is a closed end real estate investment trust. H&R REIT holds interests in a principally Canadian portfolio of 29 office, 86 industrial and 44 retail properties and 4 development projects.

Distribution History

2004 YTD (Yield)
$0.93330 (5.47%)

2003 (Yield)
$1.22400 (7.70%)

2002 (Yield)
$1.19900 (8.98%)

2001 (Yield)
$1.16400 (8.43%)

2000 (Yield)
$1.10900 (9.36%)

Halterm Income Fund

Original Unit Price
$10.00

Symbol:	TSX:HAL.UN
Address:	P.O. Box 1057
	Halifax, Nova Scotia
	Canada B3J 2X1
O/S Units:	Approx. 8,100,000
Phone:	(902) 421-1778
Fax:	(902) 469-3193
Email:	N/A
Contact:	Doug Rose, President

Business: The Halterm Income Fund is a limited purpose trust. It's wholly owned subsidiary, Halterm Limited, provides the logistical link between domestic and international shipping lines, and the rail and truck transportation systems that connect the Port of Halifax to Canadian and U.S. Midwest markets.

Distribution History

2004 YTD (Yield)
$0.34000 (5.44%)

2003 (Yield)
$0.44370 (9.54%)

2002 (Yield)
$0.97480 (11.08%)

2001 (Yield)
$0.97480 (11.15%)

2000 (Yield)
$0.97480 (12.58%)

Hardwoods Distribution Income Fund

Original Unit Price
$10.00

Symbol:	TSX: HWD.UN
Address:	27321 – 58th Crescent
	Langley, British Columbia
	Canada V4W 4W7
O/S Units:	Approx. 14,400,000
Phone:	(604) 691-9100
Fax:	(604) 688-8727
Email:	N/A
Contact:	Maurice E.Paquette, CEO

Business: Hardwoods Distribution Income Fund was created to acquire an 80% interest in a hardwood lumber and sheet goods distribution business from affiliates of Sauder Industries Limited. Hardwoods operates from 37 branches that are organized into nine geographic regions or clusters. Each cluster is comprised of a branch that serves as the primary distribution facility (or hub) which supports a number of branches within a geographic region that serve as satellite distribution facilities. Each of the distribution facilities consists of a warehouse and associated office space with yard space for deliveries. Hardwoods does not own delivery vehicles and contract virtually all deliveries with independently owned trucking operators.

Distribution History

2004 YTD (Yield)
$0.54900 (4.95%)

2003 (Yield)
$0.00000 (N/A)

2002 (Yield)
$0.00000 (N/A)

2001 (Yield)
$0.00000 (N/A)

2000 (Yield)
$0.00000 (N/A)

Harvest Energy Trust

Original Unit Price
$8.00

Symbol:	TSX:HTE.UN
Address:	#1900, 330 – 5th Avenue S.W.
	Calgary, Alberta
	Canada T2P 0L4
O/S Units:	Approx. 16,900,000
Phone:	(403) 265-1178
Fax:	(403) 265-3490
Email:	information@harvestenergy.ca
Contact:	Jake Roorda, President

Business: Harvest Energy Trust is a Calgary-based oil and natural gas trust that strives to deliver stable monthly cash distributions to its unitholders through its strategy of acquiring, enhancing, and producing crude oil, natural gas, and natural gas liquids. Harvest's assets, comprised of high-quality medium- and heavy-gravity crude oil properties in east central Alberta, and its hands-on operating strategy underpin Harvest's objective to deliver consistent returns to unitholders.

Distribution History

2004 YTD (Yield)
$1.80000 (9.52%)

2003 (Yield)
$2.40000 (17.06%)

2002 (Yield)
$0.20000 (2.11%)

2001 (Yield)
$0.00000 (N/A)

2000 (Yield)
$0.00000 (N/A)

Heating Oil Partners Income Fund

Original Unit Price
$10.00

Symbol:	TSX:HIF.UN
Address:	#3000, 79 Wellington Street West
	Toronto, Ontario
	Canada M5K 1N2
O/S Units:	Approx. 18,100,000
Phone:	(203) 655-8290
Fax:	(203) 655-9383
Email:	N/A
Contact:	J. Joseph Glick

Business: Heating Oil Partners Income Fund indirectly owns approximately 86.0 percent of Heating Oil Partners, L.P. (HOP), one of the largest residential heating oil distributors in the United States. HOP delivers heating oil and other refined liquid petroleum products to residential and commercial customers, primarily in Connecticut, Delaware, Massachusetts, New Jersey, New York, Pennsylvania, and Rhode Island. HOP's operations are conducted through 11 regional distribution and service centres. From these centres, HOP provides its customers with a full range of value-added services, including the delivery of heating oil and the installation, maintenance and service of furnaces, boilers, heating equipment and air conditioners on a 24-hours-a-day, 365-days-a-year basis.

Distribution History

2004 YTD (Yield)
$1.05000 (11.16%)

2003 (Yield)
$1.40000 (9.86%)

2002 (Yield)
$0.85167 (7.20%)

2001 (Yield)
$0.00000 (N/A)

2000 (Yield)
$0.00000 (N/A)

Home Equity Income Trust

Original Unit Price
$10.00

Symbol: TSX:HEQ.UN
Address: # 600, 45 St. Clair Avenue West
Toronto, Ontario
Canada M4V 1K9
O/S Units: Approx. 11,100,000
Phone: (416) 925-4757
Fax: (416) 925-9938
Email: info@homeq.ca
Contact: Steven K. Ranson

Business: Home Equity Income Trust's (HOMEQ) income is derived from the spread between the interest rates earned on the reverse mortgages and the interest rates paid on the AAA and investment-grade debt used to fund the reverse mortgages. Historically, the reverse mortgages have been more than 90 percent funded with AAA debt.

HOMEQ has both direct and indirect investments in reverse mortgage portfolios. The indirect investment is through its investment in the CHIP Limited Partnerships (CHIP Mortgage Limited Partnership, CHIP Four Limited Partnership, and CHIP Five Limited Partnership), which hold portfolios of reverse mortgages.

Distribution History

2004 YTD (Yield)
$0.77850 (5.88%)

2003 (Yield)
$1.03800 (7.21%)

2002 (Yield)
$0.34600 (3.04%)

2001 (Yield)
$0.00000 (N/A)

2000 (Yield)
$0.00000 (N/A)

Hot House Growers Income Fund

Original Unit Price
$10.00

Symbol: TSX: VEG.UN
Address: 4526 – 80th Street,
Delta, British Columbia
Canada V4K 3N3
O/S Units: Approx. 6,600,000
Phone: (604) 681-8811
Fax: (604) 940-6312
Email: fundinfo@hhgrowers.com
Contact: Stephen K. Fane

Business: Hot House Growers Income Fund owns 75 percent of Hot House Growers Inc., one of North America's largest producers of premium-quality greenhouse vegetables. Hot House Growers is located in British Columbia, and is one of the largest producers of premium quality greenhouse tomatoes and sweet bell peppers in North America.

Distribution History

2004 YTD (Yield)
$0.73745 (10.39%)

2003 (Yield)
$0.02740 (0.25%)

2002 (Yield)
$0.00000 (N/A)

2001 (Yield)
$0.00000 (N/A)

2000 (Yield)
$0.00000 (N/A)

IAT Air Cargo Facilities Income Fund

Original Unit Price
$10.00

Symbol: TSX: ACF.UN
Address: #2000, 5000 Miller Road
Richmond, British Columbia
Canada V7B 1K6
O/S Units: Approx. 6,600,000
Phone: (604) 273-4611
Fax: (604) 273-5624
Email: rick@iat-yvr.com
Contact: T. Richard Turner, President and CEO

Business: IAT Air Cargo Facilities Income Fund owns and
leases air cargo and related space at airports in
Vancouver, Calgary, Edmonton, Saskatchewan, and
Winnipeg. IAT owns and operates all of the buildings
it has developed for its tenants.

Distribution History

2004 YTD (Yield)
$0.52100 (6.95%)

2003 (Yield)
$0.85660 (10.38%)

2002 (Yield)
$1.12940 (11.22%)

2001 (Yield)
$1.11330 (9.47%)

2000 (Yield)
$1.14850 (9.86%)

IBI Income Fund

Original Unit Price
$10.00

Symbol: TSX: IBG.UN
Address: 230 Richmond Street West, 5th Floor
Toronto, Ontario
Canada M5V 1V6
O/S Units: Approx. 4,800,000
Phone: (416) 596-1930
Fax: (416) 596-0644
Email: N/A
Contact: Philip H. Beinhaker

Business: IBI Income Fund is an unincorporated, open-ended,
limited purpose trust. The business of the fund is
conducted indirectly through IBI Group. IBI is an
international, multi-disciplinary provider of a broad
range of professional services focused on the
physical development of cities. IBI's business is
concentrated in four main areas of development:
urban land, building facilities, transportation
networks, and systems technology. The professional
services provided by IBI include planning, design,
implementation, analysis of operations, and other
consulting services related to these four main areas
of development. IBI provides these services in major
cities across Canada, the United States, and western
Europe, as well as in other international centres.

Distribution History

2004 YTD (Yield)
$0.09375 (0.91%)

2003 (Yield)
$0.00000 (N/A)

2002 (Yield)
$0.00000 (N/A)

2001 (Yield)
$0.00000 (N/A)

2000 (Yield)
$0.00000 (N/A)

Innergex Power Income Fund

Original Unit Price
$10.00

Symbol: TSX: IEF.UN
Address: #1255, 1111 Saint-Charles St. W. East Tower
Longueuil, Québec
Canada J4K 5G4
O/S Units: Approx. 18,300,000
Phone: (514) 397-7812
Fax: (514) 875-6246
Email: info@innergex.com
Contact: Gilles LefranÁois

Business: Innergex Power Income Fund has been established
to indirectly acquire and own interests in seven
hydroelectric power generating facilities, six of which
are located in the province of Québec and one is
located in the province of Ontario. The total installed
capacity for the facilities is 65 megawatts (MW) and
has an expected annual production of 350 gigawatts
(GW) per hour of electricity. The facilities enjoy
long-term power purchase agreements with
Hydro-Québec and with the Ontario Electricity
Financial Corporation, with initial terms varying
between 20 to 30 years.

Distribution History

2004 YTD (Yield)
$0.69750 (5.58%)

2003 (Yield)
$0.45200 (3.83%)

2002 (Yield)
$0.00000 (N/A)

2001 (Yield)
$0.00000 (N/A)

2000 (Yield)
$0.00000 (N/A)

InnVest Real Estate Investment Trust

Original Unit Price
$10.00

Symbol: TSX: INN.UN
Address: 5090 Explorer Drive, 7th Floor
Mississauga, Ontario
Canada L4W 4T9
O/S Units: Approx. 41,100,000
Phone: (905) 206-7100
Fax: (905) 206-7114
Email: investor@innvestreit.com
Contact: Kenneth D. Gibson

Business: InnVest is an open-ended real estate investment
trust. InnVest REIT holds Canada's largest hotel
portfolio together with a 50 percent interest in Choice
Hotels Canada Inc., the largest franchisor of hotels in
Canada. The hotel portfolio comprises 124 limited
service and mid-market hotel properties, with over
13,000 guest rooms operated under eight
internationally recognized franchise brands such as
Comfort Inn, Quality Suites, Quality Hotels, Holiday
Inn, and Travelodge.

Distribution History

2004 YTD (Yield)
$0.84375 (7.57%)

2003 (Yield)
$1.12500 (9.87%)

2002 (Yield)
$0.48690 (5.13%)

2001 (Yield)
$0.00000 (N/A)

2000 (Yield)
$0.00000 (N/A)

Inter Pipeline Fund

**Original Unit Price
(N/A)**

Symbol: TSX: IPL.UN
Address: #2600, 237 – 4th Avenue S.W.
Calgary, Alberta
Canada T2P 0H4
O/S Units: Approx. 111,100,000
Phone: (403) 290-6000 / 1(866) 716-7473
Fax: (403) 290-6090
Email: investorrelations@interpipelinefund.com
Contact: David Fesyk, President and CEO
Robert Fotheringham, CFO

Business: Inter Pipeline Fund is a limited partnership that owns
and operates four feeder pipeline systems located in
southern Alberta and southwestern Saskatchewan.
Totalling approximately 4100 kilometres in length,
these systems comprise one of the largest crude oil
feeder pipeline businesses in Canada. In addition,
Inter Pipeline owns 85 percent of the Cold Lake
Pipeline Limited Partnership.

Distribution History

2004 YTD (Yield)
$0.48000 (5.93%)

2003 (Yield)
$0.72000 (9.28%)

2002 (Yield)
$0.68000 (11.06%)

2001 (Yield)
$0.68000 (9.93%)

2000 (Yield)
$0.66000 (11.58%)

IPC US Income Commercial REIT

**Original Unit Price
$6.40**

Symbol: TSX: IUR.U
Address: #705, 175 Bloor Street East, South Tower
Toronto, Ontario
Canada M4W 3R8
O/S Units: Approx. N/A
Phone: (416) 929-6490
Fax: (416) 929-5314
Email: investorrelations@ipcus.com
Contact: Y. Dov Meyer

Business: IPC US Income Commercial REIT beneficially owns
an 88 percent economic interest in IPC (US), Inc. IPC
has ownership interests in and manages 28 buildings
in the United States (22 office and six retail)
containing a total of 6.5 million square feet of
rentable space. Members of the Paul Reichmann
family beneficially own the remaining 12 percent
economic interest in IPC.

Distribution History

2004 YTD (Yield)
N/A

2003 (Yield)
$0.68372 (8.34%)

2002 (Yield)
$0.62740 (10.04%)

2001 (Yield)
$0.02000 (0.30%)

2000 (Yield)
$0.00000 (N/A)

IPC US Income REIT

Original Unit Price
$10.00

Symbol:	TSX: IUR.UN
Address:	#705, 175 Bloor Street East, South Tower
	Toronto, Ontario
	Canada M4W 3R8
O/S Units:	Approx. 32,300,000
Phone:	(416) 929-0514
Fax:	(416) 929-5314
Email:	investorrelations@ipcus.com
Contact:	Y. Dov Meyer

Business: IPC US Income REIT beneficially owns an 88 percent economic interest in IPC (US), Inc. IPC has ownership interests in and manages 28 buildings in the United States (22 office and six retail) containing a total of 6.5 million square feet of rentable space. Members of the Paul Reichmann family beneficially own the remaining 12 percent economic interest in IPC.

Distribution History

2004 YTD (Yield)
$0.69210 (6.53%)

2003 (Yield)
$0.93920 (8.78%)

2002 (Yield)
$0.98380 (10.04%)

2001 (Yield)
$0.03180 (0.31%)

2000 (Yield)
$0.00000 (N/A)

KCP Income Fund

Original Unit Price
$10.00

Symbol:	TSX: KCP.UN
Address:	33 MacIntosh Blvd.
	Concord, Ontario
	Canada L4K 4L5
O/S Units:	Approx. 25,900,000
Phone:	(905) 660-0444
Fax:	(905) 660-7333
Email:	sstokes@kikcorp.com
Contact:	David Cynamon

Business: KCP Income Fund, through its operating subsidiaries KIK Holdco Company and KIK Operating Partnership, is a leader in the North American private label market. With 12 vertically integrated manufacturing facilities, KCP is North America's largest producer of private label household bleach, and produces a full range of private label liquid household cleaning and laundry products. KCP's products are sold by grocery stores, mass merchandisers, and drugstore retailers in more than 45,000 stores across North America.

Distribution History

2004 YTD (Yield)
$0.79166 (8.70%)

2003 (Yield)
$1.09992 (9.02%)

2002 (Yield)
$0.38848 (3.42%)

2001 (Yield)
$0.00000 (N/A)

2000 (Yield)
$0.00000 (N/A)

KeySpan Facilities Income Fund

Original Unit Price
$10.00

Symbol:	TSX: KEY.UN
Address:	#600, 144 – 4th Avenue S.W.
	Calgary, Alberta
	Canada T2P 3N4
O/S Units:	Approx. 32,600,000
Phone:	(403) 205-8300 / 1(888) 699-4853
Fax:	(403) 205-7677
Email:	John_Cobb@keyspancanada.com
Contact:	James V. Bertram / John Cobb

Business: KeySpan Facilities Income Fund owns a 75 percent interest in the business of KeySpan Energy Canada Partnership. KeySpan's business consists of both natural gas gathering and processing as well as the processing, transportation, storage, and marketing of natural gas liquids (NGLs). KeySpan Canada's 13 gas processing plants and associated facilities are strategically located in the west-central and foothills natural gas production areas of the Western Canadian Sedimentary Basin in Alberta. They are pipeline-connected and offer a wide range of flexible services. KeySpan Canada's NGL infrastructure consists of pipelines, processing, and storage in Edmonton and Fort Saskatchewan, Alberta, a major North American NGL hub.

Distribution History

2004 YTD (Yield)
$0.84600 (6.54%)

2003 (Yield)
$0.63560 (5.08%)

2002 (Yield)
$0.00000 (N/A)

2001 (Yield)
$0.00000 (N/A)

2000 (Yield)
$0.00000 (N/A)

Labrador Iron Ore Royalty Income Fund

Original Unit Price
(N/A)

Symbol:	TSX: LIF.UN
Address:	#2600, 40 King Street West
	Toronto, Ontario
	Canada M5W 2X6
O/S Units:	Approx. 30,000,000
Phone:	(416) 863-7133
Fax:	(416) 863-7425
Email:	N/A
Contact:	Bruce C. Bone

Business: Labrador Iron Ore Royalty Income Fund has been created to acquire and hold, indirectly, a 7 percent gross overridding royalty on all iron ore products produced, sold, delivered, and shipped by the Iron Ore Company of Canada, an 11.98 percent equity interest in IOC and a 50 percent interest in Hollinger-Hanna Limited. The royalty, equity in IOC, and Hollinger-Hanna interest will be acquired through the purchase of Labrador Mining Company from Norcen Resources Limited.

Distribution History

2004 YTD (Yield)
$0.75000 (4.12%)

2003 (Yield)
$1.00000 (5.51%)

2002 (Yield)
$1.00000 (6.90%)

2001 (Yield)
$1.37500 (10.01%)

2000 (Yield)
$1.05000 (7.50%)

Lakeview Hotel REIT

Original Unit Price (N/A)

Symbol: TSX Venture: LHR.UN
Address: #600, 185 Carlton Street
Winnipeg, Manitoba
Canada R3C 3J1
O/S Units: Approx. 1,175,000
Phone: (204) 947-1161
Fax: (204) 957-1697
Email: N/A
Contact: Keith Levit, President

Business: Lakeview Hotel REIT was established for the purposes of investing in a portfolio of hotel properties, commercial and office properties ancillary to hotel properties, and extended-stay properties located across Canada and the United States with the objectives of: (i) providing unitholders with stable and growing cash distributions, to be paid quarterly, and to the maximum extent possible, tax deferred, and (ii) maximizing unit value through ongoing active management of the assets of Lakeview Hotel REIT, the acquisition of additional properties or interests therein, and the financing of new hotel developments.

Distribution History

2004 YTD (Yield)
$0.05000 (3.33%)

2003 (Yield)
$0.00000 (N/A)

2002 (Yield)
$0.00000 (N/A)

2001 (Yield)
$0.00000 (N/A)

2000 (Yield)
$0.00000 (N/A)

Lanesborough REIT

Original Unit Price (N/A)

Symbol: TSX Venture: LRT.UN
Address: 2600 Seven Evergreen Place
Winnipeg, Manitoba
Canada R3L 2T3
O/S Units: Approx. 2,600,000
Phone: (204) 475-9090
Fax: (204) 452-5505
Email: gromagnoli@scpl.com
Contact: Arni C. Thorsteinson, President
Gino Romagnoli, IR

Business: Lanesborough Real Estate Investment Trust is an unincorporated closed-ended real estate investment trust created to invest primarily in a portfolio of retail, residential, industrial, and office properties located across Canada.

Distribution History

2004 YTD (Yield)
$0.39000 (8.01%)

2003 (Yield)
$0.50000 (12.50%)

2002 (Yield)
$0.16000 (5.61%)

2001 (Yield)
$0.00000 (N/A)

2000 (Yield)
$0.00000 (N/A)

Legacy Hotels REIT

Original Unit Price
$10.00

Symbol:	TSX: LGY.UN
Address:	#1600, Canadian Pacific Tower, TD Centre
	P.O. Box 40, Toronto, Ontario
	Canada M5K 1B7
O/S Units:	Approx. 88,600,000
Phone:	(416) 874-2600 / 1(866) 627-0641
Fax:	(416) 874-2761
Email:	investor@legacyhotels.ca
Contact:	Neil J. Labatte, President

Business: Legacy Hotel REIT is a closed-ended real estate investment trust with 24 luxury and first-class hotels and resorts with approximately 10,000 guestrooms. The portfolio includes landmark properties such as Fairmont Le Château Frontenac, The Fairmont Royal York, The Fairmont Empress, and The Fairmont Olympic Hotel, Seattle. The management companies of Fairmont Hotels & Resorts Inc. operate all of Legacy's properties.

Distribution History

2004 YTD (Yield)
$0.16000 (2.38%)

2003 (Yield)
$0.18500 (2.58%)

2002 (Yield)
$0.74000 (10.21%)

2001 (Yield)
$0.87000 (10.30%)

2000 (Yield)
$0.98000 (11.60%)

Livingston International Income Fund

Original Unit Price
$10.00

Symbol:	TSX: LIV.UN
Address:	405 The West Mall
	Toronto, Ontario
	Canada M9C 5K7
O/S Units:	Approx. 15,100,000
Phone:	(416) 626-2800 / 1(800) 387-7582
Fax:	(416) 622-3890
Email:	info@livingstonintl.com
Contact:	Peter Luit

Business: The Livingston International Income Fund has been created to hold, directly or indirectly, the securities of Livingston International Inc. Livingston is Canada's leading customs brokerage company and trade-related services provider facilitating two-way trade between the United States and Canada. Livingston offers services and solutions that combine the expertise of highly specialized professionals with the advances of technology and electronic information networks.

Distribution History

2004 YTD (Yield)
$0.97900 (5.03%)

2003 (Yield)
$1.26200 (7.77%)

2002 (Yield)
$1.03300 (9.09%)

2001 (Yield)
$0.00000 (N/A)

2000 (Yield)
$0.00000 (N/A)

Macquarie Power Income Fund

Original Unit Price
$10.00

Symbol:	TSX: MPT.UN
Address:	121 King Street West
	Toronto, Ontario
	Canada M5H 3T9
O/S Units:	Approx. 21,100,000
Phone:	(416) 594-0200
Fax:	N/A
Email:	N/A
Contact:	Robert Rollinson

Business: Macquarie Power Income Fund is an open-ended, limited purpose trust investing primarily in operating power-generating assets, predominantly in Canada and the United States. The fund was created to acquire indirectly a 156 megawatt (MW) gas-fired combined cycle cogeneration plant located in Cardinal, Ontario. The facility, which is owned by Cardinal LP, is a nominal net 156 MW base load, combined cycle cogeneration plant, fuelled by natural gas. It is located in Cardinal, Ontario, which is approximately 45 kilometres east of Brockville on the St. Lawrence River. It includes the Cardinal Transmission Line, which connects the plant with the Hydro One transmission grid.

Distribution History

2004 YTD (Yield)
$0.39845 (3.86%)

2003 (Yield)
$0.00000 (N/A)

2002 (Yield)
$0.00000 (N/A)

2001 (Yield)
$0.00000 (N/A)

2000 (Yield)
$0.00000 (N/A)

Medical Facilities Corp.

Original Unit Price
$10.00

Symbol:	TSX: DR.UN
Address:	#2400, 250 Yonge Street
	Toronto, Ontario
	Canada M5B 2M6
O/S Units:	Approx. 22,200,000
Phone:	(416) 979-2211
Fax:	N/A
Email:	N/A
Contact:	Dr. Donald Schellpfeffer, CEO

Business: Medical Facilities Corp. was created to acqire a 51 percent interest in the MFC Partnerships, which own and operate three of the largest specialty hospitals in South Dakota: the Black Hills Surgery Center, LLP, Dakota Plains Surgical Center, LLP, and Sioux Falls Surgical Center, LLP. Each Hospital is a licensed speciality hospital that performs scheduled (as opposed to emergency) surgical, imaging, and diagnostic procedures. The hospitals do not offer the full range of services typically found in traditional hospitals, but instead focus on a limited number of clinical specialties, including orthopaedic; ear, nose, and throat; neurosurgery; and other surgical procedures.

Distribution History

2004 YTD (Yield)
$0.55900 (4.65%)

2003 (Yield)
$0.00000 (N/A)

2002 (Yield)
$0.00000 (N/A)

2001 (Yield)
$0.00000 (N/A)

2000 (Yield)
$0.00000 (N/A)

Menu Foods Income Fund

Original Unit Price
$10.00

Symbol:	TSX: MEW.UN
Address:	8 Falconer Drive
	Mississauga, Ontario
	Canada L5M 2C1
O/S Units:	Approx. 13,100,000
Phone:	(905) 826-3870
Fax:	(905) 826-4995
Email:	investorrelations@menufoods.com
Contact:	Robert Bras

Business: Menu Foods Income Fund is a limited purpose trust established to hold approximately 51 percent of the partnership units of Menu Foods L. P., which will, in turn, acquire all the securities and assets of Menu Foods Ltd. Menu is a leading North American manufacturer of private-label wet pet food products. It sells its products to supermarket retailers, mass merchandisers, pet specialty retailers, and other retail and wholesale outlets. Menu currently produces more than 800 million containers of wet pet food per year and is focused on the manufacture and sale of premium private-label wet pet food products.

Distribution History

2004 YTD (Yield)
$0.94500 (6.47%)

2003 (Yield)
$1.25290 (9.08%)

2002 (Yield)
$0.71690 (5.23%)

2001 (Yield)
$0.00000 (N/A)

2000 (Yield)
$0.00000 (N/A)

Morguard REIT

Original Unit Price
$10.00

Symbol:	TSX: MRT.UN
Address:	#1400, One University Avenue
	Toronto, Ontario
	Canada M5J 2P1
O/S Units:	Approx. 44,400,000
Phone:	(416) 369-1711
Fax:	(416) 369-1975
Email:	ctaccone@morguardREIT.com
Contact:	Bill Kennedy, President
	Carol Taccone

Business: Morguard REIT is a closed-ended real estate investment trust, that owns a diversified portfolio of 81 high quality retail, office, and industrial properties in Canada with a book value of $1.3 billion and approximately 10.4 million square feet of leaseable space.

Distribution History

2004 YTD (Yield)
$0.67500 (7.44%)

2003 (Yield)
$0.90000 (9.68%)

2002 (Yield)
$0.90000 (10.59%)

2001 (Yield)
$0.90000 (10.98%)

2000 (Yield)
$0.90000 (10.84%)

Movie Distribution Income Fund

Original Unit Price
$10.00

Symbol: TSX: FLM.UN
Address: 121 Bloor Street East, Suite 1500
Toronto, Ontario
Canada M4W 3M5
O/S Units: Approx. 17,900,000
Phone: (416) 967-1174
Fax: (416) 967-0971
Email: N/A
Contact: Patrice Thèroux

Business: Movie Distribution Income Fund is an open-ended, limited purpose trust that holds a 49 percent interest in Motion Picture Distribution LP. Motion Picture Distribution LP is the largest distributor of motion pictures in Canada, with a growing presence in motion picture distribution in the United Kingdom and a 24-screen chain of upscale cinemas in Canada in partnership with Famous Players, a subsidiary of Viacom Inc. The partnership distributes filmed entertainment to theatres on video and DVD, and to television broadcasters. Alliance Atlantis maintains a 51 percent interest in Motion Picture Distribution LP.

Distribution History

2004 YTD (Yield)
$0.86220 (7.64%)

2003 (Yield)
$0.24418 (2.34%)

2002 (Yield)
$0.00000 (N/A)

2001 (Yield)
$0.00000 (N/A)

2000 (Yield)
$0.00000 (N/A)

NAL Oil & Gas Trust

Original Unit Price
$10.25

Symbol: TSX: NAE.UN
Address: #600, 550 – 6th Avenue S.W.
Calgary, Alberta
Canada T2P 0S2
O/S Units: Approx. 50,500,000
Phone: (403) 294-3600 / 1(888) 223-8792
Fax: (403) 294-3601
Email: investor.relations@nal.ca
Contact: Donald Driscoll, President and CEO
Anne-Marie Buchmuller, IR

Business: NAL Oil & Gas Trust is a Calgary-based conventional oil and gas royalty trust. The trust generates monthly cash distributions by acquiring, developing, producing, and selling crude oil, natural gas, and natural gas liquids in Alberta, Saskatchewan, and Ontario.

Distribution History

2004 YTD (Yield)
$1.37000 (9.93%)

2003 (Yield)
$1.78000 (16.27%)

2002 (Yield)
$1.40000 (15.56%)

2001 (Yield)
$2.39000 (26.26%)

2000 (Yield)
$1.59500 (18.44%)

NAV Energy Trust

Original Unit Price (N/A)

Symbol:	TSX: NVG.UN
Address:	#2500, 205 – 5th Avenue S.W.
	Calgary, Alberta
	Canada T2P 2V7
O/S Units:	Approx. 11,200,000
Phone:	(403) 218-3600
Fax:	(403) 216-1572
Email:	investorrelations@navigoenergy.com
Contact:	Tom Stan, President

Business: NAV Energy Trust is a Calgary-based oil and natural gas investment trust focused on growth and delivering stable monthly cash distributions to its unitholders.

NAV Energy Trust was created as a result of the reorganization of Navigo Energy Inc. into an oil and gas investment trust and a small exploration focused oil and gas producer. The reorganization was completed through a plan of arrangement, which closed on December 29, 2003.

NAV Energy Trust is targeting to retain up to 20 percent of its cash flow to reinvest into properties through drilling or operational enhancements and to grow through acquisitions of new properties or corporate entities. By having a ready source of capital through cash flow retention, NAV Energy Trust can rely on internally sourced capital to mitigate natural production declines.

Distribution History

2004 YTD (Yield)
$1.35000 (12.24%)

2003 (Yield)
$0.00000 (N/A)

2002 (Yield)
$0.00000 (N/A)

2001 (Yield)
$0.00000 (N/A)

2000 (Yield)
$0.00000 (N/A)

Newalta Income Fund

Original Unit Price $9.30

Symbol:	TSX: NAL.UN
Address:	#1200, 333 – 11th Avenue S.W.
	Calgary, Alberta
	Canada T2R 1L9
O/S Units:	Approx. 26,800,000
Phone:	(403) 266-6556
Fax:	(403) 262-7348
Email:	info@newalta.com
Contact:	Al Cadotte

Business: Newalta Income Fund is an open-ended trust that maximizes the inherent value in industrial wastes through recovery, rather than disposal, of saleable products and recycling. Through an integrated network of 35 state-of-the-art facilities, Newalta delivers world-class solutions to a broad customer base of national and international corporations in a range of industries, including the automotive, forestry, pulp and paper, manufacturing, mining, oil and gas, petrochemical, and transportation services industries.

Distribution History

2004 YTD (Yield)
$1.08500 (5.34%)

2003 (Yield)
$0.96000 (5.95%)

2002 (Yield)
$0.00000 (N/A)

2001 (Yield)
$0.00000 (N/A)

2000 (Yield)
$0.00000 (N/A)

Noranda Income Fund

Original Unit Price
$10.00

Symbol:	TSX: NIF.UN
Address:	181 Bay St., Suite 200, P.O. Box 755, BCE Place
	Toronto, Ontario
	Canada M5J 2T3
O/S Units:	Approx. 37,500,000
Phone:	(416) 982-7111
Fax:	(416) 982 7423
Email:	request@norandaincomefund.com
Contact:	Lucy Rosato
IR Counsel:	Renmark Financial Communications Inc.

Business: Noranda Income Fund was created to acquire, indirectly through Noranda Operating Trust and Noranda Income Limited Partnership, Noranda's CEZinc zinc processing facility located in Salaberry-de-Valleyfield, Québec and ancillary assets. The fund distributes all of the available cash generated by the processing facility, after payments of its costs and expenses, to unitholders. The processing facility is the second largest zinc-processing facility in North America.

Distribution History

2004 YTD (Yield)
$0.76500 (6.63%)

2003 (Yield)
$1.01833 (8.75%)

2002 (Yield)
$0.66126 (6.71%)

2001 (Yield)
$0.00000 (N/A)

2000 (Yield)
$0.00000 (N/A)

North West Company Fund Trust Units

Original Unit Price
(N/A)

Symbol:	TSX: NWF.UN
Address:	77 Main Street
	Winnipeg, Manitoba
	Canada R3C 2R1
O/S Units:	Approx. 16,100,000
Phone:	(204) 934-1481
Fax:	(204) 934-1455
Email:	nwc@northwest.ca
Contact:	Ian Sutherland

Business: The North West Company, operating in Canada as Northern and in Alaska as AC Value Centers, is the leading retailer of food, family apparel, and general merchandise in small northern communities.

Distribution History

2004 YTD (Yield)
$1.35000 (5.42%)

2003 (Yield)
$1.90000 (7.67%)

2002 (Yield)
$1.56000 (7.50%)

2001 (Yield)
$1.45500 (8.96%)

2000 (Yield)
$1.44000 (12.47%)

Northern Property Real Estate Investment Trust

Original Unit Price
$10.00

Symbol: TSX: NPR.UN
Address: #110, 6131 – 6th Street S.E.
Calgary, Alberta
Canada T2H 1L9
O/S Units: Approx. 9,100,000
Phone: (403) 531-0720
Fax: (403) 531-0727
Email: info@npreit.com
Contact: James Britton

Business: Northern Property REIT is an unincorporated open-end real estate investment trust that invests in a portfolio of mainly residential income-producing properties located in the Northwest Territories, Nunavut and the Province of Alberta, much of which is leased to government and large corporations to meet staff housing needs. The REIT also invests in commercial premises in Northern Canada leased to government and corporate interests.

Distribution History

2004 YTD (Yield)
$0.88830 (6.35%)

2003 (Yield)
$1.15250 (7.56%)

2002 (Yield)
$0.67690 (5.69%)

2001 (Yield)
$0.00000 (N/A)

2000 (Yield)
$0.00000 (N/A)

Northland Power Income Trust

Original Unit Price
$10.00

Symbol: TSX: NPI.UN
Address: 17th Floor, 30 St. Clair Avenue West
Toronto, Ontario
Canada M4V 3A2
O/S Units: Approx. 37,800,000
Phone: (416) 962-6262
Fax: (416) 962-6266
Email: info@NPIFund.com
Contact: Tony Anderson

Business: Northland Power Income Fund is a Canadian trust that owns a cogeneration power plant located in Iroquois Falls, Ontario, and an interest in a cogeneration plant located near Kingston, Ontario. The facilities supply electricity to Ontario Electricity Financial Corporation and steam to neighbouring industries under long-term contracts. The fund is administered by the manager, Iroquois Falls Power Management Inc., a wholly owned subsidiary of Northland Power Inc., which also manages the Iroquois Falls facility.

Distribution History

2004 YTD (Yield)
$0.24750 (1.87%)

2003 (Yield)
$0.98000 (8.28%)

2002 (Yield)
$0.98000 (8.91%)

2001 (Yield)
$0.98000 (8.45%)

2000 (Yield)
$0.94000 (10.62%)

O&Y Real Estate Investment Trust

Original Unit Price
$10.00

Symbol: TSX: OYR.UN
Address: #3300, 1 First Canadian Place, P.O. Box 72
Toronto, Ontario
Canada M5X 1B1
O/S Units: Approx. 42,500,000
Phone: (416) 862-6183
Fax: (416) 862-6908
Email: ir@oyp.com
Contact: Frank M. Hauer

Business: O&Y Real Estate Investment Trust is a closed-ended
real estate investment trust created to invest in
quality office buildings in major markets across
Canada. It owns a national portfolio of 21 high-quality
Class A and Class B multi-tenant and government
office buildings across Canada, totalling 5.5 million
square feet, and an indirect interest in
First Canadian Place, a 2.7 million square foot Class
AAA, 72-storey office complex in downtown Toronto.
In addition, O&Y REIT has an option to purchase
from O&Y Properties Corporation the Maritime Life
Tower, the first office tower to be developed in
downtown Toronto.

Distribution History

2004 YTD (Yield)
$0.82530 (6.31%)

2003 (Yield)
$1.08540 (9.24%)

2002 (Yield)
$1.06870 (10.63%)

2001 (Yield)
$0.53650 (4.94%)

2000 (Yield)
$0.00000 (N/A)

Oceanex Income Fund

Original Unit Price
$10.00

Symbol: TSX: OAX.UN
Address: #2550, 630 Rene-Levesque Blvd. West
Montreal, Québec
Canada H3B 1S6
O/S Units: Approx. 8,700,000
Phone: (514) 875-9244
Fax: (514) 877-0226
Email: dbelisle@oceanex.com
Contact: Peter Henrico
Daniel Bèlisle

Business: Oceanex Income Fund owns and operates an
inter-modal transportation company that operates
Roll-on/Roll-off vessels, marine terminals, and a
large fleet of containers and trailers. It provides
door-to-door frieght services from any point of origin
in North America to destinations in Newfoundland
and Labrador.

Distribution History

2004 YTD (Yield)
$0.74960 (5.03%)

2003 (Yield)
$1.12440 (8.03%)

2002 (Yield)
$1.12440 (9.95%)

2001 (Yield)
$1.12440 (9.53%)

2000 (Yield)
$1.12440 (12.36%)

Osprey Media Income Fund

Original Unit Price
$10.00

Symbol:	TSX: OSP.UN
Address:	#110, 100 Renfrew Drive
	Markham, Ontario
	Canada L3R 9R6
O/S Units:	Approx. 37,400,000
Phone:	(905) 752-1132
Fax:	(905) 752-0989
Email:	jleader@ospreymedia.ca
Contact:	Michael Sifton, President

Business: Osprey Media Income Fund is one of Canada's leading publishers of daily and weekly newspapers, magazines, and specialty publications. Its publications include 21 daily newspapers and 35 weekly newspapers together with shopping guides, magazines, telephone directories, and other publications.

Distribution History

2004 YTD (Yield)
$0.41250 (4.16%)

2003 (Yield)
$0.00000 (N/A)

2002 (Yield)
$0.00000 (N/A)

2001 (Yield)
$0.00000 (N/A)

2000 (Yield)
$0.00000 (N/A)

Paramount Energy Trust

Original Unit Price
(N/A)

Symbol:	TSX: PMT.UN
Address:	#500, 630 – 4th Avenue S.W.
	Calgary, Alberta,
	Canada T2P 0J9
O/S Units:	Approx. 44,600,000
Phone:	(403) 269-4400
Fax:	(403) 269-4499
Email:	info@paramountenergy.com
Contact:	Clayton H. Riddell, CEO

Business: Paramount Energy Trust is a natural gas-focused Canadian energy trust. The trust was created to hold, through Paramount OperatingTrust, certain mature natural gas assets in northeastern Alberta.

Distribution History

2004 YTD (Yield)
$1.58000 (10.23%)

2003 (Yield)
$2.88400 (24.69%)

2002 (Yield)
$0.00000 (N/A)

2001 (Yield)
$0.00000 (N/A)

2000 (Yield)
$0.00000 (N/A)

Parkland Income Fund

Original Unit Price (N/A)

Symbol:	TSX: PKI.UN
Address:	#236 Riverside Office Plaza
	4919 – 59th Street, Red Deer, Alberta
	Canada T4N 6C9
O/S Units:	Approx. 6,700,000
Phone:	(403) 357-6400
Fax:	(403) 346-3015
Email:	corpinfo@pkif.com
Contact:	Andrew Wiswell
IR Counsel:	Cavalcanti Hume Funfer Inc.

Business: Parkland Income Fund operates a retail and wholesale fuels and convenience store business under its marketing brands Fas Gas, RT Fuels, and Short Stop. Parkland has developed a strong market niche in western and northern Canada by focusing on non-urban markets.

Distribution History

2004 YTD (Yield)
$1.28000 (5.95%)

2003 (Yield)
$1.68000 (8.86%)

2002 (Yield)
$0.84000 (6.75%)

2001 (Yield)
$0.00000 (N/A)

2000 (Yield)
$0.00000 (N/A)

PBB Global Logistics Income Fund

Original Unit Price $10.00

Symbol:	TSX: PBB.UN
Address:	33 Walnut Street, P.O. Box 40
	Fort Erie, Ontario
	Canada L2A 5M7
O/S Units:	Approx. 6,100,000
Phone:	(905) 871-1606
Fax:	(905) 991-0404
Email:	Chalmers@pbb.com
Contact:	Michael D. Scott

Business: PBB Global Logistics Income Fund is a trust that owns all of the issued and outstanding securities of PBB Global Logistics Inc., one of Canada's leading providers of third-party international logistics services. Founded in 1946, PBB provides supply chain solutions and global service to its approximately 26,000 clients, including customs brokerage, freight, warehousing, and distribution, and trade, regulatory, and other services.

Distribution History

2004 YTD (Yield)
$1.21249 (6.36%)

2003 (Yield)
$1.50000 (10.24%)

2002 (Yield)
$0.81850 (7.65%)

2001 (Yield)
$0.00000 (N/A)

2000 (Yield)
$0.00000 (N/A)

PDM Royalties Income Fund

Original Unit Price
$10.00

Symbol:	TSX: PDM.UN
Address:	#2100, 40 King Street West, Scotia Plaza
	Toronto, Ontario
	Canada M5H 3C2
O/S Units:	Approx. 5,000,000
Phone:	(506) 853-0990
Fax:	(506) 853-4131
Email:	blane@pizzadelight.ca
Contact:	Bernard Imbeault

Business: PDM Royalties Income Fund has been created to acquire, indirectly through PDM Royalties Limited Partnership and PDM Holdings Trust, the trade-marks, trade names, operating procedures and systems, and other intellectual property and proprietary rights, and all goodwill associated therewith, owned by Pizza Delight Corporation and Mikes Restaurants Inc. and their subsidiaries, and used in connection with Pizza Delight and Mikes restaurants operated by the company and its franchisees.

Distribution History

2004 YTD (Yield)
$0.29600 (2.85%)

2003 (Yield)
$0.00000 (N/A)

2002 (Yield)
$0.00000 (N/A)

2001 (Yield)
$0.00000 (N/A)

2000 (Yield)
$0.00000 (N/A)

Peak Energy Services Trust

Original Unit Price
$10.00

Symbol:	TSX: PES.UN
Address:	#1800, 530 – 8th Ave S.W.
	Calgary, Alberta
	Canada T2P 3S8
O/S Units:	Approx. 29,500,000
Phone:	(403) 543-7325
Fax:	(403) 543-7320
Email:	mjhuber@pesl.com
Contact:	Christopher Haslam, President and CEO

Business: Peak Energy Services Trust is a diversified energy services organization providing oilfield equipment and related services to the energy industry in western Canada.

Distribution History

2004 YTD (Yield)
$0.37500 (4.88%)

2003 (Yield)
$0.00000 (N/A)

2002 (Yield)
$0.00000 (N/A)

2001 (Yield)
$0.00000 (N/A)

2000 (Yield)
$0.00000 (N/A)

Pembina Pipeline Income Fund

Original Unit Price
$10.00

Symbol: TSX: PIF.UN
Address: 700 – 9th Avenue S.W., P.O. Box 1948
Calgary, Alberta
Canada T2P 2M7
O/S Units: Approx. 98,000,000
Phone: (403) 231-7500 / 1(888) 428-3222
Fax: (403) 237-0254
Email: investor-relations@pembina.com
Contact: Robert B. Michaleski
Glenys Hermanutz

Business: Pembina Pipeline Income Fund is a publicly traded
Canadian income fund engaged, through its wholly
owned subsidiary Pembina Pipeline Corporation, in
the transportation of synthetic and conventional
crude oil, condensate, and natural gas liquids in
western Canada. The fund pays distributions on a
monthly basis and, since formation in 1997, has
established a record of consistent cash payments to
unitholders.

Distribution History

2004 YTD (Yield)
$0.78750 (6.59%)

2003 (Yield)
$1.05000 (8.02%)

2002 (Yield)
$1.05000 (9.63%)

2001 (Yield)
$1.05000 (9.28%)

2000 (Yield)
$0.96000 (10.97%)

Pengrowth Energy Trust Units

Original Unit Price
(N/A)

Symbol: TSX: PGF.UN
Address: #700, 112 – 4th Avenue S.W.
Calgary, Alberta
Canada T2P 0H3
O/S Units: Approx. 81,400,000
Phone: (403) 233-0224 / 1(800) 223-4122
Fax: (403) 294-0051
Email: pengrowth@pengrowth.com
Contact: James S. Kinnear
Janice Young

Business: Pengrowth Energy Trust, started in 1988, is one of
the largest royalty trusts in North America, providing
investors with superior cash-on-cash returns and
growth in value. Unitholders invest in a large portfolio
of oil and gas properties and receive the net cash
flow after expenses on a monthly basis.

Distribution History

2004 YTD (Yield)
N/A

2003 (Yield)
$2.67000 (12.56%)

2002 (Yield)
$2.00000 (13.58%)

2001 (Yield)
$3.28000 (23.07%)

2000 (Yield)
$3.64500 (18.98%)

Petrofund Energy Trust

Original Unit Price (N/A)

Symbol:	TSX: PTF.UN
Address:	#600, 444 – 7th Avenue S.W.
	Calgary, Alberta
	Canada T2P 0X8
O/S Units:	Approx. 99,200,000
Phone:	(403) 218 8625 / 1(866) 318 1767
Fax:	(403) 539-4300
Email:	info@petrofund.ca
Contact:	Jeffery E. Errico, President and CEO

Business: Petrofund Energy Trust is a Calgary based royalty trust that acquires and manages producing oil and gas properties and payout out a portion of resulting cash flow to investors on a monthly basis.

Distribution History

2004 YTD (Yield)
$1.44000 (9.08%)

2003 (Yield)
$2.09000 (11.12%)

2002 (Yield)
$1.71000 (15.76%)

2001 (Yield)
$4.24000 (35.42%)

2000 (Yield)
$1.33000 (22.17%)

Peyto Energy Trust

Original Unit Price (N/A)

Symbol:	TSX: PEY.UN
Address:	#2900, 450 – 1st Street S.W.
	Calgary, Alberta
	Canada T2P 5H1
O/S Units:	Approx. 45,400,000
Phone:	(403) 261-6077
Fax:	(403) 261-8976
Email:	dgray@peyto.com
Contact:	Don T. Gray, President and CEO

Business: Peyto Energy Trust is an investment trust engaged in oil and gas acquisitions and exploration primarily focused in western Canada.

Founded in November 1998, Peyto converted to an income trust in mid-2003 to further enhance company performance, maintaining its internal management structure and strategies. Peyto works on a low-cost basis, funding distributions and exploration from operations.

Distribution History

2004 YTD (Yield)
$1.47000 (4.25%)

2003 (Yield)
$0.90000 (3.30%)

2002 (Yield)
$0.00000 (N/A)

2001 (Yield)
$0.00000 (N/A)

2000 (Yield)
$0.00000 (N/A)

Phoenix Technology Income Fund

Original Unit Price (N/A)

Symbol:	TSX: PHX.UN
Address:	#630, 435 – 4th Avenue S.W.
	Calgary, Alberta
	Canada T2P 3A8
O/S Units:	Approx. 17,000,000
Phone:	(403) 543-4466
Fax:	(403) 543-4485
Email:	N/A
Contact:	John Hooks, President

Business: Phoenix provides horizontal and directional drilling services to the oil and natural gas industry in Canada and the United States. JAG Rentals, a division of Phoenix, provides innovative drilling and completion solutions for the oil and natural gas industry in western Canada with its rental fleet of drilling jars, shock tools, stabilizers, and down-hole performance drilling motors.

Distribution History

2004 YTD (Yield)
$0.16000 (3.99%)

2003 (Yield)
$0.00000 (N/A)

2002 (Yield)
$0.00000 (N/A)

2001 (Yield)
$0.00000 (N/A)

2000 (Yield)
$0.00000 (N/A)

Prime Restaurants Royalty Income Fund

Original Unit Price $10.00

Symbol:	TSX: EAT.UN
Address:	#600, 10 Kingsbridge Garden Circle
	Mississauga, Ontario
	Canada L5R 3K6
O/S Units:	Approx. 6,100,000
Phone:	(905) 568-0000
Fax:	(905) 568-0080
Email:	jrothschild@primerestaurants.com
Contact:	Nicholas M. Perpick

Business: Prime Restaurants Royalty Income Fund currently has 130 pooled restaurants contributing to the revenue on which the royalty is based.
Prime Restaurants of Canada Inc. operates and franchises one of Canada's leading chains of casual dining restaurants and premium pubs with a diversified portfolio of concepts that include: East Side Mario's, Casey's Bar & Grill, a Belgian-style brasserie operating under the trademark Esplanade Bier Market, and a family of authentic Irish pubs operating under the trademarks Fionn MacCool's Irish Pub, D'Arcy McGee's Irish Pub, Paddy Flaherty's, Tir nan Og, and Slainte as well as RD's BBQ and Blues, and Pat and Mario's.

Distribution History

2004 YTD (Yield)
$0.84600 (8.70%)

2003 (Yield)
$1.12780 (12.07%)

2002 (Yield)
$0.50200 (5.79%)

2001 (Yield)
$0.00000 (N/A)

2000 (Yield)
$0.00000 (N/A)

Primewest Energy Trust

Original Unit Price
$10.00

Symbol:	TSX: PWI.UN
Address:	#4700, 150 - 6th Avenue S.W.,
	Calgary, Alberta,
	Canada T2P 3Y7
O/S Units:	Approx. 47,900,000
Phone:	(403) 234-6600 / 1(877) 968-7878
Fax:	(403) 266-2825
Email:	investor@primewestenergy.com
Contact:	Kent MacIntyre

Business: PrimeWest Energy Trust is a Calgary-based conventional oil and gas royalty trust actively managed for the benefit of unitholders. The trust generates monthly cash distributions by acquiring, developing, producing and selling crude oil, natural gas and natural gas liquids in Western Canada. With assets exceeding $1 billion, PrimeWest is one of Canada's largest energy trusts.

Distribution History

2004 YTD (Yield)
$2.39500 (9.21%)

2003 (Yield)
$4.32000 (15.67%)

2002 (Yield)
$4.80000 (18.90%)

2001 (Yield)
$9.24000 (36.32%)

2000 (Yield)
$7.08000 (19.78%)

Priszm Canadian Income Fund

Original Unit Price
$10.00

Symbol:	TSX: QSR.UN
Address:	101 Exchange Avenue
	Vaughan, Ontario
	Canada L4K 5R6
O/S Units:	Approx. 15,000,000
Phone:	(416) 739-2900
Fax:	(416) 361-6018
Email:	info@priszm.com
Contact:	Rupert Altschuler, President

Business: Priszm Canadian Income Fund, through its 60.2 percent interest in KIT LP, operates 470 KFC and multi-branded restaurants, accounting for approximately 70 percent of all KFC product sales in Canada based on the number of restaurants. Priszm is one of the largest KFC franchisees in the world. KFC is one of the most recognized brands in the world, and is the Canadian quick-service restaurant industry leader in chicken sales. In total, Priszm owns and operates 470 restaurants in 7 provinces across Canada. Of the 470 restaurants, 415 are KFC restaurants, while 55 are multi-branded restaurants combining KFC, Pizza Hut™, and Taco Bell™.

Distribution History

2004 YTD (Yield)
$0.90000 (7.47%)

2003 (Yield)
$0.17000 (1.63%)

2002 (Yield)
$0.00000 (N/A)

2001 (Yield)
$0.00000 (N/A)

2000 (Yield)
$0.00000 (N/A)

Progress Energy Trust

Original Unit Price (N/A)

Symbol: TSX: PGX.UN
Address: #1400, 440 – 2nd Avenue S.W.
Calgary, Alberta
Canada T2P 5E9
O/S Units: Approx. 33,400,000
Phone: (403) 216-2510
Fax: (403) 216-2514
Email: ir@progressenergy.com
Contact: Michael Culbert, President

Business: Progress Energy Trust is a Calgary based natural gas and crude oil exploration and production trust currently producing approximately 20,000 barrels of oil equivalent per day. Its main operating areas include the deep basin of northwest Alberta and the foothills and plains regions of northeast British Columbia.

Distribution History

2004 YTD (Yield)
$0.42000 (2.84%)

2003 (Yield)
$0.00000 (N/A)

2002 (Yield)
$0.00000 (N/A)

2001 (Yield)
$0.00000 (N/A)

2000 (Yield)
$0.00000 (N/A)

Provident Energy Trust

Original Unit Price (N/A)

Symbol: TSX: PVE.UN
Address: #700, 112 – 4th Avenue S.W.
Calgary, Alberta
Canada T2P 0H3
O/S Units: Approx. 128,100,000
Phone: (403) 296-2233 / 1(800) 587-6299
Fax: (403) 294-0111
Email: info@providentenergytrust.com
Contact: Randall J. Findlay

Business: Provident Energy Trust is a Calgary based oil and gas trust that acquires, develops, produces and markets crude oil, natural gas and natural gas liquids and makes monthly cash distributions to its unitholders.

Distribution History

2004 YTD (Yield)
$1.08000 (9.64%)

2003 (Yield)
$2.06000 (18.02%)

2002 (Yield)
$2.03000 (18.88%)

2001 (Yield)
$2.54000 (31.01%)

2000 (Yield)
$0.00000 (N/A)

PRT Forest Regeneration Income Fund

Original Unit Price
$10.00

Symbol:	TSX: PRT.UN
Address:	#4, 1028 Fort Street
	Victoria, British Columbia
	Canada V8V 3K4
O/S Units:	Approx. 7,200,000
Phone:	(250) 381-1404 / 1(866) 553-8733
Fax:	(250) 381-0252
Email:	investor_relations@prtgroup.com
Contact:	John Kitchen
	Robert Miller

Business: The PRT Forest Regeneration Income Fund is a publicly traded income fund, which was created to hold all common shares and certain notes of PRT. PRT is the largest producer of container-grown forest seedlings in North America, operating 13 nurseries in Ontario, Saskatchewan, Alberta, and British Columbia, and managing over 130 million seedlings annually.

Distribution History

2004 YTD (Yield)
$0.65700 (6.77%)

2003 (Yield)
$0.91240 (10.14%)

2002 (Yield)
$1.01420 (10.13%)

2001 (Yield)
$0.96020 (8.65%)

2000 (Yield)
$1.05010 (12.00%)

Public Storage Canadian Properties Ltd.

Original Unit Price
(N/A)

Symbol:	TSX: PUB
Address:	#6600, 100 King St. W., 1 First Canadian Place
	Toronto, Ontario
	Canada M5X 1B8
O/S Units:	Approx. 4,800,000
Phone:	(310) 317-1443 / 1(866) 772-2623
Fax:	(310) 774-5194
Email:	investor@publicstoragecanada.com
Contact:	David P. Singelyn, President

Business: Public Storage Canadian Properties is a publicly held limited partnership that has invested in mini-warehouse storage facilities, of which 13 are located in Ontario and three are located in British Columbia. It is a full-service real estate company engaged in the acquisition, development, syndication, and management of real property.

Distribution History

2004 YTD (Yield)
N/A

2003 (Yield)
$1.80000 (8.13%)

2002 (Yield)
$1.95000 (9.63%)

2001 (Yield)
$1.75000 (9.94%)

2000 (Yield)
$1.33000 (9.85%)

Rainmaker Income Fund

Original Unit Price
(N/A)

Symbol:	TSX: RNK.UN
Address:	50, 2nd Avenue West
	Vancouver, British Columbia
	Canada V5Y 1B3
O/S Units:	Approx. 10,700,000
Phone:	(604) 874-8700 / 1(800) 616-4433
Fax:	(604) 872-8296
Email:	ir_rnk@rainmaker.com
Contact:	Hugh McKinnon

Business: Rainmaker is an unincorporated open-ended limited purpose trust that is located in Vancouver, British Columbia. Rainmaker, through its predecessors, was established in 1979 and is one of North America's leading film and video post-production organizations. Rainmaker uses innovative technology, superior service, and world-class talent to design, build, and shape content for film, television, and new media productions.

Distribution History

2004 YTD (Yield)
$0.36000 (9.00%)

2003 (Yield)
$0.68000 (17.44%)

2002 (Yield)
$0.39000 (17.57%)

2001 (Yield)
$0.00000 (N/A)

2000 (Yield)
$0.00000 (N/A)

Retirement Residences REIT

Original Unit Price
$10.00

Symbol:	TSX: RRR.UN
Address:	175 Bloor Street East, South Tower, 6th Floor
	Toronto, Ontario
	Canada M4W 3R8
O/S Units:	Approx. 77,800,000
Phone:	(416) 929-5450
Fax:	(416) 323-3818
Email:	contactus@retirementreit.com
Contact:	Barry Reichmann

Business: Retirement REIT is the largest private accommodation and care provider for seniors in Canada. REIT owns 205 retirement and long-term care facilities, including 30 facilities in select U.S. markets, and provides management services at 12 homes for other parties, with an aggregate resident capacity in excess of 24,500. Retirement REIT also provides nursing placement and in-home health care through its Central Health Services and Central Med units, and provides third-party management services to an additional 12 retirement and long-term care homes.

Distribution History

2004 YTD (Yield)
$0.76720 (7.01%)

2003 (Yield)
$1.15080 (8.96%)

2002 (Yield)
$1.11720 (9.50%)

2001 (Yield)
$0.75500 (6.19%)

2000 (Yield)
$0.00000 (N/A)

Retrocom Mid-Market REIT

Original Unit Price
$10.00

Symbol:	TSX: RMM.UN
Address:	#400, 89 The Queensway West
	Mississauga, Ontario
	Canada L5B 2V2
O/S Units:	Approx. 11,000,000
Phone:	(905) 848-2430
Fax:	(905) 848-2869
Email:	dwilkinson@retrocom.ca
Contact:	R. Michael Steplock

Business: Retrocom Mid-Market Real Estate Investment Trust will focus on owning and acquiring income-producing mid-market commercial properties in primary and secondary cities across Canada. The objectives of the REIT are to: (i) generate stable and growing cash distributions on a tax-efficient basis; (ii) enhance the value of the REIT's assets and maximize long-term unit value through the active management of its assets; and (iii) expand the asset base of the REIT and increase its distributable income through an accretive acquisition program. The REIT intends to pay unitholders stable and growing monthly cash distributions, and is initially expected to provide an annual yield that compares favourably to the yields available from other Canadian real estate investment trusts.

Distribution History

2004 YTD (Yield)
$0.08540 (0.93%)

2003 (Yield)
$0.00000 (N/A)

2002 (Yield)
$0.00000 (N/A)

2001 (Yield)
$0.00000 (N/A)

2000 (Yield)
$0.00000 (N/A)

Richards Packaging Income Fund

Original Unit Price
$10.00

Symbol:	TSX: RPI.UN
Address:	3115 Lenworth Drive
	Mississauga, Ontario
	Canada L4X 2G5
O/S Units:	Approx. 10,200,000
Phone:	(905) 624-3391
Fax:	(905) 624-2288
Email:	gglynn@richardspackaging.com
Contact:	David Prupas, President

Business: Richards Packaging is a full-service rigid packaging distributor targeting small and medium-sized North American businesses. Richard Packaging provides its customers with a wide range of packaging solutions to help those customers differentiate their products, as well as with design and development services and comprehensive logistics management. The company serves a wide customer base that is comprised of over 6000 regional food, wine and spirits, cosmetic, specialty chemical, pharmaceutical, and other companies.

Distribution History

2004 YTD (Yield)
$0.48960 (4.72%)

2003 (Yield)
$0.00000 (N/A)

2002 (Yield)
$0.00000 (N/A)

2001 (Yield)
$0.00000 (N/A)

2000 (Yield)
$0.00000 (N/A)

RioCan Real Estate Investment Trust

Original Unit Price (N/A)

Symbol:	TSX: REI.UN
Address:	#700, Box 378, 130 King Street West
	Toronto, Ontario
	Canada M5X 1E2
O/S Units:	Approx. 177,600,000
Phone:	(416) 866-3000 / 1(800) 465-2733
Fax:	(416) 866-8567
Email:	ir@riocan.com
Contact:	Ed Sonshine, President
	Maggie Sagadore, IR
Business:	RioCan owns and operates a portfolio of income properties and joint venture properties under development across Canada. RioCan's primary investment objective is the long-term maximization of cashflow and capital appreciation of its portfolio. RioCan has ownership interests in a portfolio of 171 retail properties across Canada containing an aggregate of well over 35 million square feet.

Distribution History

2004 YTD (Yield)
$0.89250 (5.45%)

2003 (Yield)
$1.13750 (7.43%)

2002 (Yield)
$1.10500 (8.86%)

2001 (Yield)
$1.07500 (8.86%)

2000 (Yield)
$1.07125 (11.40%)

Rogers Sugar Income Fund

Original Unit Price $10.00

Symbol:	TSX: RSI.UN
Address:	4026 Notre-Dame Street East
	Montreal, Québec
	Canada H1W 2K3
O/S Units:	Approx. 88,700,000
Phone:	(514) 527-8686
Fax:	(514) 527-1610
Email:	N/A
Contact:	Dan Lafrance
IR Counsel:	Maison Brison
Business:	Rogers Sugar Income Fund is an open-ended, limited purpose trust established to hold all of the common shares and notes of Rogers Sugar Ltd. Rogers is the leading refiner, processor, distributor and marketer of sugar products in western Canada.

Distribution History

2004 YTD (Yield)
$0.30060 (7.63%)

2003 (Yield)
$0.46020 (12.78%)

2002 (Yield)
$0.45500 (9.68%)

2001 (Yield)
$0.40000 (9.30%)

2000 (Yield)
$0.78500 (17.84%)

ROW Entertainment Income Fund

Original Unit Price
$10.00

Symbol:	TSX: ROW.UN
Address:	255 Shields Court
	Markham, Ontario
	Canada L3R 8V2
O/S Units:	Approx. 14,100,000
Phone:	(905) 475-3550
Fax:	(905) 475-4163
Email:	cjamieson@rowentertainment.ca
Contact:	Darren Throop, President and CEO

Business: ROW Entertainment Income Fund indirectly acquired the wholesale/fullfillment business previously carried on by Records on Wheels and the retail music and movie business previously carried on by CD Plus. The fund is the successor to one of the leading participants in the home entertainment industry in Canada, which currently focuses on the wholesale/fullfillment and retail sale of pre-recorded music and movies. ROW's business currently includes a wholesale/fullfillment business, as well as a retail business that includes 99 traditional storefront retail locations and an Internet retail site, www.cdplus.com.

Distribution History

2004 YTD (Yield)
$0.97470 (8.30%)

2003 (Yield)
$0.27600 (2.59%)

2002 (Yield)
$0.00000 (N/A)

2001 (Yield)
$0.00000 (N/A)

2000 (Yield)
$0.00000 (N/A)

Royal Host REIT

Original Unit Price
$10.00

Symbol:	TSX: RYL.UN
Address:	#500, 5940 Macleod Trail South
	Calgary, Alberta
	Canada T2H 2G4
O/S Units:	Approx. 24,700,000
Phone:	(403) 259-9800
Fax:	(403) 259-8580
Email:	investorinfo@royalhost.com
Contact:	Randy Royer
	Peter Sikora

Business: Royal Host REIT owns 39 hotels, manages 143 properties, and franchises 120 locations for over 20,000 guestrooms in the mid-market to upscale segments. Royal Host also owns the Travelodge Master Franchise in Canada, provides hotel and resort management services for the portfolio and to third-party properties, markets vacation intervals in hotels and resorts, and operates a facility for customers to trade and bank prepaid vacation weeks.

Distribution History

2004 YTD (Yield)
$0.18000 (3.52%)

2003 (Yield)
$0.48000 (9.27%)

2002 (Yield)
$0.72000 (12.20%)

2001 (Yield)
$0.90000 (15.00%)

2000 (Yield)
$0.96000 (15.24%)

Royal LePage Franchise Services Fund

Original Unit Price
$10.00

Symbol:	TSX: RSF.UN
Address:	39 Wynford Drive
	Toronto, Ontario
	Canada M3C 3K5
O/S Units:	Approx. 9,983,000
Phone:	(416) 510-5853
Fax:	(416) 446-0050
Email:	selenafiacco@royallepage.ca
Contact:	Philip D. Soper, President
	Selena Fiacco, IR
Business:	The Royal LePage Franchise Services Fund is a leading provider of services to residential real estate brokers and their agents. The Fund generates cash flow from franchise royalties and service fees derived from a national network of real estate brokers and agents in Canada operating under the Royal LePage, Johnston and Daniel and Realty World brand names.

Distribution History

2004 YTD (Yield)
$0.82530 (6.82%)

2003 (Yield)
$0.45410 (4.19%)

2002 (Yield)
$0.00000 (N/A)

2001 (Yield)
$0.00000 (N/A)

2000 (Yield)
$0.00000 (N/A)

SCI Income Trust

Original Unit Price
$10.00

Symbol:	TSX: SMN.UN
Address:	#251, 6900 Airport Road
	Mississauga, Ontario
	Canada L4V 1E8
O/S Units:	Approx. 7,700,000
Phone:	(905) 671-1033
Fax:	(905) 671-0669
Email:	sci-investor-relations@simmonscanada.com
Contact:	Terence H. Pace, President and CEO
Business:	SCI Income Trust is a trust owns the business currently carried on by Simmons Canada Inc. SCI Income Trust through its wholly-owned operating subsidiary, Simmons Canada, is a manufacturer of mattresses and foundations in Canada. The company manufactures four nationally-known brand names of mattresses, Beautyrest, BackCare, Beautysleep and Dreamscapes. The company also contracts the manufacture of Hide-A-Bed convertible sofas and other upholstery products and high quality furniture. The company supplies its products to a broad range of customers, including national department store chains, specialty sleep stores, furniture buying groups, independent furniture retailers as well as the health care and hospitality industries.

Distribution History

2004 YTD (Yield)
$0.72000 (6.62%)

2003 (Yield)
$1.02000 (9.53%)

2002 (Yield)
$1.30000 (11.50%)

2001 (Yield)
$1.02000 (10.30%)

2000 (Yield)
$1.55000 (14.35%)

SFK Pulp Fund

Original Unit Price $10.00

Symbol:	TSX: SFK.UN
Address:	4000 Saint-Eusëbe Road
	Saint-Fèlicien, Québec
	Canada G8K 2R6
O/S Units:	Approx. 44,400,000
Phone:	(418) 679-4545
Fax:	(418) 679-0666
Email:	N/A
Contact:	Andrè Bernier
IR Counsel:	Renmark Financial Communications Inc.
Business:	Through SFK Pulp General Partnership, SFK Pulp Fund operates a mill located in Saint-Fèlicien, Québec, approximately 450 kilometres north of Montreal in the Lac-Saint-Jean region. The mill has an annual production capacity of 350,000 metric tonnes of NBSK pulp and is one of the lowest-cost producers of NBSK pulp in Canada. The mill supplies NBSK pulp to various sectors of the paper industry in Canada, the United States, and in Europe for use in products such as lightweight coated papers, groundwood specialities, supercalendered grades, high-quality woodfree coated rades, uncoated papers, and premium tissues.

Distribution History

2004 YTD (Yield)
$0.49750 (5.99%)

2003 (Yield)
$1.00000 (13.16%)

2002 (Yield)
$0.50000 (4.90%)

2001 (Yield)
$0.00000 (N/A)

2000 (Yield)
$0.00000 (N/A)

Shiningbank Energy Income Fund

Original Unit Price $10.00

Symbol:	TSX: SHN.UN
Address:	#1310, 111 – 5th Avenue S.W.
	Calgary, Alberta
	Canada T2P 3Y6
O/S Units:	Approx. 44,100,000
Phone:	(403) 268-7477 / 1(866) 268-7477
Fax:	(403) 268-7499
Email:	irinfo@shiningbank.com
Contact:	David M. Fitzpatrick
	Bruce Gibson
Business:	Shiningbank is a conventional oil and gas royalty trust that purchases, develops, and operates producing properties for the direct benefit of the unitholder on a tax-advantaged basis. Shiningbank has the highest weighting of natural gas volumes among its peers. The fund acquires producing properties, improves field performance, and markets its production. These activities offer investors exposure to commodity prices, while maintaining a low-risk investment in the oil and gas industry.

Distribution History

2004 YTD (Yield)
$2.07000 (9.81%)

2003 (Yield)
$2.62000 (14.06%)

2002 (Yield)
$2.16000 (14.26%)

2001 (Yield)
$3.40000 (24.34%)

2000 (Yield)
$2.76000 (16.24%)

SIR Royalty Income Fund

Original Unit Price
$10.00

Symbol: TSX: SRV.UN
Address: #200, 5360 South Service Road
Burlington, Ontario
Canada L7L 5L1
O/S Units: Approx. 5,300,000
Phone: (905) 681 2997
Fax: (905) 681 0394
Email: info@sircorp.com
Contact: David M. Fitzpatrick
Peter Fowler

Business: SIR Corp. is a company incorporated under the laws of the Province of Ontario and, together with its subsidiaries that carry on business or own property in Canada, is in the business of creating, owning and operating full service restaurants in Canada. SIR, which stands for Service Inspired Restaurants, is a strategically driven organization with an impressive portfolio of restaurants that have been characterized by SIR as Concept Restaurants and Signature Restaurants. Concept Restaurants (i.e., Jack Astorís Bar and Grill, Canyon Creek Chop House and Alice Fazooliís! Italian Crabshack) are the brands that have been rolled out to multiple locations because of their broader appeal, earning potential and strategic growth opportunity.

Distribution History

2004 YTD (Yield)
$0.00000 (N/A)

2003 (Yield)
$0.00000 (N/A)

2002 (Yield)
$0.00000 (N/A)

2001 (Yield)
$0.00000 (N/A)

2000 (Yield)
$0.00000 (N/A)

Sleep Country Canada Income Fund

Original Unit Price
$10.00

Symbol: TSX: Z.UN
Address: 140 Wendell Avenue
Toronto, Ontario
Canada M9N 3R2
O/S Units: Approx. 13,500,000
Phone: (416) 242-4774
Fax: (416) 242-9644
Email: investor@sleepcountry.ca
Contact: Christine Magee

Business: Sleep Country Canada Income Fund is an open-ended limited purpose trust that owns 100 percent of the voting securities of Sleep Country Canada Inc. The company owns and operates Canada's largest chain of retail mattress stores. It is one of the two leading retailers of mattresses in Canada, commanding a 16 percent national market share and an average regional market share of approximately 40 percent across the six regional markets it serves. The company now operates in six regional markets, including Vancouver, Toronto, southwestern Ontario, Calgary, Edmonton, and Ottawa.

Distribution History

2004 YTD (Yield)
$0.84400 (4.53%)

2003 (Yield)
$0.76460 (5.66%)

2002 (Yield)
$0.00000 (N/A)

2001 (Yield)
$0.00000 (N/A)

2000 (Yield)
$0.00000 (N/A)

Specialty Foods Group Income Fund

Original Unit Price
$10.00

Symbol:	TSX: HAM.UN
Address:	603 Pilot House Road
	Newport News, Virginia
	23604, USA
O/S Units:	Approx. 20,100,000
Phone:	(757) 952-1200
Fax:	N/A
Email:	investorrelations@sfgtrust.com
Contact:	Thomas Davis, President
	William Dunham, IR

Business: Specialty Foods Group Income Fund is an open-ended, limited purpose trust established under the laws of the province of Ontario, which indirectly holds an interest of approximately 55 percent in Specialty Foods Group, Inc. (SFG). SFG is a leading independent U.S. producer and marketer of premium branded and private-label processed meat products. SFG produces a wide variety of products such as franks, hams, bacon, luncheon meats, dry sausage, and delicatessen meats. These products are sold to a diverse customer base in the retail and food-service sectors. SFG sells products under a number of leading national and regional brands, such as Nathan's, Swift Premium, Field, Fischer's, Mosey's, Liguria, Alpine Lace and Scott Petersen as well as on a private-label basis.

Distribution History

2004 YTD (Yield)
$0.42500 (13.28%)

2003 (Yield)
$0.91164 (11.54%)

2002 (Yield)
$0.00000 (N/A)

2001 (Yield)
$0.00000 (N/A)

2000 (Yield)
$0.00000 (N/A)

Sterling Leaf Income Trust

Original Unit Price
$10.00

Symbol:	TSX: SLM.UN
Address:	2100 Allard Street,
	Montreal, Quebec,
	Canada H4E 2L6
O/S Units:	Approx. 10,000,000
Phone:	(514) 262-5066
Fax:	(514) 262-5066
Email:	N/A
Contact:	Joseph Pettinicchio

Business: Sterling Leaf Income Trust has been established to acquire, through Sterling Leaf Income Services Ltd., a company wholly owned by the trust, with interests in consumer installment sales contracts generated in the publishing industry. The corporationís business will be managed by Mount Real Financial Management Services Corporation, a wholly owned subsidiary of Mount Real Corporation.

The corporation will enter into the business of acquiring consumer instalment sales contracts. Initially it is expected that almost all of the consumer instalment sales contracts acquired by the corporation will be pursuant to the sales of magazine subscriptions.

Distribution History

2004 YTD (Yield)
$0.35400 (3.54%)

2003 (Yield)
$0.00000 (N/A)

2002 (Yield)
$0.00000 (N/A)

2001 (Yield)
$0.00000 (N/A)

2000 (Yield)
$0.00000 (N/A)

Summit Real Estate Investment Trust

Original Unit Price (N/A)

Symbol: TSX: SMU.UN
Address: 9th Floor, 5991 Spring Garden Road
Halifax, Nova Scotia
Canada B3H 1Y6
O/S Units: Approx. 50,800,000
Phone: (902) 421-1222
Fax: (902) 420-0559
Email: pdykeman@summitreit.com
Contact: Lou Maroun
Paul Malcolm Dykeman

Business: Summit Real Estate Investment Trust provides investors with the opportunity to participate in a diversified portfolio of primarily income-producing real property investments located principally in Canada and in the southeastern United States. The trust's investments consist of shopping centres, industrial buildings, and apartments.

Distribution History

2004 YTD (Yield)
$0.89250 (5.08%)

2003 (Yield)
$1.53000 (8.43%)

2002 (Yield)
$1.53000 (10.11%)

2001 (Yield)
$1.53000 (10.13%)

2000 (Yield)
$1.53000 (13.30%)

Sun Gro Horticulture Income Fund

Original Unit Price $10.00

Symbol: TSX: GRO.UN
Address: #100, 15831 N.E. 8th Street
Bellevue, Washington
USA 98008
O/S Units: Approx. 22,000,000
Phone: (425) 373-3601
Fax: (425) 450-9587
Email: investorcontact@sungro.com
Contact: Mitchell J. Weaver

Business: The fund is a limited purpose trust established to acquire and hold the securities of Sun Gro Horticulture Canada Ltd. Sun Gro is the largest producer of sphagnum peat in North America and the largest distributor of peat moss and peat-based growing media to professional plant growers in the United States and Canada. The company operates a network of 13 production facilities, comprising six peat and peat-mixing plants in Canada and seven mix plants in the United States.

Sun Gro sells its professional products primarily to greenhouse, nursery, and specialty crop growers as well as to golf course developers and landscapers. The company also sells peat moss and peat-based growing mixes to retail customers, either by way of private label partnerships or under its own brand names.

Distribution History

2004 YTD (Yield)
$0.74080 (9.01%)

2003 (Yield)
$1.08030 (13.94%)

2002 (Yield)
$0.88110 (8.43%)

2001 (Yield)
$0.00000 (N/A)

2000 (Yield)
$0.00000 (N/A)

Superior Plus Income Fund

Original Unit Price (N/A)

Symbol:	TSX: SPF.UN
Address:	#408 Canterra Tower, 400 – 3rd Avenue S.W.
	Calgary, Alberta
	Canada T2P 4H2
O/S Units:	Approx. 67,400,000
Phone:	(403) 218-2970 / 1(866) 490-7587
Fax:	(403) 218-2973
Email:	info@superiorplus.ca
Contact:	Peter Green

Business: Superior Plus Income Fund holds 100 percent of Superior Plus Inc., which has three operating divisions. Superior Propane is Canada's largest distributor of propane, related products, and services. ERCO Worldwide is a leading supplier of chemicals and technology to the pulp and paper, and water treatment industries. Superior Energy Management provides natural gas supply services, predominantly to commercial and industrial markets in Ontario.

Distribution History

2004 YTD (Yield)
$1.86500 (6.77%)

2003 (Yield)
$2.28000 (8.89%)

2002 (Yield)
$1.98800 (10.10%)

2001 (Yield)
$1.67000 (9.86%)

2000 (Yield)
$1.38000 (8.82%)

Swiss Water Decaffeinated Coffee Income Fund

Original Unit Price $10.00

Symbol:	TSX: SWS.UN
Address:	3131 Lake City Way
	Burnaby, British Columbia
	Canada V5A 3A3
O/S Units:	Approx. 5,500,000
Phone:	(604) 420-4050
Fax:	(604) 420-8711
Email:	idwong@swisswater.com
Contact:	Frank Dennis, President and CEO
	Dave Wong

Business: Swiss Water Decaffeinated Coffee Income Fund owns Swiss Water Decaffeinated Coffee Company Inc., a premium green coffee decaffeinator located in Burnaby, British Columbia, Canada. The SWISS WATER® process is a 100 percent chemical free, proprietary decaffeinating process used by premium roasters and demanded by discerning decaf drinkers around the world. Swiss Water decaffeinates premium coffees to a 97 percent caffeine removal—U.S. standard guaranteed. Swiss Water is the world's only branded decaffeinating process and supports its brand through ongoing consumer research and focused consumer advertising.

Distribution History

2004 YTD (Yield)
$0.97650 (6.73%)

2003 (Yield)
$1.30200 (9.40%)

2002 (Yield)
$0.57400 (5.13%)

2001 (Yield)
$0.00000 (N/A)

2000 (Yield)
$0.00000 (N/A)

Taylor NGL Limited Partnership

Original Unit Price
$10.40

Symbol:	TSX: TAY.UN
Address:	#2200, 800 – 5th Avenue S.W.
	Calgary, Alberta
	Canada T2P 3T6
O/S Units:	Approx. 18,000,000
Phone:	(403) 781-8181
Fax:	(403) 777-1907
Email:	bpritchard@taylorngl.com
Contact:	Bob Pritchard, President

Business: Taylor NGL Limited Partnership owns interests in, and operates, the Younger Extraction Plant in British Columbia, the Joffre Extraction Plant in Alberta, and the RET Complex also in Alberta. Both the Younger and Joffre plants are natural gas liquids extraction facilities that produce ethane, propane, butane, and condensate. The RET Complex consists of three interconnected natural gas processing facilities and their associated gathering systems.

Distribution History

2004 YTD (Yield)
$0.43000 (5.91%)

2003 (Yield)
$0.52000 (8.52%)

2002 (Yield)
$0.44000 (9.69%)

2001 (Yield)
$0.54000 (11.49%)

2000 (Yield)
$0.56000 (12.58%)

TerraVest Income Fund

Original Unit Price
N/A

Symbol:	TSX: TI.UN
Address:	4901 Bruce Road
	Vegreville, Alberta
	Canada T9C 1C3
O/S Units:	Approx. 6,700,000
Phone:	(403) 640-7339
Fax:	(403) 640-7390
Email:	laniuk@telusplanet.net
Contact:	Dale H. Laniuk

Business: TerraVest Income Fund is an unincorporated open-ended investment trust established for the purposes of investing in a diversified group of income-producing businesses. The fund initially has two operating divisions, R.J.V. Gas Field Services and Ezee-On Manufacturing, which are currently wholly owned subsidiaries of Laniuk. RJV is one of the largest providers of wellhead processing equipment for the Canadian natural gas industry. Ezee-On manufactures heavy-duty equipment for large acreage grain farms and livestock operations.

Distribution History

2004 YTD (Yield)
$0.15095 (1.73%)

2003 (Yield)
$0.00000 (N/A)

2002 (Yield)
$0.00000 (N/A)

2001 (Yield)
$0.00000 (N/A)

2000 (Yield)
$0.00000 (N/A)

TGS North American REIT

Original Unit Price
$10.00

Symbol:	TSX: NAR.UN
Address:	#1010, 1520 – 4th Street S.W.
	Calgary, Alberta
	Canada T2R 1H4
O/S Units:	Approx. 16,800,000
Phone:	(403) 264-4310
Fax:	(403) 264-9824
Email:	investorrelations@tgsreit.com
Contact:	Jeffrey D. Kohn, CEO
	Lloyd A. Wiggins, CFO

Business: TGS North American Real Estate Investment Trust is an unincorporated, open-ended limited purpose real estate investment trust formed to invest in office, retail, and industrial real estate located in western North America. TGS NA REIT currently owns retail and office properties in Alberta, Colorado, and Texas, having approximately 3.2 million square feet of rentable area.

Distribution History

2004 YTD (Yield)
$0.56925 (6.43%)

2003 (Yield)
$0.75900 (7.79%)

2002 (Yield)
$0.08331 (0.83%)

2001 (Yield)
$0.00000 (N/A)

2000 (Yield)
$0.00000 (N/A)

The Brick Group Income Fund

Original Unit Price
$10.00

Symbol:	TSX: BRK.UN
Address:	16930 – 114 Avenue
	Edmonton, Alberta
	Canada T5M 3S2
O/S Units:	Approx. 42,900,000
Phone:	(780) 930-6000
Fax:	(780) 454-0969
Email:	N/A
Contact:	Kim Yost, President

Business: The Brick Group Income Fund is an unincorporated, open-ended, limited purpose trust. The Brick Group is one of Canada's largest volume retailers of household furniture, mattresses, appliances, and home electronics. In addition, the Brick Group operates distribution centres in Vancouver, Edmonton, Winnipeg, Toronto, and Montreal. The Brick Group's retail operations are unique in their ability to offer products in three different price segments under three distinct banners: The Brick, United Furniture Warehouse, and HomeShow Canada. In addition, the Brick Group derives revenues from franchise sales, extended warranty and credit insurance services, and its Website.

Distribution History

2004 YTD (Yield)
$0.13871 (1.15%)

2003 (Yield)
$0.00000 (N/A)

2002 (Yield)
$0.00000 (N/A)

2001 (Yield)
$0.00000 (N/A)

2000 (Yield)
$0.00000 (N/A)

The Consumers' Waterheater Income Fund

Original Unit Price
$10.00

Symbol: TSX: CWI.UN
Address: #1400, 25 Sheppard Avenue West
Toronto, Ontario
Canada M2N 6S6
O/S Units: Approx. 39,700,000
Phone: (416) 590-3462
Fax: (416) 250-2977
Email: amelia.young@ngwi.com
Contact: Larry Ryan

Business: The Consumers' Waterheater Income Fund owns a
portfolio of 1.3 million installed water heaters and
other assets, leased primarily to residential
customers in Ontario. Direct Energy Essential Home
Services provides service support to the portfolio in
exchange for 35 percent of aggregate rental
revenues, thereby significantly reducing the fund's
operating risk. The asset base has been generating
stable and growing cashflows since Its inception in
the late 1950s.

Direct Energy Essential Home Services is the brand
name for Enbridge Services Inc. and is a subsidiary
of Centrica Canada Limited.

Distribution History

2004 YTD (Yield)
$0.79940 (5.67%)

2003 (Yield)
$1.05000 (7.83%)

2002 (Yield)
$0.00000 (N/A)

2001 (Yield)
$0.00000 (N/A)

2000 (Yield)
$0.00000 (N/A)

The Keg Royalties Income Fund

Original Unit Price
$10.00

Symbol: TSX: KEG.UN
Address: #1900, 355 Burrard Street
Vancouver, British Columbia
Canada V6C 2G8
O/S Units: Approx. 8,150,000
Phone: (604) 682-7137
Fax: (604) 682-7131
Email: N/A
Contact: David Aisenstat

Business: The fund has been created to acquire, indirectly
through The Keg Rights Limited Partnership and The
Keg Holdings Trust, the trademarks, trade names,
operating procedures and systems and related items,
and all goodwill owned by Keg Restaurants Ltd. Keg
is a leading operator and franchisor of steakhouse
restaurants in Canada and also has a substantial
presence in the United States.

Distribution History

2004 YTD (Yield)
$0.81000 (6.92%)

2003 (Yield)
$1.08000 (11.02%)

2002 (Yield)
$0.54000 (5.84%)

2001 (Yield)
$0.00000 (N/A)

2000 (Yield)
$0.00000 (N/A)

TimberWest Timber Trust Stapled Units

**Original Unit Price
(N/A)**

Symbol:	TSX: TWF.UN
Address:	#2300, 1055 West Georgia Street
	Vancouver, British Columbia
	Canada V6E 3P3
O/S Units:	Approx. 76,200,000
Phone:	(604) 654-4600
Fax:	(604) 654-4571
Email:	invest@timberwest.com
Contact:	Paul McElligott

Business: TimberWest Forest Corp. is positioned as the largest owner of private forest lands in western Canada. The company's 334,000 hectares, providing a sustainable annual harvest of 2.1 million to 2.5 million m(3) of logs, are largely located on Vancouver Island and contain some of the best coniferous forest growing sites in the world. The American Forest & Paper Association has certified that the company is committed to managing these private lands according to sustainable forestry standards under its Sustainable Forestry Initiative (SFI)(SM) Program. TimberWest also owns annual Crown harvest rights for 1.2 million m(3) of logs, a lumbermill, and about 6000 hectares of properties that are progressively being made available for higher uses.

Distribution History

2004 YTD (Yield)
$1.07600 (7.48%)

2003 (Yield)
$1.07746 (8.48%)

2002 (Yield)
$1.07746 (8.98%)

2001 (Yield)
$1.07746 (8.29%)

2000 (Yield)
$1.07746 (9.93%)

TransAlta Power L.P.

**Original Unit Price
$10.00**

Symbol:	TSX: TPW.UN
Address:	#110, 12th Avenue S.W.
	Calgary, Alberta
	Canada T2P 2M1
O/S Units:	Approx. 34,000,000
Phone:	(403) 267-2520 / 1(800) 387-3598
Fax:	(403) 267-2590
Email:	investor_relations@transalta.com
Contact:	Ian Bourne
	Ken Wetherell

Business: TransAlta Power owns and operates three Ontario cogeneration facilities and a 60 percent interest in the Fort Saskatchewan cogeneration plant in Alberta. Electricity from the Ontario plants is sold to Ontario Electricity Financial Corp. under long-term contract; steam and other thermal energy produced is supplied to manufacturing plants and other facilities. Electricity and steam from the Fort Saskatchewan plant are sold to Dow Chemical under a long-term contract.

Distribution History

2004 YTD (Yield)
$0.52320 (5.86%)

2003 (Yield)
$0.76740 (7.68%)

2002 (Yield)
$0.74300 (7.94%)

2001 (Yield)
$0.73450 (7.98%)

2000 (Yield)
$0.70000 (10.29%)

TransCanada Power L.P.

Original Unit Price
$25.00

Symbol:	TSX: TPL.UN
Address:	450 – 1st Street S.W.
	Calgary, Alberta
	Canada T2P 5H1
O/S Units:	Approx. 39,300,000
Phone:	(403) 920-7980
Fax:	(403) 920-2353
Email:	investor_inquiries@transcanada-powerlp.com
Contact:	Sean McMaster, David Moneta, Debbie Persad

Business: TransCanada Power, L.P. owns 11 power plants in Canada and the United States with total generating capacity of 744 megawatts. Subsidiaries of TransCanada Corporation manage the partnership and the operation of assets owned by the partnership. These subsidiaries own 30.6 percent of the partnership.

Distribution History

2004 YTD (Yield)
$1.89000 (5.62%)

2003 (Yield)
$0.81900 (2.26%)

2002 (Yield)
$0.25200 (0.82%)

2001 (Yield)
$0.24900 (0.78%)

2000 (Yield)
$0.24000 (0.87%)

TransForce Income Fund

Original Unit Price
$8.50

Symbol:	TSX: TIF.UN
Address:	6600 Chemin Saint Francois
	Saint Laurent, Québec
	Canada H4S 1B7
O/S Units:	Approx. 48,000,000
Phone:	(514) 856-7540 / 1(800) 856-5559
Fax:	(514) 332-9527
Email:	administration@transforce.ca
Contact:	Alain Bedard, President and CEO
IR Counsel:	Maison Brison

Business: TransForce Income Fund is one of Canada's leading transport and logistics companies. TransForce Income Fund, through its businesses, operates in four well-defined business segments: less than truckload (LTL) and parcel delivery, truckload (TL), specialized truckload and logistics and warehousing services. TransForce Income Fund offers its services across North America with a focus on eastern Canada.

Distribution History

2004 YTD (Yield)
$0.86750 (7.32%)

2003 (Yield)
$1.14000 (11.94%)

2002 (Yield)
$0.28500 (3.75%)

2001 (Yield)
$0.00000 (N/A)

2000 (Yield)
$0.00000 (N/A)

Tree Island Wire Income Fund

Original Unit Price
$10.00

Symbol: TSX: TIL.UN
Address: 3933 Boundary Road
Richmond, British Columbia
Canada V6V 1T8
O/S Units: Approx. 16,400,000
Phone: (604) 524-3744
Fax: (604) 524-2657
Email: gflesher@treeisland.com
Contact: N/A

Business: The Fund is an open ended trust to provide
unitholders with cash distributions derived from the
ownership of the Notes and Common Shares of Tree
Island Industries Ltd.
Tree Island Industries Ltd. is one of North
America's largest producers of steel wire and
fabricated wire products. Its principal products are
nails, bright wire (including wire for the bedding and
upholstery industries), stainless steel and galvanized
wire (including baling wire), stucco reinforcing
products, fence products, and other fabricated wire
products. These products are all manufactured from
wire rod, sourced from a variety of steel producers
around the world.

Distribution History

2004 YTD (Yield)
$0.97502 (6.33%)

2003 (Yield)
$1.27503 (11.18%)

2002 (Yield)
$0.17355 (1.85%)

2001 (Yield)
$0.00000 (N/A)

2000 (Yield)
$0.00000 (N/A)

Trinidad Energy Services Income Trust

Original Unit Price
(N/A)

Symbol: TSX: TDG.UN
Address: #888, 665 – 8th Street S.W.
Calgary, Alberta
Canada T2P 3K7
O/S Units: Approx. 27,900,000
Phone: (780) 875-1414
Fax: (780) 875-1930
Email: twood@trinidaddrilling.com
Contact: Michael E. Heier, CEO

Business: Trinidad Energy Services is a growth-oriented income
trust.Trinidad's divisions operate in the drilling and
well servicing sectors of the Canadian oil and gas
industry. Trinidad has 31 drilling rigs ranging in
depths from 1000 - 5500 metres. In addition to its
drilling rigs, Trinidad has 8 service rigs geographically
concentrated in northeastern Alberta. Trinidad is
focused on providing modern, reliable, expertly
designed equipment operated by well-trained and
experienced personnel.

Distribution History

2004 YTD (Yield)
$0.49000 (5.47%)

2003 (Yield)
$0.41500 (6.09%)

2002 (Yield)
$0.06750 (3.14%)

2001 (Yield)
$0.00000 (N/A)

2000 (Yield)
$0.00000 (N/A)

UE Waterheater Income Fund

Original Unit Price
$10.00

Symbol:	TSX: UWH.UN
Address:	2 Lansing Square
	North York, Ontario
	Canada M2G 4P8
O/S Units:	Approx. 41,500,000
Phone:	(416) 499-7600
Fax:	(416) 499-5085
Email:	psteffen@unionenergy.com
Contact:	Roger Rossi, President
	Paul Steffensen, Controller

Business: UE Waterheater Income Fund is an unincorporated, open-ended limited purpose trust established under the laws of Ontario to indirectly acquire and hold the water heater rental business of Union Energy Limited Partnership and its related commercial activities. Union Energy owns and services Canada's second largest portfolio of rental water heaters in a program that was started in the 1960s. Union Energy's water heater rental portfolio has over one million water heaters, representing approximately 40% of the water heater rental market in Ontario, and operates under two principal brand names of Union Energy and Ontario Hydro Energy.

Distribution History

2004 YTD (Yield)
$0.63747 (5.47%)

2003 (Yield)
$0.03027 (0.26%)

2002 (Yield)
$0.00000 (N/A)

2001 (Yield)
$0.00000 (N/A)

2000 (Yield)
$0.00000 (N/A)

Vermilion Energy Trust

Original Unit Price
(N/A)

Symbol:	TSX: VET.UN
Address:	#2800, 400 – 4th Avenue S.W.
	Calgary, Alberta
	Canada T2P 0J4
O/S Units:	Approx. 58,700,000
Phone:	(403) 269-4884 / 1(866) 895-8101
Fax:	(403) 264-6306
Email:	info@vermilionenergy.com
Contact:	Lorenzo Donadeo / Paul Beique

Business: Vermilion Energy Trust is led by two of the three founders of Vermilion Resures Ltd, the trust's predecessor company, and provides investors with a high-quality asset base, proven leadership, and exposure to an exciting international natural gas discovery through the trust's 72 percent ownership of Aventura Energy Inc. Vermilion Energy Trust is an international energy trust with geographically diverse production. While 74 percent of production volumes come from high-quality oil and gas reserves in Canada, the trust also produces high-value, light oil in France. These core properties generate strong cash flow, 80–85 percent of which the trust plans to distribute to unitholders. The trust also holds a 72.3 percent interest in Aventura Energy Inc. a Trinidad-based operation.

Distribution History

2004 YTD (Yield)
$1.53000 (7.67%)

2003 (Yield)
$1.87000 (12.19%)

2002 (Yield)
$0.00000 (N/A)

2001 (Yield)
$0.00000 (N/A)

2000 (Yield)
$0.00000 (N/A)

Versacold Income Fund

Original Unit Price
$8.50

Symbol:	TSX: ICE.UN
Address:	2115 Commissioner Street
	Vancouver, British Columbia
	Canada V5L 1A6
O/S Units:	Approx. 21,300,000
Phone:	(604) 255-4656
Fax:	(604) 255-4330
Email:	jsmith@versacold.com
Contact:	H.Brent Sugden
	Joel M. Smith

Business: Versacold Income Fund is an unincorporated, open-ended limited purpose trust. The trust was created to invest in public refrigerated warehousing, distribution, and related businesses in Canada and the United States, initially through the acquisition of Versacold Corporation. Versacold Corporation operates 24 temperature-controlled facilities and a fully integrated national refrigerated distribution network in Canada. Versacold serves customers including food producers and processors, and wholesale and retail distributors.

Distribution History

2004 YTD (Yield)
$0.69750 (7.12%)

2003 (Yield)
$0.93000 (9.78%)

2002 (Yield)
$0.84000 (10.43%)

2001 (Yield)
$0.00000 (N/A)

2000 (Yield)
$0.00000 (N/A)

Viking Energy Royalty Trust Units

Original Unit Price
$10.00

Symbol:	TSX: VKR.UN
Address:	#400, 330 – 5th Avenue S.W.
	Calgary, Alberta
	Canada T2P 0L4
O/S Units:	Approx. 96,700,000
Phone:	(403) 268-3175 / 1(877) 292-2527
Fax:	(403) 266-0058
Email:	vikingin@viking-roy.com
Contact:	John E. Zahary, President

Business: Viking Energy Royalty Trust is an open-ended investment Trust that holds a royalty in certain long-life oil and natural gas producing properties in Alberta and Saskatchewan. The beneficiaries of the trust are the holders of the trust's units who receive monthly distributions of the cash flow from the income generated by the trust's properties.

Distribution History

2004 YTD (Yield)
$0.72000 (11.37%)

2003 (Yield)
$1.28000 (22.65%)

2002 (Yield)
$1.16000 (16.41%)

2001 (Yield)
$1.91000 (29.75%)

2000 (Yield)
$1.71000 (20.00%)

Volume Services America Holdings, Inc.

Original Unit Price
$19.71

Symbol:	TSX: CVP.UN
Address:	201 East Broad Street
	Spartanburg, South Carolina
	29306, USA
O/S Units:	Approx. 16,800,000
Phone:	(864) 598-8600
Fax:	(864) 598-8695
Email:	info@centerplate.com
Contact:	Lawrence E. Honig, Chairman and CEO

Business: Volume Services America Holdings, Inc. (VSAH) is a leading provider of food and beverage concessions, high-end catering and merchandise services for sports facilities, convention centres, and other entertainment facilities throughout the United States. Based on the number of facilities served, VSAH is one of the largest providers of food and beverage services to a variety of recreational facilities in the United States.

Distribution History

2004 YTD (Yield)
$1.21300 (6.48%)

2003 (Yield)
$0.00000 (N/A)

2002 (Yield)
$0.00000 (N/A)

2001 (Yield)
$0.00000 (N/A)

2000 (Yield)
$0.00000 (N/A)

Wellco Energy Services Trust

Original Unit Price
$5.00

Symbol:	TSX: WLL.UN
Address:	#3100, 500 – 4th Avenue S.W.
	Calgary, Alberta
	Canada T2P2V6
O/S Units:	Approx. 8,000,000
Phone:	(403) 232-6334
Fax:	(403) 232-6338
Email:	info@wellcoenergy.com
Contact:	R.D. (Rick) Patmore, President
	Gregory J. Longphee, IR

Business: Wellco Energy Services Trust provides various products and services to the Canadian oil and gas industry. These include (i) directional and horizontal drilling services; (ii) the rental of professional wellsite accommodation, water and wastewater treatment systems, and patented Altex flare tanks; and (iii) environmental assessment services.

Distribution History

2004 YTD (Yield)
$0.72000 (7.66%)

2003 (Yield)
$0.98000 (14.02%)

2002 (Yield)
$0.41000 (7.88%)

2001 (Yield)
$0.00000 (N/A)

2000 (Yield)
$0.00000 (N/A)

Westshore Terminals Income Fund

Original Unit Price
$10.00

Symbol: TSX: WTE.UN
Address: #1600, 1055 West Hastings Street
Vancouver, British Columbia
Canada V6E 2H2
O/S Units: Approx. 70,400,000
Phone: (604) 688-6764
Fax: (604) 687-2601
Email: N/A
Contact: David F. Phillips

Business: Westshore Terminals Income Fund is an
open-ended, single-purpose trust, that owns all of the
common shares and $470 million aggregate principal
amount of subordinated notes of Westshore
Terminals Ltd. Westshore operates a coal storage
and export terminal located in Greater Vancouver
(Delta). The terminal operates on a throughput basis
and receives a handling charge from its customers
based on the type and volumes of coal exported.
Westshore does not take title to the coal. Income
derived by the fund from these securities (minus
expenses) is distributed quarterly to unitholders.

Distribution History

2004 YTD (Yield)
$0.58000 (6.59%)

2003 (Yield)
$0.81228 (11.20%)

2002 (Yield)
$0.61600 (12.62%)

2001 (Yield)
$0.70248 (12.43%)

2000 (Yield)
$0.64304 (15.88%)

Yellow Pages Income Fund

Original Unit Price
$10.00

Symbol: TSX: YLO.UN
Address: 16 Place du Commerce, Île des Soeurs
Verdun, Québec
Canada H3E 2A5
O/S Units: Approx. 229,700,000
Phone: (514) 934-5817 / 1(877) 956-2003
Fax: (514) 934-0721
Email: IR.info@ypg.com
Contact: Marc P. Tellier, President & CEO
Patrick Nadeau, IR

Business: Yellow Pages Income Fund is an unincorporated,
open-ended, limited purpose trust established to
invest in Yellow Pages Group. The fund indirectly
holds a 70.28 percent ownership interest in Yellow
Pages Group. Yellow Pages Group is Canada's
largest telephone directories publisher and the official
publisher of Bell Canada's directories. Yellow Pages
Group publishes annually more than 200 print Yellow
Pages™ directories and alphabetical pages. The
Company also manages Canada's most visited
commercial online directories YellowPages.ca™,
Canada411.ca, CanadaTollFree.ca, as well as the
CanadaPlus.ca network, a leader in the local city
sites market. Yellow Pages Group is one of Canada's
leading media companies.

Distribution History

2004 YTD (Yield)
$0.67620 (5.62%)

2003 (Yield)
$0.35300 (3.04%)

2002 (Yield)
$0.00000 (N/A)

2001 (Yield)
$0.00000 (N/A)

2000 (Yield)
$0.00000 (N/A)

Zargon Energy Trust

Original Unit Price (N/A)

Symbol:	TSX: ZAR.UN
Address:	#700, 333 – 5th Avenue S.W.
	Calgary, Alberta
	Canada T2P 3B6
O/S Units:	Approx. 14,600,000
Phone:	(403) 264-9992
Fax:	(403) 265-3026
Email:	zargon@zargon.ca
Contact:	Craig H. Hansen

Business: Zargon Energy Trust is an upstream oil and gas company with assets located in Alberta, British Columbia, Manitoba, and Saskatchewan.

Distribution History

2004 YTD (Yield)
$0.28000 (1.31%)

2003 (Yield)
$0.00000 (N/A)

2002 (Yield)
$0.00000 (N/A)

2001 (Yield)
$0.00000 (N/A)

2000 (Yield)
$0.00000 (N/A)

Index of Funds

Index

About the Authors

PETER BECK

Peter Beck is a well-known financial expert and President of Swift-Trade Inc., Canada's leading proprietary trading firm.

A European-trained chef, Mr. Beck immigrated to Canada in 1979 and set up a number of successful businesses, including a coffee shop, a water bottling company, a pet food delivery service, and ITN Corporation, the first legally operating long distance company in Canada. In 1998, he founded SwiftTrade, which was #7 on *Profit Magazine's* "10 Hottest Startups in Canada" for 2001, and was named #2 on the "Top 100 Fastest Growing Businesses in Canada" for 2004, also by *Profit*, with an astounding five-year growth rate of almost 9000%.

Mr. Beck has been featured in media across the country, including *The Globe and Mail*, the *Toronto Star*, CTV News, ROB TV, and *Canadian Business*. He regularly appears on television to offer commentary on the markets, writes articles for financial publications across the country, and is the co-author of *Hedge Funds for Canadians: New Investment Strategies for Winning in Any Market* (John Wiley & Sons).

SIMON ROMANO

Simon Romano is a partner at Stikeman Elliott LLP, a 440-lawyer firm with an international reputation in all areas of business law, most notably securities, tax, banking, corporate finance, M&A, securitizations and derivatives, commercial litigation, competition law, commercial real estate, labour/employment and pension law, environmental law, intellectual property and related fields. Mr. Romano practices principally in the area of securities, M&A and finance, as well as acting for private equity funds, income trusts, and alternative trading systems.

Mr. Romano has practiced in both Toronto and New York, and was formerly a clerk at the Supreme Court of Canada. During 1995 and 1996, he was Special Counsel to the Ontario Securities Commission, where he dealt with take-over bids as well as other projects. He has written a number of articles, is a frequent speaker at seminars, and was a member of the Ontario Securities Commission's Securities Advisory Committee.

He is particularly active in the area of income trusts, having advised the Livingston International Income Fund and the SIR Royalty Income Fund, among others. He has been recognized by Lexpert/American Lawyer as one of Canada's top 500 lawyers, and by Chambers Global as one of the world's leading lawyers